YOU CAN'T BE WHAT
YOU CAN'T SEE

Community Youth Creative Learning Experience (CYCLE), Cabrini-Green, Chicago, Illinois

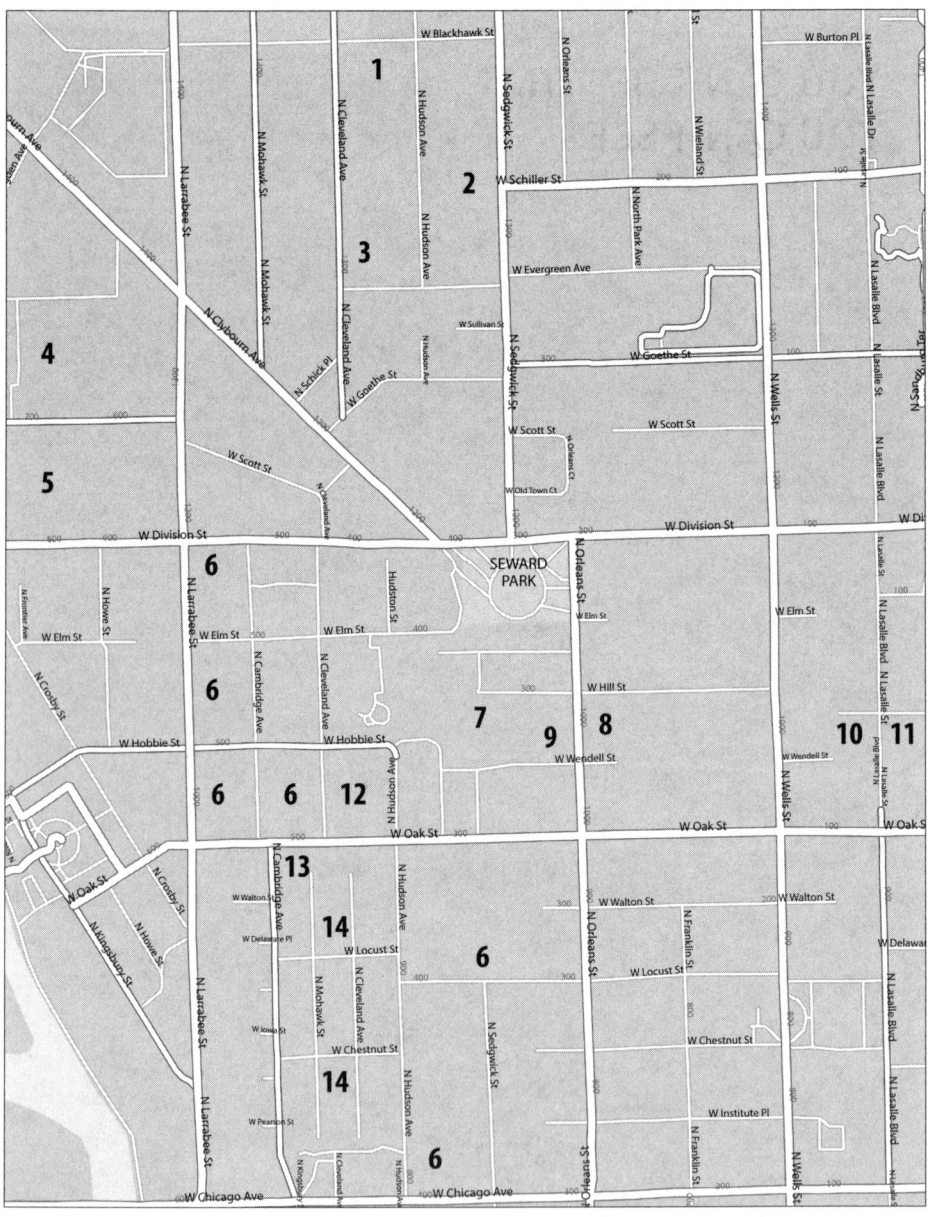

1. CYCLE building at 1441 N. Cleveland (the Olivet Center)
2. Town and Garden Apartments
3. Manierre Elementary School
4. Schiller Elementary School
5. William Green Homes ("the Whites")
6. Cabrini Extension ("the Reds")
7. Byrd Elementary School
8. St. Joseph Elementary School
9. St. Matthew's Church (CYCLE summer day camp site)
10. La Salle Street Church (CYCLE headquarters until 1982)
11. Ascension Church (CYCLE summer day camp site)
12. Jenner Elementary School
13. CYCLE building at 515 Oak St. (formerly St. Philip Benizi School)
14. Francis Cabrini Homes ("the row houses")

YOU CAN'T BE WHAT YOU CAN'T SEE

The Power of Opportunity to Change Young Lives

MILBREY W. McLAUGHLIN

Harvard Education Press
Cambridge, Massachusetts

Copyright © 2018 by the President and Fellows of Harvard College

All rights reserved. No part of this publication may be reproduced or transmitted in any form or by any means, electronic or mechanical, including photocopy, recording, or any information storage and retrieval systems, without permission in writing from the publisher.

Paperback ISBN 978-1-68253-152-5
Library Edition ISBN 978-1-68253-153-2

Library of Congress Cataloging-in-Publication Data
Names: McLaughlin, Milbrey Wallin, author.
Title: You can't be what you can't see : the power of opportunity to change young lives / Milbrey W. McLaughlin.
Description: Cambridge, Massachusetts : Harvard Education Press, 2018. | Includes bibliographical references and index.
Identifiers: LCCN 2017055260| ISBN 9781682531525 (pbk.) | ISBN 9781682531532 (library edition)
Subjects: LCSH: After-school programs--Illinois--Chicago. | Community and school--Illinois--Chicago. | Urban youth--Education--Illinois--Chicago. | Youth--Services for. | Social work with youth--Illinois--Chicago. | Social interaction in youth. | Educational change--Illinois--Chicago. | Urban youth--Illinois--Chicago. | Youth development--Illinois--Chicago. | Self-esteem in adolescence.
Classification: LCC LC34.5.I5 M35 2018 | DDC 372.42/5--dc23 LC record available at https://lccn.loc.gov/2017055260

Published by Harvard Education Press,
an imprint of the Harvard Education Publishing Group

Harvard Education Press
8 Story Street
Cambridge, MA 02138

Frontispiece map of Chicago by MarketMAPS
Cover Design: Ciano Design
Cover Photo: crazycroat/iStock.com
The typefaces used in this book are Glober and ITC Legacy Serif.

CONTENTS

FOREWORD by Arne Duncan		vii
INTRODUCTION		1
CHAPTER 1:	Growing Up in Cabrini-Green	11

PART I: THE CYCLE PROGRAM

CHAPTER 2:	Starting CYCLE	41
CHAPTER 3:	Tutoring: Opportunities for Growth	57
CHAPTER 4:	Junior Staff: Opportunities for Leadership	73
CHAPTER 5:	Scholarships: Opportunities for Success	95
CHAPTER 6:	The I Have A Dream Scholarship Program	107
CHAPTER 7:	The College Opportunity Scholarship Program: Class of 1995	125

PART II: TURNING POINTS FOR CYCLE YOUTH

CHAPTER 8:	Exposure: You Can't Be What You Can't See	143
CHAPTER 9:	Mentors: Someone to Walk With	155
CHAPTER 10:	A Community of Belonging: A Good Gang	165

PART III: LEARNING FROM CYCLE

CHAPTER 11:	A Community of Practice	181
CHAPTER 12:	The Power of Opportunities to Change Lives	197
AFTERWORD by Greg Darnieder		219

Notes	223
About the Research	243
Acknowledgments	251
About the Author	255
Index	257

FOREWORD

I have spent my entire life working with low-income youth, and I have never wavered in my belief that anything is possible when time, opportunity, and love come together. I grew up in an afterschool program, run by my mother, serving poor African American children on Chicago's South Side. Some of the kids in the program defied the odds and went on to great careers in fields like engineering, education, and entertainment.

My mother offered them nothing more than a place to gather, read, do homework, play, sing, and feel safe and secure. There was nothing mysterious about it. But for many of these kids, my mother was an adult they could talk to and trust. For some of them, she was a surrogate parent. I have often wondered what it would take to go to scale and give every young person more opportunities outside of school to learn, play, and work together.

The answer is right here in Milbrey McLaughlin's book about CYCLE, a remarkable program founded by Greg Darnieder that worked with hundreds of young people in one of America's most challenging communities, Chicago's Cabrini-Green housing complex. The book begins with these young people as adolescents in the 1980s. Now in their forties and fifties, most of the CYCLE graduates have achieved middle-class success, built careers, and raised families, while so many of their counterparts outside the program fell through the cracks.

CYCLE's approach was straightforward: give young people positive, structured opportunities with clear, unambiguous expectations, and they will rise to meet them. One of the program's graduates now works with me to help young people avoid gangs, drugs, and street life and find work in the legal economy—paying forward his debt to the next generation.

As the book's title suggests, the essential problem for low-income urban youth is that they can't imagine a world they can't see. The only life they see is the one in front of them—single-parent families, drug dealing, street gangs, few if any men going to work each morning and coming home each night, police patrols, and violence. Asking them what they want to do with their lives and how they might fit in the larger world is like asking a fish to imagine what it's like to fly. If you've never worked in an office building and don't know anyone who does, you can't imagine doing it yourself.

Programs like CYCLE understand that poverty is not the defining obstacle to success. The real barrier is the lack of opportunity to see and experience the larger world. Children from families with means already have life-enriching opportunities in the nonschool hours: music lessons, summer camp, family travel, relationships with adults from a variety of fields. If we are to build a more equitable and just society, we need to make better use of that out-of-school time for low-income children. They need mentors, relationships, internships, work and play opportunities, and sometimes just friends from outside their immediate environment.

At a time when more than half of Chicago Public School students failed to complete high school, CYCLE participants had graduation rates in the range of 90 percent, which is higher than the national average *today* and well above Chicago's current record-setting rate. They didn't all go to college, but many of their children have, suggesting the enduring intergenerational impact of the program.

The best part of the book are the stories of the people and their lives told in their words and through their experiences. Also valuable are the thoughtful insights from McLaughlin and, in the afterword, Greg Darnieder, who was a mentor to me when I first got involved in public education.

Having worked in public education at the local and the national levels, I can tell you that the system we have created today does not systematically provide these kinds of opportunities to the children who need them the most. Whether it's lack of resources, bureaucratic inertia, or simply a failure of imagination, none of us has made the commitment at scale to provide the kinds of support that CYCLE pioneered in Chicago. And as with so many other challenges in public education, we lack the political will to find the resources.

I continue to believe that public education is the best antipoverty program in our country. But schools can't do it on their own. There are too many nonschool hours in the life of a child and too many burdens facing our teachers and parents. Guiding children to a successful adulthood is a shared responsibility for our entire society. As many others have said, "It takes a village," and in these polarizing times, the village needs to come together for our most vulnerable kids. My deepest hope is that policy makers everywhere take time to read this book and find the will to bring programs like this to low-income communities all across America. It's the smart thing to do. It's the right thing to do. And we know that it works.

Arne Duncan
US Secretary of Education, 2009–16

INTRODUCTION

In the mid-1980s, colleagues and I conducted research on six reportedly successful out-of-school time programs operating in high-poverty neighborhoods of three diverse US cities. Our 1994 book *Urban Sanctuaries* reports the results of that research.[1] However, while *Urban Sanctuaries* could celebrate the promising outcomes associated with these initiatives, it could say nothing about whether the positive consequences we observed would last as the young people who participated in these programs went on to experience various life changes and shifting circumstances. *You Can't Be What You Can't See: The Power of Opportunity to Change Young Lives*, adopts a long-term perspective to consider participants' life outcomes and the role of one such program, CYCLE.[2]

CYCLE operated from the 1980s through the mid-1990s in Chicago's notorious Cabrini-Green public housing project, one of the nation's most violent, most impoverished neighborhoods. To support the development of poor African American youth living in or near Cabrini-Green, CYCLE offered free comprehensive afterschool and summer supports primarily through closely interrelated tutoring, Junior Staff, and scholarship programs. *You Can't Be What You Can't See* follows up with these CYCLE participants thirty years later and in doing so provides a rare opportunity to see outcomes of a youth program over an extended period of time and over a generation. The "kids" we met in the mid-1980s and early 1990s now are in their forties and fifties, and most have children of their own.[3]

Between 2012 and 2017, Greg Darnieder, CYCLE's founder, and I conducted extensive interviews with former participants to hear if, how, or why CYCLE shaped their core attitudes, careers, and life choices. We focused on those cohorts that were most involved in the program: the more than 600 youth who became part of the Junior Staff, a program that provided youth with paid positions as coaches, tutors, and program leaders; and those who participated from grades 7 to 12 in two scholarship programs that guaranteed financial support for college or other postsecondary programs. We also interviewed key staff, funders, and trustees to gather their reflections on the program and reviewed data kept by the program and its coordinators.[4] We conducted in-depth interviews with more than 40 individuals and, with the assistance of program staff and social media, were able to account for the education outcomes of more than 700 former CYCLE participants, specifically whether they had graduated high school, attended college, or completed college. Because the life stories of the participants were so integral to documenting the success of this program, this book features the stories of about a dozen individuals to illuminate, in their own words, how and why CYCLE mattered to them and shaped their life trajectory.

CYCLE served hundreds of African American kids growing up in Cabrini-Green. Nearly all of them lived in a single-caregiver, welfare-eligible household headed by a mom, an aunt, an older sister, or a grandmother. Few had a dad living at home; most saw their fathers rarely, if at all, either because of disconnection with the mom, participation in "the [gang] life," incarceration, addiction, or death. All grew up in concentrated poverty, thanks to the Chicago Housing Authority's income guidelines, and most went to the public grammar schools serving the housing project, schools deemed by some observers of the Chicago Public School (CPS) system as the worst of the worst.[5] The majority of Cabrini-Green youth dropped out of high school; many of the young men fell victim to violence or drugs, were killed, or went to jail, and early pregnancy was the norm for the young women.

However, CYCLE participants' lives took a dramatically different course. The vast majority earned their high school diplomas, and of those graduates, more than one-third went on to gain acceptance at a college or university, from which approximately half graduated. In addition to earning associate and bachelor's degrees, among the CYCLE participants from the 1980s and early 1990s, eleven earned doctorates, two MDs, and several MAs in programs such as architecture, accounting, social work, education, communication, and business. Impressive accomplishments in any context, these outcomes are remarkable when placed against figures for the city's schools then and even now. During the time of our original research, CPS's overall high school graduation rate was approximately 35 percent; CYCLE senior staff report that graduation rates for young men growing up in Cabrini-Green hovered at around 20 percent and for young women around 30 percent.[6]

CYCLE executive director Greg Darnieder and former Junior Staffers gathered in 2015 to celebrate the awarding of Carleta Alston's doctoral degree, and to pose for this photo taken by Carleta. Top row (left to right): Greg Darnieder, Craig Nash, Don Smith, Johnny Calerway, Cyril Nichols, Brian Alston. Bottom row (left to right): Andre Stokes and Lloyd Rogers.

Today most CYCLE alums and their children enjoy middle-class lifestyles. They pursue such careers as educators, doctors, administrators, social workers, managers, youth leaders, tradesmen, law enforcement officers, among many other professions. They have stable family lives and see to it that their children get good educations, which for most involves college. They remain in close touch with one another, maintaining the relationships forged at CYCLE all those years ago. Arguably, these life outcomes represent a significant return on investment, especially when one considers that at its peak enrollment in 1992, the program, funded primarily by private donors, operated on an annual budget of $1.4 million (around $2.2 million in 2017 dollars).

GOALS

Three broad goals shape this book:

- *to look inside the black box of program processes and principles.* Although research considering the operation and outcomes of afterschool programs or out-of-school opportunities has begun to provide details on program activities and strategies, few accounts provide concrete details about what goes on inside effective programs—or what's inside the black box, the space between program inputs and participant outputs.[7] Much research on afterschool programs remains either variable based and purely correlational (time spent on mentoring activities, staff-youth ratios, race/ethnicity) or is focused on general features (program site, youth involvement opportunities, staffing practices) as they relate to various youth outcomes (retention rates, academics, health). Largely missing in this literature are close-grained descriptions of *how* activities are carried out and structured.[8] For instance, what do mentors and mentees do together? How do youth and adults interact in supportive relationships? What are core principles guiding behavior for both youth and adults? The narratives in this book take up these black box questions from the perspective of both former staff and former participants.

- *to understand factors affecting sustained positive outcomes.* CYCLE youth appeared to be headed for productive lives when they left the program in the late 1980s or early 1990s. Twenty-five and thirty years later, nearly all stayed on the positive paths they chose. Few long-term accounts exist to consider questions of sustainability, questions important to any youth program. But these issues are especially significant in the context of concentrated poverty and around worries that at-risk youth will fall back into predicted behaviors of dependence, crime, or substance abuse. CYCLE participants not only kept alive the values, perspectives, and ambitions they acquired in the program, but they passed them on to their children. What happened at CYCLE that supported this extraordinary departure from the expected Cabrini-Green youth trajectory? Former CYCLE participants provide persuasive, consistent explanations of what mattered most to their lives and why. These accounts provide compelling evidence in favor of youth-centered, relationship-based, out-of-school programs focused on providing opportunities for adolescents.
- *to move CYCLE's experience from being exceptional to a new norm for youth program approaches.* Founder Greg Darnieder has often said that putting together a program like CYCLE "is not rocket science"; nor does a CYCLE-like opportunity need to break the bank. What would it take to create more programs reflecting CYCLE's core design principles? What are the implications of CYCLE's experience for funders, policy makers, and practitioners?

The individual reports that make up this book consider participants' journeys from CYCLE and Cabrini-Green to their lives as adults.[9] These alums' life accounts provide powerful and important stories of how a youth program operated with such effectiveness in a setting of extreme poverty, violence, and crime and fostered positive change that was sustained for a lifetime and across generations. A life course perspective departs from research or evaluation approaches that tally accounts of program effects at completion or one or three or five years later. It considers the significance of an experience such as CYCLE participation as seen in individuals' choices and actions over time and in different contexts. This viewpoint invites questions of how and why an experience affected individuals' choices and action and consideration of whether or not those consequences continued across time.[10]

However, several somewhat different approaches gather under the life course umbrella.[11] This book takes a *life story* approach, attending to how young people's choices and actions reflected relations with the various environments through which they moved to create a life pathway.

WHY THIS BOOK NOW?

The growing inequalities in the education and economic outcomes of poor urban youth alarm educators, social planners, and civic leaders, but efforts to stem or reverse them generally have fallen short. With few exceptions, public and private investments in areas such as education, housing, or mentoring mostly have failed to disrupt the high rates of school failure, violence, and incarceration for low-income urban youth of color.

Not a single-focus youth program, CYCLE took a whole-child, comprehensive view of what Cabrini-Green youth needed in order to imagine, reach for, and attain lives different from those forecast for them. Program leaders believed that all children, regardless of the conditions in which they grow up, share the same foundational needs and that the concentrated poverty of the Cabrini-Green environment undermined families' ability to meet those needs. In response, CYCLE developed a portfolio of youth development supports typically unavailable to families living in distressed neighborhoods.

Although the program operated in the Cabrini-Green neighborhood, CYCLE took a *place-conscious* rather than a place-based approach to identifying and providing these supports for the hundreds of young people who came through its doors. Staff pursued connections and opportunities across Chicago, the region, and even the nation. They worked to integrate and supplement the resources of multiple organizations and public and private institutions—schools, social services, recreational opportunities, nonprofit agencies, and employers—to create an array of opportunities for CYCLE youth. The program's regional perspective aimed not just to provide a neighborhood-based refuge but to connect young people with resources outside the psychological and practical constraints of Cabrini-Green.

The practices CYCLE alums said enabled their positive life outcomes and the design principles staff deemed foundational to program operations provide important lessons for policy makers, educators, community activists, funders, youth agency directors, and others who want to learn what makes a youth organization effective in changing the lives of low-income, marginalized youth today.

This long-term account also raises questions for researchers and evaluators about *when* and *how* to consider program effects. The usual impact assessment conducted after program involvement ended would have missed many important CYCLE-shaped outcomes; it would have missed, for instance, how one participant who became a teen mom in the mid-1990s finished her EdD in 2015. The life stories told here challenge researchers to attend to more than quantitative tallies of program outcomes, such as graduation rates and college degrees, to consider evidence of program values enacted in life choices, such as family stability, careers, and community engagement.

A lot has happened in the out-of-school time (OST) arena since we set out to learn about effective programs for urban youth in the mid-1980s. The field has expanded exponentially, and much has been learned about the characteristics of effective OST initiatives. Other sources offer narrative accounts and research reviews of youth programs that made a difference for poor youth and discuss elements associated with high-quality programs.[12] This book, however, is distinctive in its follow-up account of participants' lives more than three decades later and their reflections on how and why program elements enabled them to attain their positive futures and build important supports for their children.

Finally, *You Can't Be What You Can't See* makes a significant argument about how to frame policies intended to benefit youth living in high-poverty settings. It pushes explicitly against culture of poverty explanations for the distressing social, education, and economic outcomes reported for poor youth of color, most especially black males. According to a culture of poverty perspective, not only does poverty largely determine an individual's life outcomes, but the negative outcomes associated with growing up in concentrated poverty predictably persist across generations. This book puts forth importantly different assumptions to guide youth policy and practice. These compelling life accounts show that these inequities result not from a culture of poverty but, rather, as the title of the book suggests, from a *poverty of opportunities* that could allow young people to see and take a different path.[13]

ORGANIZATION

You Can't Be What You Can't See proceeds in three parts. Following a portrait of life in Cabrini-Green based on accounts of social historians and on the lived experiences of CYCLE kids and senior staff, Part I describes the CYCLE program—its activities, core design principles, and the opportunities offered participating youth. Part II takes up the three factors alums named as reasons why their involvement with CYCLE constituted a turning point in their lives and set them on a positive, productive pathway out of poverty: exposure, mentoring, and community. Part III considers what made CYCLE effective and discusses implications for practice, policy, and research.

Because CYCLE operated in an especially difficult, dangerous, and toxic environment for children and adolescents, it is important to understand how CYCLE functioned in this context, what made it so effective, and why its accomplishments are extraordinary.

CHAPTER 1

Growing Up in Cabrini-Green

The Cabrini-Green public housing project stood just a mile from the elegant shops, prestigious offices, and luxury hotels of Chicago's Magnificent Mile and the nearby expensive lakefront residential properties known as the Gold Coast. The bleak contrast between Cabrini-Green and the wealth and power just a few blocks away prompted many of its residents to make mocking reference to their low-income, African American neighborhood as the Soul Coast.[1]

The Chicago Housing Authority (CHA) constructed the Cabrini-Green public housing project to replace the crime-ridden slum widely known as Little Hell with clean, family-friendly, affordable housing. Opened in 1942, the Frances Cabrini Homes was a 586-unit row home complex named after a renowned nun who gave medical care to the North Side Italian immigrants. Jammed into just two square blocks, the Cabrini low-rise apartments resembled army barracks, and by the late 1940s the Cabrini row homes were full, primarily with white families. As those families began to leave for the suburbs in the 1950s, low-income black families, many on public assistance, moved in.

As black migration from the South to Chicago continued during the 1950s, housing needs grew pressing. Although CHA planners thought that the two-story row houses were the best option for families with children, they concluded that costs made them unfeasible. In 1958 the CHA completed the Cabrini Extension: 1,896 units in fifteen high-rise structures that ranged from seven to nineteen stories. In 1962 a second eight-building high-rise project opened, the 1,096-unit William Green Homes, named after the depression-era president of the American Federation of Labor.

In the beginning, Cabrini-Green offered a hopeful setting for low-income Chicago families. Craig Nash, a CYCLE alum who became coordinator of the I Have A Dream scholarship program, remembered his family's enthusiasm on moving to Cabrini-Green in the late 1960s: "It was paradise compared to what you had before. When the high-rises first went up, they were beautiful. There were trees, there were families—mother, father, children, working families. I can tell you this from firsthand experience. We lived in a co-op tenement [before moving to Cabrini-Green] where there was one bathroom on the floor. And that's what people were used to. Then the projects went up, they were like, 'Oh, we got a bathroom and we got bedrooms and all this kinda stuff. It's paradise.'" Sharon Williams, the mother of former CYCLE Junior Staffer Gloria Purifoy, lived in the Reds high-rise for more than fifty years. She also recalled her youth in Cabrini in the 1960s: "We had a mom and a dad in the home... It was a nice place to live. There was a sense of family." Many long-time residents remembered a pride in the neighborhood in those days; homes and apartments were well maintained, and the CHA levied fines for littering.

Yet, CHA regulations created the economic segregation in Cabrini-Green that over time shifted the make-up of Cabrini-Green from the 1960s-era community of two-parent, working families to a community in the 1980s largely comprised of single mothers struggling to make ends meet. Sharon noted, "As time went on that balance changed. It became a community at odds with itself... It just became like a lawless community... So you had that sense of family, but then on the other side of that, some of those same people who were out getting into things that they shouldn't, drugs, gangs, they were some of the most loving people with their families and their neighbors."

In 1981–82 the income eligibility for residency in the housing project ranged from $13,750 for a unit housing one person to $24,500 for a unit housing eight or more.[2] The monthly rent equaled

20 percent of gross adjusted income, major deductions being 10 percent of gross income for an elderly resident in the household, 5 percent for a nonelderly adult, and $300 for each child. Rents during this period averaged less than $100 a month. As a result of this CHA policy, 100 percent of Cabrini-Green residents were low-income, and the majority were unemployed and on some form of public assistance. And most residents were black.

By the late 1970s and early 1980s, Cabrini-Green stood as an economically, racially, and socially segregated residential setting. The second-largest public housing project in Chicago—only Robert Taylor Homes was bigger—it included 81 high-, mid-, and low-rise buildings and covered 70 acres. Approximately 10,000 children lived in the nearly all-black project in the early 1980s, making up around 70 percent of the registered population of 13,000, though many more people—by some estimates between 3,000 and 5,000—lived there unofficially. Over 90 percent of registered Cabrini-Green households were headed by a single female, and 84 percent were on welfare, of which 81 percent were families with children.[3] In addition to struggling with difficult social problems, Cabrini-Green residents generally were poorly educated; on average, adults read on a sixth-grade level and had weak job-related skills.

The housing project soon became as dangerous as the slum it replaced. Although Cabrini-Green was intended for families with children, the high-rise project introduced structural disadvantages for child rearing. The challenges of supervising children from seven or fifteen or nineteen stories up were soon apparent, as was the community's inability to superintend and control teenage groups, most especially gangs. One account of Cabrini-Green's social context likened the high-rises to a "hive swarming with children."[4] Jesse White, the official and unofficial coach to hundreds of males growing up in Cabrini-Green, and later an Illinois state representative and secretary of state, observed how difficult it was for parents to discipline their kids in the housing project: "A mother cleaning house on the 16th floor has a hard time knowing what her child is up to outside.

And outside, of course, are gangs and drug dealers."[5] Commentators concluded that "far from being a solution to the complex urban problems of poverty and racial segregation, the Cabrini-Green high-rises are the modern version of the 'relief shanties' which plagued Little Hell."[6]

For residents, the Cabrini-Green housing community, bounded by four blocks, formed three distinct neighborhoods: the red-brick high-rise Cabrini Extension units, known as "the Reds"; the William Green Homes, called "the Whites" because of their white-brick exterior; and the Francis Cabrini Homes, referred to as "the row houses." Residents considered the row houses the most prestigious neighborhood. Cyril Nichols, who was a CYCLE Junior Staffer, remembered his family's move from the Reds to the row houses when he was three: "Moving to the row houses then was like a big deal. If the projects were seen as the lower class, the row houses were seen as middle class 'cause you had a front door, back door, yard, upstairs, downstairs, and a parking spot." CYCLE alums recounted a clear pecking order in this community of poverty. As one said, "Living in the row houses was way cooler, better than living in the high rises. Kids would tease about that."

Some CYCLE youth, such as Shree Green and Tamiko Jones, grew up in the Town and Garden Apartments, residences not officially part of Cabrini-Green but connected socially through family and friendship networks. Tamiko said that living across Division Street in Town and Garden "wasn't an easy walk either . . . it was tough over there too. But there was the idea that the high rises were a little tougher because you had to get on that elevator or walk those stairs—those kids had a different edge about themselves, a toughness about them."

Originally named the Marshall Field Garden Apartments, built by philanthropist Marshall Field III in 1929, this complex was comprised of 628 low-income units in five-story walk-up buildings that ran the equivalent of two city blocks along North Sedgwick Street.

The residential project changed ownership and names several times as repeated efforts to attract more middle-income, racially diverse families proved unsuccessful. By the mid-to-late 1960s, the ten buildings, renamed Town and Gardens, were badly deteriorating and were occupied primarily by black households on public assistance. Though not directly adjacent to the Cabrini-Green development during CYCLE's existence, Town and Garden was considered part of the Cabrini neighborhood by its residents and as not much safer than the Cabrini-Green project.

Division Street divided the Cabrini-Green community physically and socially. Crossing Division was perilous because of warring gangs on each side. Residents in the Reds and the row houses attended different schools than residents in the Whites on the other side of Division. Gang affiliations also determined the lived geography of Cabrini-Green. The Reds were dominated by the Black Stones, Cobra Stones, and Vice Lords. The Disciples controlled the Whites and the row houses. Town and Garden was Black Stones/El Runkn territory. Mohawk, a street that circled the row houses, was the Vice Lords' domain. Gang affiliations also dictated clothing color choices: the Disciples wore blue that could be mixed with black, Black Stones red and black, and Vice Lords gold and black. All residents avoided public spaces—parks, blacktops—on both sides of Division Street fearing gang warfare, snipers, or physical assault.

Media at the time widely denigrated Cabrini-Green, claiming it was "notorious, infamous . . . a sad and dangerous place spoiled with poverty, crime, violence, drugs and gangs."[7] And when the housing project's end seemed inevitable in the mid-1970s and early 1980s, the CHA disinvested and pulled back maintenance support. The Reds and the Whites became home to roaches and rats, broken pipes, windows and elevators, vandalized wiring and plumbing, unreliable heating and indifferent garbage collection. Cabrini-Green, once considered a blessing by poor Chicago residents, became an emblem of urban desolation.

"Neighborhoods are not accidents. They are the products of systematic sorting processes."[8] Tim Huizenga, an early CYCLE board member and board chair in the mid-1980s, agreed.

> I realized how difficult life was in these public housing high-rises and how CHA had built them mostly to effectively seal off low-income black people from the rest of the city. For a while, the high-rises were decent places to live. But for a variety of reasons, eventually they became the place where people that just had no options were living and all the problems that were associated with life there . . . Managing public housing was way down the list of [the CHA's] goals or their priorities. So, really, I think they gave up around 1975 in terms of actually trying to make public housing work. And after that, it was just going through the motions.

Indeed, as Cabrini-Green's high-rise buildings degenerated, vacancies rose. In 2000 the CHA developed plans to demolish the existing high-rise buildings and replace them with mixed-income and upscale condominiums.[9] The last high-rise came down in 2011.

LIFE IN CABRINI-GREEN

CYCLE alums had much to say about what it was like to grow up in Cabrini-Green in the 1970s and 1980s, and they provided consistent accounts of their schools and day-to-day life in the neighborhood. Nearly all went to public grammar (K–8) schools in Cabrini-Green, all of their families struggled to make ends meet, few had a consistent or attentive father in their lives, and all grew up aware of dangers of violence and drug dealing on the streets and in their buildings. Tragedy was endemic in their neighborhood.

The Schools

CYCLE alums agreed that the public schools serving Cabrini-Green youth at that time were substandard and signaled low-expectations for their futures. And even those alums who attended private schools through CYCLE's scholarship programs or more selective public schools experienced overt racial discrimination.

"Schools that serve low-income kids of color don't always have the highest expectations of them," said Bernard McCune, urban educator and director of CYCLE's Education Assistance Limited (EAL) scholarship program. The schools attended by most Cabrini-Green youth were "borderline functional," in the opinion of one CYCLE alum. "I was considered at the top of my class but I came out of the Chicago Public School system borderline illiterate," noted another. And one alum said that the schools serving Cabrini-Green "were among the worst of the worst," echoing US Secretary of Education William Bennett, who declared in 1987, "I am not sure there's a system as bad as the Chicago system."[10]

Most Cabrini-Green youth attended Jenner, Manierre, or Byrd grammar schools, and those living in the Whites went to Schiller. Some, like Tamiko, attended St. Joseph's, a private Catholic school across North Orleans Street from the Byrd Academy and the Whites; and a few were bused to a Lutheran school on the West Side. On graduating grammar school, Cabrini-Green youth were assigned to one of two high schools: those living south of Oak Street went to Wells, and those living north of Oak went to Lincoln Park. These high schools ranked among the lowest performing in Chicago. For example, throughout the early 1990s, graduation rates at Lincoln Park High School hovered at around 50 percent, and Wells High School graduated only about 40 percent of its students.

Though several CYCLE alums, especially those who were academically successful, had positive memories of particular teachers, most recalled Cabrini-Green public grammar schools as poorly maintained, uninspired settings staffed by teachers who cared but expected little of them. It seemed to them that CPS had disinvested in the neighborhood schools, just as the CHA had disinvested in the Cabrini-Green housing project. A 2007 account of the conditions at Byrd Community Academy differed little from descriptions of the school CYCLE kids made two decades earlier: "Classrooms were no place to learn. Lights worked sporadically. No natural light entered foggy, cracked windows pocked with bullet holes . . . Bathrooms were dysfunctional and filthy . . . the school had no lunchroom, no gym, and no auditorium."[11]

Graduates of all the Cabrini-Green grammar schools, even St. Joseph's, recalled teachers' generally low expectations. Reflecting on her experience at St. Joe's, Tamiko said, "I don't think I learned much of anything . . . And we were out of control . . . the principal didn't have any control of us." Some described racial slurs and race-based sorting. Former Junior Staffer Cyril Nichols remembered his white seventh-grade teacher referring to him as "a monkey with a tail. My brother said another teacher in Jenner made exactly the same comment to him. I didn't know what it meant, but [in college I] read something about Africans having tails, like it was the sign of the beast." Richard Blackmon, who lived in the Whites and went to Schiller, remembered teachers at Lane Technical High School making embarrassing references to both his race and his Cabrini-Green address. Richard said that when he asked about purchasing drafting paper for the class, one teacher said, "We don't accept food stamps." And on seeing Richard come in on a Monday with new clothes, another teacher quipped, "The check must have come on Friday."

The few CYCLE alums who attended Chicago's more competitive high schools, such as Lane Tech, found that they were far behind academically, especially in math, when they entered high school. Blackmon, who went on to graduate from Notre Dame Law School, remembered, "Basically I was still in elementary school when I got to high school. I realized quickly coming from Schiller to Lane Tech I was behind academically. When I left Schiller we were still doing fractions. At Lane Tech all of my classmates had already taken algebra and started on geometry. You just didn't get the same foundation [in Cabrini schools]." Tamiko Jones, who attended the competitive Providence–St. Mel private high school on a Schuessler/CYCLE scholarship, recalled struggling at St. Joe's: "I missed a lot of stuff in sixth, seventh, eighth grade. I remember my mom having to teach me fractions at maybe the eighth grade. I should have learned that stuff [before then]!"

CYCLE alums contend that the poor quality of the grammar schools serving Cabrini-Green youngsters contributed significantly to the neighborhood's high school dropout rates. Bernard McCune, who excelled in school, estimated that between 75 percent and 80 percent of his grammar school classmates dropped out, and he saw the path to dropping out of school as having started early: "Probably around third grade you figure out if [school is for you]. I really do believe that a lot of kids drop out in the third, fourth, fifth grade. They just hang around for another eight to ten years. They think that game isn't for me and they don't have people who can reinforce that they can achieve." Tamiko also noted how, "by the time you're in fourth grade—I hate to say it—you are kinda really on your route. That's [when they got] their expectations for themselves. Fourth, fifth, those are tough grades."

CYCLE's director of volunteers, Michelle McConnell, recalled comments made by volunteer tutors that "sometime around third or fourth grade, the light in their eyes goes out and they disconnect from school" because they were getting little affirmation that they can succeed in school. Alumnus David Gates, now an executive in the Community and Economic Development Association of Cook County, thought that teachers paid attention only to the very best students, leaving the rest to manage the "total shambles" of the school: "At Jenner they had like a ranking system when they rank every student and basically the top test kids get recognition. The rest, well, you know."

In addition to place, race was also a factor in these youths' education options and choices. For instance, one high-achieving CYCLE alum, Shree Green, turned down a scholarship to the prestigious Latin School of Chicago because "people didn't look like me there. It's like, how did this black person show up? You know what I mean, feeling racially insecure? And I started to hear more about 'they' and 'them' and, you know, 'blacks.' So it wasn't right. Not for me."

Concern about gangs figured in every trip to and from school for Cabrini-Green kids. Shree Green, a graduate of DePaul University and an entrepreneur, remembered being dropped off at her aunt's row house so she could walk to Byrd with her cousins: "We couldn't walk from where we lived in Town and Garden [because it was] gang territory." She remembered many times being "rushed back into school because of gunfire . . . It almost seemed that they would wait for us to get out of school to start gang activity . . . We look at the news and see things happening in other countries, developing countries, but that type of stuff was literally happening right in the heart of Chicago."

Bernard McCune's memories of Manierre also involved gang shootings and death: "I would go to school, it'd be like, 'they found Dubaz's body there, they found this person's body there, and in that field they found somebody's body there' . . . I remember that just being ordinary. It was not uncommon for me to go to school and come across a crowd and a dead body." Like others, he also recalled gangbangers' brazen presence in and around school grounds:

> I have a vivid memory of playing basketball at Manierre—just out there shooting baskets by myself. A bunch of guys in a gang, older guys, and so they were like the gang leaders, just walked through the basketball court. One of them has a shotgun at his side, the other one has a pistol, the other one looks like he has a machine gun. And this is in broad daylight, 12:00, 1:00 in the afternoon, and they looked at me and said, "What's up, shorty?" and kept walking. They're going towards North Avenue, so I know they're going to shoot some Disciples. I really felt like I was in a warzone. 'Cause it's broad daylight and they just walked past like it was nothing. And I mean, they didn't fear that the police would be around or anything. They looked at me and said, "Hey," nodded at me. I nodded at them and [thought] "this is crazy."

Expectations and Social Norms

If their schools held low expectations for them, many youth growing up in Cabrini-Green during the 1980s also had low expectations for themselves, which contributed to the challenges in achieving personal growth and social mobility. One example of this is how more than one CYCLE graduate characterized expected futures for black males in the neighborhood as "dead or in jail by twenty-one. Yeah, or done on drugs."

Another indication of low expectations for the future was the high rate of teen pregnancy. One Cabrini-Green pastor saw pregnancies among young girls as a "tremendous problem; it is the single largest occupation in Cabrini."[12] Single teen mothers—children having children—were common in Cabrini-Green, as were grandmothers or older siblings taking care of the babies. Early pregnancy was commonplace. For some, having a baby was seen as a way to "get out of the house . . . get your own check, and do your own thing."[13] Many young women saw having a child as bringing meaning to lives that otherwise lacked direction or significance. Child-bearing at a young age responds to a deep longing for something positive to do, a way to make a difference. To this point, sociologists Kathryn Edin and Maria Kefalas interviewed low-income single mothers over a period of five years; they heard that impoverished women view childlessness as "one of the greatest tragedies in life . . . For the poor, childbearing often rises to the top of the list of potential meaning-making activities for mere lack of competition."[14]

Birth control of any form was uncommon. Young men in Cabrini generally did not use condoms because they were not considered "manly." And expectations about a short life defused concerns about STDs. Young women seldom used birth control because of the cost of the necessary doctor visits and pills. The norm of teen pregnancy figured prominently, along with the status pregnancy afforded both the young women and the young men. Some young men saw young women's use of birth control as an affront and as a signal of unfaithfulness. Disturbing accounts of young women living in places similar to those of Cabrini-Green tell of boyfriends' or husbands' rage and accusations of "being a ho" or a "slut" at any suggestion of using birth control.[15] Pat Ford, a CYCLE alum who became its academic director, saw early pregnancy as routine in Cabrini-Green because so many of the single moms living there had themselves been teen mothers.

> A lot of things are normalized [in the Cabrini-Green community], like an early pregnancy, if the mom got pregnant early and other people in the neighborhood got pregnant early, it's not seen as a setback in certain families. It's like, "Oh, okay, so and so is pregnant," and it's just a matter of fact. Even if a mom got pregnant early [herself], some mothers are able to use that as a lesson and really tell the story, like, "Hey, this wasn't the way to do it." Other moms think, "Everybody is comfortable, this is just our life. This is just how it is and this is what happens and we just keep moving forward." So, I think that it's a mind-set, too.

College rarely figured into the futures of the Cabrini-Green youth. Gang-life claimed many boys, and girls who did graduate from high school were expected to get a job and contribute to family finances. "My mom and others were from the South," Shree Green said. "They work. That's it."

Everyday Violence

Violence permeated the lives of children growing up in Cabrini-Green and was recalled by the CYCLE graduates in the starkest terms. "I don't know a [Cabrini-Green] family that has not had a wounded soldier." And Cyril Nichols said, "Cabrini-Green is an evil place . . . it just takes lives."

National news trumpeted Cabrini-Green violence during the 1980s and 1990s: the 1992 sniper killing of seven-year-old Dantrell Davis as he walked to Jenner School holding his mother's hand; the

1997 savage rape and torture of nine-year-old "Girl X" in a Cabrini stairwell, an assault that left her paralyzed, blind, and unable to speak. These horrific events were unexceptional; Cabrini-Green residents navigated such violence and danger every day. Richard Blackmon related how his football coaches came onto the field to tell him that his brother was dead—"I said, 'Which one?' They looked at me like that's an odd response. I said, 'Well, I've got two that are living that life.'" CYCLE alum reflected on the violence, saying, "Community members almost became desensitized to it." "You learn to expect it," said a woman who grew up in Cabrini-Green, be it a snatched purse, a beating, or a rape.

Violence occurred not just in the parks and on the blacktops of Cabrini-Green but also in the stairs and elevators of the high-rises. It was common knowledge that lightbulbs would be unscrewed to darken stairwells to facilitate "jumps" as residents climbed the stairs to their apartments. The elevators, when they worked, also were settings for attacks. One former resident remembered seeing his first dead body in a Cabrini-Green elevator.[16] As someone darkly noted, "The most dangerous public transportation system in Chicago is the Cabrini-Green elevator."[17]

Youth growing up in the housing project had to adopt critical survival skills, including knowing what to do when the shooting started. Snipers were an ever-present threat in Cabrini-Green—the Black Stones occupied the Reds, the Disciples the Whites. Only brave souls crossed the blacktop between the two high-rise complexes. Bernard McCune recalled how nobody played on the basketball courts in Cabrini near the blacktop and in Seward Park because of the sniper fire and said that "people getting killed was part of just ordinary everyday life, and so was knowing what to do when there was shooting—to get down or get low. It was so part of the life that you could sense it, you knew when it was about to happen, when it was about to go down." Don Smith, a CYCLE alum who became a Chicago law enforcement officer, recalled, "You hit the floor, and when [the shooting stopped], you checked to see if anyone you were with was shot."

In the late 1980s, Cabrini-Green was also a hotspot for nonlethal and drug-related crimes. Crime data from Cabrini-Green looked strikingly different than reports from other gang territories during this time. Many Chicago neighborhoods, such as North and South Lawndale, were troubled primarily with either nonlethal or drug-related crimes. In contrast, Cabrini-Green's gang-related crimes involved a high concentration of both drug and nonlethal crimes as well as a higher incidence of gang-related homicides.[18]

The CYCLE community suffered losses from gang violence. Fifth grader Latisha Crosby was one. She was shot and killed in 1984 by a stray bullet from rival gang fire while jumping double Dutch in the first-floor breezeway of her high-rise. Greg kept one of her drawings in his office, a picture of herself and her family with the words "God loves us all." It was the last art project she completed at CYCLE's summer day camp.

Cabrini-Green parents taught their kids street survival skills at an early age, including finding alternative routes to various destinations. The safe way to avoid snipers, recalled one alum, was to "walk the L-shaped path through the neighborhood" to get to school, friends, or neighborhood activities. Tamiko Jones said, "You learned how to take the roundabout way to get to 515 Oak, where CYCLE was, as opposed to walking through" Cabrini and the blacktop. For many youth, some parts of Cabrini-Green were just off limits. For instance, David Gates remembered that he and others growing up in the row houses were not allowed to go into the high-rises or to play in Seward Park.

Older siblings, too, taught their brothers and sisters the ways of the streets. Tamiko recalled how she trained her younger siblings to run: "'When I say run, I want you to run!' We had to cross Division Street to come back from mass at St. Joseph's . . . One day some boys decided to start to start throwing bottles, and I knew eventually they were gonna fight me. I said, 'Run!' They took off running . . . The three boys just started punching me. I think I had a busted lip or something like that . . . I also decided I'm done wearing gold chains [after having them snatched several times]." Sometimes gangbangers themselves looked out for the "shorties" (the younger kids) when trouble was about to start. One chronicler of life in Cabrini wrote, "I remember how they use to tell me, 'Lil James, go in the house . . . We 'bout to be shooting.'"[19] Bernard McCune learned never to acknowledge his brother, who was a leader in the Black Stones, since the Disciples dominated parts of Cabrini he traveled through every day. "He told me if I am south of Division, where I spent a lot of time playing basketball in Seward Park, and I see him, never to speak to him. This is the closest person in the world to me, and most people didn't know we were related 'cause we lived in different worlds."

Social Stigma

Living in Cabrini-Green "was like the bottom of the ladder socially in Chicago," said Don Smith. CYCLE participants who attended private or competitive public high schools recounted the strategies they used to conceal that they were from Cabrini-Green. Tamiko Jones told us that she used to miss the CYCLE van intentionally, "so that I wouldn't have to be dropped off at Providence–St. Mel, because of the stigma—everybody would know that van was from Cabrini . . . I would never say I was from Cabrini. I would say I was from Near North Side . . . My girlfriend, who was from over there, she was like, 'Girl, you ain't tell me you live in the projects.'" Similarly, a CYCLE alum who was a successful student at a magnet school remembered being challenged by two white girls as she prepared to board the bus headed back to Cabrini: "'You're on that bus? You don't look like you come from there.' I'm like, 'How am I supposed to look?' They were used to Cabrini kids being in the lower-ability reading and math groups . . . Being on the Cabrini bus negatively typed me."

For many Cabrini-Green youth, the social stigma of living in Cabrini-Green seemed insurmountable. A crafts program leader at CYCLE recalled one teen's frustration when she asked, "How am I ever gonna get out of here? When I go to a job and put down my address, my app goes in the junk pile."

Urban designer and planner Lawrence Vale contends that, with the possible exception of prisons and mental hospitals, no place stigmatizes people in as many ways as do distressed, deteriorating inner-city housing projects.[20] Low-income "project" residents are often characterized in the media, political speeches, and living room exchanges as lazy, free-loading, substance-addicted, sexually promiscuous, criminally inclined individuals taking advantage of public largesse. According to historian and social theorist Michael Katz, "The undeserving poor, the culture of poverty, and the underclass are moral statuses identified by the source of dependence, the behavior with which it is associated, its transmission to children, and its crystallization into cultural patterns."[21] And these characteristics, typically attributed to welfare recipients, especially those corralled into bleak public inner-city housing such as Cabrini-Green, negatively shape young people's sense of worth and their dreams for the future.

The Lure of the Gangs

Virtually every CYCLE participant we interviewed had a gang-involved sibling, relative, or friend who became a "wounded soldier," was killed, or went to prison. The high unemployment rates of black youth and young adults during the 1970s and 1980s fueled gangs' growth and power. During this time, more than 25 percent of Chicago's factories closed, and various fiscal crises trimmed all public services.[22] This bleak economic environment contrasted starkly with the postwar boom that had drawn black families from the South to Chicago.

For many youth, the pull of the gangs and the streets was just too hard to resist. Bernard McCune watched his beloved older brother become deeply involved with the Black Stones as a sniper and receive a forty-year prison sentence. He understood the lure both from personal experience and as an urban educator.

> I think that all children want attention and reinforcement that they are valuable. I was able to find mine in a lot of different ways that are considered positive. My brother was able to find that through people

in the gangs. The older guys in the gangs will mentor somebody. They will say, "Hey, little fella, I'll show you how to do this, that, and the other. Come join my family, be a part of my family. We have nothing but love for each other, our brothers. I'm gonna show you how to make money or do whatever." So they will really mentor somebody. So my brother was able to get the strokes and reinforcement of being a big guy in the gang.

For many Cabrini youth, joining a gang provided them with a sense of belonging, worth, and identity. Many of the participants also pointed to boredom and the absence of positive alternatives as major reasons why young boys got involved in gangs. Bernard described the dreadful consequences of boredom:

If you're on the street, kids would get bored and be hanging out, saying, "Hey, we don't have anything to do, let's go beat up somebody." So I literally remember kids doing that to one of the really smart guys in my classroom—"Let's go beat up him and his brother and his sister." And they just went and they beat this kid up. This kid ended up joining the gang a little bit later after that, I guess because he didn't want to get beat up. And he was a really, really smart kid. He ended up joining that gang and he went to jail for a robbery or something. Then he went back to jail for being a serial rapist or something. He'll spend the rest of his life in jail.

As this highlights, gang membership often was forced on youth, since resistance usually was met with intimidation, confrontation, or bodily harm. CYCLE alums' accounts of gang recruitment and activities in Cabrini-Green reinforce the conclusion of one observer of Chicago's black street gangs that, in "some communities, it got to a point where being a gang member was the safest thing to do."[23]

Benefits of membership mattered as well. Craig Nash stressed how hard it was for Cabrini-Green youth to walk away from the gangs once they had a taste of "the life": "Because at first, okay, you're doing that and you do this, too. And then, it's like, 'man, come on, we're getting ready to go do this.' And then you're experimenting with stuff, whether it's alcohol, whether it's marijuana, whether it's harder drugs. Now it's even more of a pull because you see this as excitement, as fun, and that pull is serious." Schools served as major sites for gang recruitment. Turf identification and declaring gang affiliation was a rite of passage for many Cabrini-Green boys as they graduated from grammar school. For many, affiliating with a gang was about protection now that "childhood" was over: "At thirteen years old I had to get on some type of side so I could be protected in school [and not] get beat up."[24] Craig's younger brother turned to a gang for protection when Craig was no longer there to walk with him to school. "Up until then it was really just a normal childhood for me."

> So when I left grammar school and then he was left to the neighborhood, he would get in fights. And whereas I could pretty much handle myself, at first he couldn't handle himself, so he would get beat up by girls. He would come home and his face would be all scratched up, because that's what they did back then. And I guess, finally, he just got tired of it and he started running with some guys and developing a little reputation. So, the reputation was big for him. "Nobody's ever going to do this to me again. My big brother's not here to protect me. I'm going to get some other big brothers."

For some males growing up in Cabrini-Green, gang membership provided status and protection not only for themselves but also for their younger siblings. CYCLE alum Lloyd Rogers, who now is a law enforcement officer in an Illinois youth detention center, explained the expectations held in the projects for the oldest brother: "It's hard. You're supposed to be the responsible one. My brother said that he joined a gang so I wouldn't have to. Nobody bothered me either. My brother just took up for me; that was his role . . . He had to fight because he was the oldest." Bernard McClure's older brother saw his role in those same terms. So did Richard Blackmon's: "Nobody ever bothered me. I never could understand why. My brother called me a couple of months ago. I said, 'I wanna ask you something: Why did nobody ever bother me going back and forth?' He said, 'I made it clear to them if they touched a hair on your head, I would not only kill them, but I'd kill everybody in their families.' So that's why I had kind of free passage back and forth."

For others, keeping with "the life" was primarily about economic survival. Richard Blackmon recalled, "I'll never forget my brother—the one that's still alive—said to me, 'You gotta understand, this is about shoes.' I said, 'What?' He said, 'You get shoes on your feet the way you can get them. I'm not smart like you. I'm not at school like you. I can't play football like you. I've gotta figure out a way to get shoes on my feet and keep shoes on my kids' feet. This is the way I do it.' So we never had that conversation again."

A Sense of Community

Yet, all was not violence and despair in Cabrini-Green. "There was a major sense of community in Cabrini," remembered Michelle McConnell. Despite the troubled terrain and daily challenges, and even though some parents were addicted to drugs or alcohol or absent altogether, many felt, and continue to feel, strong ties to the community, the social networks and "family" that sustained them growing up. "People can say what they wanna say about Cabrini, but it was a community of people that cared."

The strong sense of mutual support and community that many youth and families experienced within Cabrini-Green went a long way to helping the young people cope with the daily stresses of violence and economic hardship. Greg Darnieder estimates that around 80 percent of the youth who attended CYCLE had that kind of stable support network from mothers, aunties, grandmothers, friends, and neighbors. Indeed, the women played a key role. Families sometimes moved between apartments so that mothers and daughters and extended families could be near each other and form their own community for safety, child rearing, shopping, and socializing. Moms could be counted on to provide a meal or shelter to a neighbor child when another mother was not able to. A number of CYCLE alum recounted how their mothers managed to provide for them despite meager economic resources. David Gates recalled family expeditions to buy shoes:

> When I was growing up, we were poor, but I never knew it. You know, I had no idea that I was poor. First day of school I always had new clothes. I don't know how my mom did it, having three brothers and two sisters and my mom by herself... But she always managed to get us whatever we needed... There was a sporting goods store called Morrie's Sports. It was maybe about ten blocks from our house. It was maybe once or twice a year my mom would march us, line us up, we would all walk over to Morrie's, and she would buy us shoes. But... our old shoes were so bad that we would literally put our new shoes on in the store and just leave our old shoes there.

Gloria Purifoy, whose mother raised three kids in the Reds, described the feeling of communal caretaking and normalcy she felt as a child:

> There was no sense of being poor. There was no sense of being lost and destitute... even in growing up in a community that was, for all intents and purposes, notorious to many, it did not always feel notorious to us. We had those experiences of being on the play lot, or riding your bike down your block. We had people see after you. On a warm summer day, or warm summer night meant that kids got to go ahead and get out and be under safe watch with the mothers of the community. Everybody knew when you weren't supposed to be out, because they knew that your mother had expectations. So there was a [rounding up of kids] at a certain time when the streetlights come on, there was a call.

In some neighborhoods, older youth came together to support younger kids and keep them from harm's way. Many who went through CYCLE remembered the group of successful high school athletes that called itself the UFOs (Unidentified Flying Objects). Cyril Nichols remembered:

> They weren't a gang. They were just a group of about eight guys that was like, "We're gonna look out for each other, but we're gonna look out for Cyril and them too in the neighborhood. We're not gonna allow them to be in the gang." Those guys wanted to be role models and leaders. And they were like our surrogate big brothers. They came and played basketball all the time. After the games were over we always sat there and talked and laughed and joked. And that was the thing, no matter where you were at, if one of them was around it was, "We're from the neighborhood, man."

Social and Institutional Isolation

But these close personal ties and protective support networks did not translate into assets that could connect youth to what they called "mainstream" society and its institutions. The close social organization supporting many CYCLE participants did not create a resource at the community level that young people and their families could use to shape their institutional contexts or futures. While many had tight connections *within* their neighborhoods, they had little social capital *outside* them.

Churches and schools were the only institutions operating in the housing project. Few of the elements that traditionally mark a neighborhood and foster communication existed in or around Cabrini-Green during the 1970s and 1980s. There were no department stores, supermarkets, movie houses, drug stores, banks or reputable small businesses that could provide neighborhood stability and jobs. Because of this, spatial distances reflected social distances. Residents had to travel outside the neighborhood to shop, find a job, go

The UFOs in 2017. This original group of Junior Staffers, who called themselves the UFOs (Unidentified Flying Objects), took it upon themselves to watch over younger CYCLE participants. The men in this group have maintained their friendship over thirty-plus years. From left to right: Andre Stokes, Don Smith, Johnny Calerway, Anthony Zin. At top: Brian Alston.

to work, have a meal (other than fast food). Cyril Nichols remembered the commercial destitution of Cabrini-Green: "You have unemployment. You don't have any community businesses. The only community businessman we knew was Mr. Nogales with the candy truck or Leon's Barbecue, which raised up everyone's blood pressure. Mr. Turner's corner store. But they started losing their businesses. The whole community structure was deteriorating every day." CHA's decision to locate poor, black families in a neighborhood of concentrated poverty produced social isolation for Cabrini-Green residents.[25] The 13,000 (or 15,000, depending on the source) residents of Cabrini-Green had limited opportunities to interact with people holding steady jobs or with Chicago's formal or informal employment networks. Furthermore, the economic segregation precipitated by CHA's housing eligibility rules created a community where youth had few models of successful pathways to high school graduation or postsecondary education, steady jobs, or resources for getting there. Joblessness and a lack of access, both social and physical, to the mainstream economy undermined their motivation to take school seriously and acquire the job-related skills, attitudes, and behaviors needed in the contemporary workplace.[26]

The social isolation of Cabrini-Green residents promoted an underground economy of drugs, school dropouts, lawlessness, and cynicism among youth about their futures. It meant that parents had limited access to institutional and material resources for themselves or their children. Gangs made crossing Division Street to go downtown a dangerous undertaking; many of the youth seldom ventured out of their neighborhood, not even to see Lake Michigan, little more than a mile away. As a result, the children of Cabrini-Green, exposed to greater risks growing up, also had fewer traditional supports for their healthy development.

Therefore, the social infrastructure and community-based resources that existed for families and children in Cabrini-Green had to be home grown and took the form of the informal social networks that enabled residents to get by but not to get ahead. These neighborhood assets did not translate into residents' ability to exercise social control over the institutions through which they moved or to influence the broader character of neighborhood life. As urban sociologist Robert Sampson notes, "Even if personal ties are strong in areas of concentrated disadvantage, they may be weakly tethered to collective action."[27]

CYCLE—DEVELOPMENTAL SUPPORTS AND BRIDGES TO THE MAINSTREAM

CHA housing policies assigned Cabrini-Green youth to concentrated poverty. But by itself, poverty serves as a less powerful impediment to healthy youth development than do the social and structural factors often associated with it. For instance, researchers examining neighborhoods as developmental contexts conclude that "forms of disadvantage other than poverty, such as the concentration of single-parent families, female-headed households, crime, and substandard housing, may constitute the most potent sources of risk for children and adolescents."[28] Developmental psychologists have compiled a similar catalog of environmental factors that place children at risk of poor cognitive and behavioral outcomes: low parental education, a household with four or more young children, residential mobility, being or having a single mother, teen parenthood, an unemployed parent, economic hardship.[29]

Researchers examining structural and compositional effects of neighborhoods on development also agree about other neighborhood and community characteristics that constitute powerful influences on the lives of children and families, most especially the quality of the physical environment and housing stock, housing density, and the availability of institutional resources.[30] These are associated with a "family" of problematic developmental outcomes—low birth weight, reduced cognitive ability and low verbal skills, teen pregnancy, school failure and dropout, violence and crime.[31]

Studies suggest that the *number* of risk factors may be more important for youth development than the precise nature of risk factors and that their negative effects on development are most powerful during infancy and early childhood and again in mid-to-late adolescence. All Cabrini-Green kids would have scored high on any tally of developmental risk factors, even with such positives as an involved parent or extended family networks considered.

Understanding the context of growing up in Cabrini-Green informs an understanding of why and how CYCLE mattered for the hundreds of young people who came through its doors. CYCLE was not a once-a-week program aimed primarily at addressing problems, such as poor academic performance. Nor was it a seasonal sports team focused on athletics but little else. CYCLE's programs and staff operated seven days a week, taking a comprehensive, positive youth development approach in tending to participants' success in school as well as to their involvement with fun activities, new things, and new places and the youths' personal lives.

CYCLE staff and mentors ensured emotional and physical safety; they made long-term commitments to supporting participants through whatever challenges they confronted in their schools or neighborhoods or at home. CYCLE staff intentionally provided the connections, knowledge, and supports absent in the youths' families and Cabrini-Green community—assets and expectations that enabled the young people to imagine and reach for futures different from those they saw in the corridors, schools, and streets around them. For almost all CYCLE participants, involvement with the program disrupted the grim futures of school failure, gang membership, or poverty predicted for them by virtue of growing up in Cabrini-Green. As more than one CYCLE alum said, "I would not have made it through Cabrini-Green without CYCLE."

PART I
THE CYCLE PROGRAM

Out-of-school time programs operate in communities across the country to provide school-aged youth with engaging activities and opportunities. The terms *out-of-school time* and *afterschool* often are used interchangeably, yet they describe programs that address different purposes and populations. Afterschool programs generally serve elementary and middle school children, most often on their school site from 3:00 to 6:00 p.m., whereas out-of-school time programs include before school, afterschool, and weekend programs as well as summer learning and recreational offerings. OST initiatives typically include formal, structured programs; some offer less-structured activities and drop-in settings.

OST program goals and content differ considerably, but most seek to provide learning, enrichment, and leadership opportunities to support academic success and overall positive development. Many programs designed for older youth have a specific focus, such as sports, the arts, service learning, mentoring, or internships, but few provide comprehensive supports for teens.

OST programs vary in how goals are framed. Those targeting middle and high school youth, for instance, sometimes focus on prevention (dropout, delinquency, pregnancy) or remediation (academic proficiency), and participation is often mandatory. In contrast, youth compete for spots in selective OST programs that identify participants based on distinguished performance in areas such as academics, the arts, or sports.[1]

OST program sponsorship and funding differ. Most often programs are provided by schools, community and faith-based groups, youth-serving organizations, cultural institutions, and city, state, or federal agencies. Some OST initiatives represent grassroots investments in and priorities limited to a specific community or neighborhood. National organizations, such as the Boys and Girls Clubs, Scouts, YMCA/YWCA, and Big Brothers Big Sisters, offer opportunities to youth in every state. Foundations with a national scope, such as Charles Stuart Mott, Wallace, and MetLife, have invested heavily in OST initiatives around the country, while state and local foundations most often support regional or community programs.

Youth programs of these various stripes operate in a diverse, uncoordinated, sporadically funded universe that provides opportunities unevenly to young people. Few exist in the nation's inner-city, high-poverty neighborhoods, which means that the youth most vulnerable to involvement in risky behaviors have the fewest constructive options. And, nationwide, youth programs for teens tend to aim for "the in-between group of urban youth, those who are neither the handful of high-achieving academic stars nor those who are deeply gang-involved."[2]

Within the youth program universe, CYCLE remains distinctive—then and now. It functioned as a community-based, comprehensive youth development program open to all Cabrini-Green youth from kindergarten through college. Academic supports formed the foundation of every age group's experience and were enhanced by fun activities and exposure to new experiences. CYCLE aimed to keep the youth involved with the program seven days a week, twelve months a year, and activities followed a tight schedule and structure.

CYCLE's careful attention to program structure and kids' active participation finds strong support in research looking at the benefits of organized youth activities for adolescents: teens learn more, have greater school success, and participate at higher levels in programs that provide goal-directed, engaging activities. Adolescent participation in activities with low activity structure, such as a community drop-in center or recreational facility, is often associated with negative or antisocial behaviors, such as dropping out of school or delinquency. Based on an extensive review of the literature on school-based extracurricular activities, Amy Feldman and Jennifer Matjasko conclude that "school-based, structured, extra-curricular activity participation, in contrast to participation in unstructured activities . . . is associated with positive adolescent developmental outcomes."[3]

CYCLE did not select youth; anyone could join, but continued membership depended on consistent participation. The initiative was almost entirely privately funded by Chicago-area philanthropies, business and community leaders, and individuals supportive of its goals and the youth. These attributes defined CYCLE's organizational approach and differentiate it in scope and stance from other efforts, even contemporary ones, directed at a similar youth population.

CHAPTER 2

Starting CYCLE

CYCLE began in 1978 as a small tutoring program serving thirty kids in the basement of Cabrini-Green's LaSalle Street Church. The academic-year program quickly expanded to include many more kids, a full-day six-week summer program, five different scholarship programs, a youth leadership initiative, and two additional sites, the former St. Philip Benizi School and the Olivet Center site, rented from Chicago Commons. The program's numbers quickly exploded, and by the mid-1980s more than 450 kids and 250 volunteer tutors and mentors participated weekly, and even more were involved in the summer.

The idea that led to CYCLE began with Greg Darnieder, who, in 1965, as a junior from a Catholic high school in Oshkosh, Wisconsin, volunteered with Brother Tom O'Brien's St. Theresa's Providence summer youth program in St. Louis. A teacher at Providence, Brother Tom made sure that educational enhancement was at the center of the school's summer program design. The program was highly relational and used castaway school district buses to cart hundreds of young people out of St. Louis's North Grand Boulevard neighborhood, an inner-city African American neighborhood, to camps located in rural areas. In the mid-1960s, when there was no air conditioning in the rat-infested and dilapidated housing, the summer camps offered an escape from St. Louis's oppressive summer heat and gave the kids the chance to enjoy some healthy outdoor activity.

High school student volunteers like Greg kept the old buses running, including making sure a bag of ice was in each bus before it set off from the stifling St. Louis heat. With assistance from volunteers, Brother Tom used his carpentry skills to rehab two camps and in doing so taught dozens of teens the building trades. As Greg remembered it, he and the other volunteers "ate cheerios, Bugles and Kool-Aid for breakfast six days a week, along with peanut butter and jelly sandwiches for lunch and dinner. On Sundays, we stuffed ourselves with a chicken dinner provided by Brother Tom's mother."

Greg's eventual transfer to St. Louis University from St. Mary's College in Winona, Minnesota, enabled him to remain involved in Brother Tom's youth program. It also cemented his commitment to addressing equity issues in urban education, which developed after he experienced racial intimidation firsthand when a barn attached to a youth camp in the foothills of the Ozarks was torched while he was supervising a winter weekend experience for forty primary-age students. A couple of years later, a second camp was similarly set on fire, and nearly twenty dormitories and gathering places were burnt to the ground the night before the camp's dedication. Brother Tom and Greg had led the rehabbing of these buildings only to have their efforts turned to ashes.

Brother Tom's work with low-income black youth capitalized on the energy and idealism that middle and high school students bring to working with younger children. This summer volunteer work planted the seed for the program that would eventually become CYCLE, which focused on building strong relationships; having high expectations; creating fun, constructive, meaningful activities; and putting high school students in key leadership positions and youth in supervisory roles.

Greg graduated from St. Louis University in 1971 with a bachelor's degree in sociology and a teaching certificate. He taught middle grade students in St. Louis and then in Riverdale, Maryland, before returning to the Midwest and Wheaton College, where he earned a master's degree in Christian education. In 1978 he put Brother

Tom's lessons into practice when he was hired by Chicago pastor Bill Leslie to head up the LaSalle Street Church's (LSC) tutoring program, which was a response to Chicago Public Schools' dysfunction and an attempt to address the academic struggles of nearby Cabrini-Green youth. The program had operated out of the Sunshine Gospel Mission on Larrabee Street, a dingy old warehouse in the backyard of the row houses, but in 1979 relocated to the LSC building, a far better space for young people. The move proved to be beneficial to the program. The February 1979 LSC newsletter documented the tutoring program's popularity and growth: "Tutoring program is mushrooming in every way. Under the extremely capable direction of Greg Darnieder, the tutoring program (now in its 15th year) is at its best." The budget that year was $25,000, with $10,000 of that allocated to the director's salary. The program's annual budget came from LSC funds and private donors.

It didn't take long for Greg to recognize that he would need different, and more, support and resources in order to develop the modest tutoring program into a comprehensive youth development program such as the one he worked with in St. Louis: "I realized at the end of the 1979 fiscal year that I would not get any assistance from the tutoring program's board, which I affectionately called the Sewing Circle. After all, they were serving at the request of the pastor, and he had guaranteed the annual $25,000 budget. That was good enough for them but not for me!" He promised Pastor Leslie that he would stay five years and then got busy building the tutoring program.

Greg's attention focused initially on the structural components needed to support activities beyond tutoring. Affiliation with Young Life and LSC enabled the sharing of physical resources such as space and vans, and volunteers allowed Greg to introduce program enhancements to build age-appropriate programming beyond middle grades, with high school tutoring as the first official enhancement. Elementary school students from Cabrini-Green came after school and some early evenings for tutoring from CYCLE's Junior Staff, Cabrini-Green middle and high school students who were paid for their time. Volunteers from nearby colleges, such as Wheaton and Trinity, tutored the middle and high school students. As a former math teacher, Greg was comfortable designing quick math assessments, and eventually the Gates-McGinitie reading tests became the crude appraisal of reading levels.

The early years required much creativity and making do. Because the Chicago Public Schools prohibited its students from taking books home, CYCLE's instructional materials were limited to mimeographed workbooks. Books came to CYCLE's library from many different sources—donations from churches and local nonprofits as well as old textbooks donated by college students and new books purchased by volunteers. The CYCLE library expanded to occupy five tall, hinged bookshelves on wheels (made by Junior Staffers). With these resources, the staff rolled out a narrow assembly of age-appropriate materials for each tutoring session.

It didn't take long for Greg to realize that, to make a difference in the lives of Cabrini-Green kids, a program had to involve more than academics. And so in 1980 the program became the LaSalle Street Community Youth Creative Learning Experience (CYCLE), a 501c3 entity. The nonprofit status opened the door for philanthropic resources to be sought for cultural, social, camping, arts, entrepreneurial, and postsecondary programs.

And in the summer of 1980, CYCLE launched a full-day, six-week summer day camp held in the LSC basement. The program grew to include camp sites at Ascension Episcopal Church across the street and nearby St. Matthew's Church. Summer day camp enhanced participants' learning opportunities through the incorporation of the arts into themed learning projects. Whether it was painting one of the vans with scenes from ethnic neighborhoods or building and painting portable murals or making papier-mâché facial imprints of every student, kids' learning took powerful new directions.

LSC offered much more than startup funds, pastoral support, and space to launch a program. Young Life, a national parachurch program for high schoolers (not affiliated with any one denomination but philosophically aligned with Christian beliefs and principles) met at the church on Wednesday nights and provided a group of engaged Cabrini-Green high school students CYCLE built on. This partnership, and that with the Fellowship of Friends, a Quaker meeting group of about fifty people, demonstrated the power of nonprofit youth organizations, acknowledging the strengths of each partner to build a seamless and integrated youth development strategy. They shared offices, vans, staff, program resources, and even philanthropic support.

In 1982, the Chicago Archdiocese sold the abandoned St. Philip Benizi grade school to the Fellowship of Friends and CYCLE for $100. This building at 515 Oak became CYCLE's main home. Also, the Variety Club of Chicago donated two new vans to CYCLE to be used jointly with Young Life. This intentional collaboration wasn't without conflict, but, for the most part, it proved to be a huge benefit

St. Philip Benizi School at 515 Oak, circa 1954. The Chicago Archdiocese sold the property to CYCLE for $100 in 1982, and it served as CYCLE's main home for the next fifteen-plus years.

to Cabrini-Green youth by increasing resources for tutoring and other activities.

CORE PRINCIPLES

From the beginning, CYCLE focused on providing Cabrini-Green youth opportunities for academic success, leadership development, and career awareness. "The core principles on which CYCLE was built nearly forty years ago are the same ones I'd use today in building a youth organization," said Greg. "And there's nothing mysterious about them: a safe environment with caring adults containing constructive and educational activities that embrace young people as the most significant resource available."

Two overarching values shaped the organization's culture and approach. One, activities reflected the constructs of the evolving youth development movement that saw young people as resources to be developed rather than problems to be fixed. Two, Judeo-Christian tenets of respect, love, and trust formed the value system that shaped the ways in which youth, staff, and volunteers treated each other. Joining these foundational beliefs were five principles of practice that described CYCLE's culture and programming:

- *an open door.* CYCLE welcomed all Cabrini-Green youth—no application, screening process, or fee required. Young people could stay in the program as long as they wanted to as long as they participated regularly and did not miss tutoring sessions more than twice in one school year or in the summer. Participants' good standing enabled them to participate in club and field trips on weekends during the school year. The summer program also required consistent attendance.
- *a safe environment.* Concerns about physical safety were ever present in Cabrini-Green. Not a day passed without gunfire or other gang violence threatening neighborhood residents and

visitors. CYCLE staff went to great lengths to assure young people (and their parents) that they would be safe in the program. Senior staff also paid careful attention to the emotional safety of the participants and laid out clear ground rules, expectations, and norms for communication based in values of mutual respect.

- *minimum rules, maximum impact.* CYCLE's few rules were clear and consistently enforced. In line with the program's value system, swearing, fighting, and any kind of inappropriate verbal interaction were absolutely prohibited. No signifying or gang representation was tolerated. And participants in the youth leadership program, Junior Staff, faced a dock in pay if they were even a minute late.
- *commitment to the individual.* "Never give up on a kid" was a CYCLE mantra. The program was built around commitment to the individual, and its practice reflected this in several ways. For instance, staff directed students who were struggling in comprehensive high schools to alternate settings where they could succeed. Junior Staff and volunteer tutors created plans specific to their young charges' academic progress and personal circumstances. The program operated according to the core Young Life principle: it is adults' responsibility to "earn the right to be heard" by kids.
- *structured, developmentally appropriate activities and scaffolded responsibilities.* All CYCLE activities—tutoring, cultural outings, fun adventures—were carefully structured to ensure youths' active participation and engagement. Academics, career exploration, and leadership development were at the heart of the programs, which operated throughout the year to surround youth with constructive, educational, age-appropriate activities. Junior Staff tutoring and program implementation assignments featured near-peer relationships and levels of responsibility.

FUND-RAISING AND BOARD DEVELOPMENT

From 1979 to 1992, CYCLE's annual budget grew from $25,000 to $1.4 million, and its board evolved from a group of six volunteer LSC parishioners to one composed of civic leaders, successful businessmen, and philanthropists.

Once CYCLE was incorporated, Greg set about raising funds to expand the program beyond tutoring supports. Greg sought out LSC members who worked for banks and other downtown Chicago corporations with the hope that they would open doors to grants and wealthy individuals—"There wasn't any great plan beside using the connections of CYCLE's volunteers, staff and LSC members. I was always cultivating leads, one lead at a time." The first grant, for $5,000, came in 1980 from the Joyce Foundation. By the mid-1980s, the annual budget had grown to $450,000. The tutoring programs that reached about 425 kids annually relied on 250 college and professional volunteers and around 30 Junior Staffers. For several summers Amoco Oil made its deep resources available and funded junior staff positions, summer positions at its corporate headquarters, and college internships at its Naperville research facility. Amoco built a multiage hands-on science project curriculum and trained several Junior Staffers, who then trained the summer staff on how to do each of the experiments with campers. This opportunity exposed these students to science in ways they had never experienced and then tasked them with translating the experiments into action for first through sixth graders.

The Chicago Donors Forum became another helpful resource, with its cache of annual reports, funding guidelines, and contacts with trustees for every foundation in the Midwest. Darnieder capitalized on concerns among Chicago-area philanthropists and civic leaders about the negative conditions and life outcomes associated with the city's public housing, and particularly Cabrini-Green, which became the poster for all that was wrong with public housing not only in Chicago but around the country. He said, "I knew I had several advantages other nonprofit leaders didn't necessarily have with CYCLE's mission exclusively focused on the most dangerous neighborhood in the city, its close proximity to the Loop and Gold Coast, our academic/leadership mission, affiliation with LSC. And maybe most important, I was white and the perfect bridge between the Cabrini community and the white corporate/philanthropic worlds." From the beginning, Greg focused on engaging private Chicago-area donors who were sympathetic toward CYCLE's mission.

> My philosophy from the beginning was that private investments from corporations, private foundations, civic organizations, the faith-based community, and individuals would give us the freedom to create the programs which would have maximum impact without engulfing staff with ridiculous, time-wasting government grant paperwork. There was too much to do, too many kids who needed guidance and love. Forcing unwarranted paperwork as a means of accountability was misguided. We could point to outcomes that weren't just sign-in sheets, test scores, detailed lesson plans, checklist things associated with government grants.

His approach to raising private funds resembled a "trust me" model. He did not approach potential funders with a formal strategic plan, enumerated benchmarks, or outcome indictors. He did have a compelling vision, based on his St. Louis experience, of how CYCLE would and could make a difference for youth growing up in Cabrini-Green. And he had a passionate commitment to providing those opportunities and supports.

Greg grew the board to support and advocate for that vision and worked to find individuals through LSC members who might be able to bring in corporate donations and add to the board's racial diversity. "I was particularly looking for African American businessmen and women because I had to counter in substantive ways the reality of my being a white guy affiliated with a predominantly white church and pastor and attracting several hundred white college students and business folks as tutors when we served a 100 percent African American clientele."

As the organization expanded, he moved to establish organizational processes and procedures to support that growth. He also began to hire promising graduates of CYCLE programs, such as Pat Ford, whose mother, Sarah, and sister Jackie, moved from Birmingham, Alabama, to settle in the Cabrini-Green Housing Development in the late 1960s.

The fifth of Sarah's seven children, Pat watched as her mom spent endless hours in the kitchen after working days cleaning people's homes. A regular CYCLE participant, Pat graduated from Whitney Young High School in 1983 and went on to graduate from Bradley University as the first Schuessler/CYCLE scholarship recipient. In 1987 Greg tapped her to be the first academic director in charge of CYCLE's programs.

Through his own efforts and those of his small staff, LSC parishioners, friends, and volunteers, Greg managed to piece together hundreds of private and in-kind donations. It was safer, in his view, to integrate numerous funding sources for CYCLE than to rely on a few big checks that could be abruptly discontinued. He recalled being "enamored" of how The Door, a youth agency in New York City, integrated "seemingly hundreds" of funding streams and thinking, "Yes! That's the way to do it!" He recognized that it wasn't an easy task, "but it was the appropriate way to structure things to effectively meet each participant's emotional, academic, social, spiritual, and career needs."

As CYCLE continued to grow in the mid-1980s, with an annual budget of $600,000, Greg recognized that the organization needed a different board to help support and manage the program. "I realized I had to find a board that had access to money. A final stage in CYCLE's development was the need to create mechanisms that would lead to donations from wealthy individuals and the identification of new individuals and philanthropic entities to support CYCLE's infrastructure and seemingly endless program expansion." At this time the scholarship programs gained the support of prominent families—the Kaplans, Dittmers, Roskams, Schuesslers, and Winebergs—and well-known civic and corporate leaders began giving generously to CYCLE and contributing other resources to the program. Greg said, "The amazing thing is we never filed an application, and I still don't know how that happened. To have the business community begin to truly believe in the talent of Cabrini-Green youth and raise substantial funds—possibly around $1 million in annual scholarships—to support them was quite a statement."

And the number of individual donors continued to grow. By 1992, the annual report listed more than 180 individual contributors to CYCLE, many of whom were connections made by staff and volunteers. The annual economic value easily represented hundreds of thousands of dollars.

Despite his strong preference for supporting CYCLE activities with private funds, Greg did seek federal monies for one youth initiative, the flagship Junior Staff leadership program. The Job Training and Partnership Act (JTPA), established in the early 1980s, provided federal funds to community-based programs to hire and pay minimum wages to young people aged 16 to 21 during the school year and 14 and up during the summer. These wages made it possible for Cabrini-Green youth to participate in the Junior Staff program, since many families expected them to contribute to household costs through part-time jobs, or the teens themselves felt an obligation to help out with expenses. And eventually state and federal monies also funded CYCLE's evolving adult education program.

COSTS AND EXPENSES

CYCLE's costs were relatively modest, since there were few administrative expenses. The 1992 Annual Report showed approximately

$1.4 million in income and expenses and detailed source/expenditure percentages:

INCOME

Foundations/Corporations	50%
Government	26%
Individuals	9%
United Way	5%
Scholarship program interest	4%
Special events	3%
Churches	1%
Other	1%

EXPENSES

Programs	76%
Administration & building expenses	14%
Scholarship awards	5%
Fund raising	5%

The tutoring program benefited from donated time, space, and materials. Because CYCLE owned space or could use local churches for free, had nearly 250 weekly volunteers, and a library of donated books, tutoring expenses were limited to paying senior staff, building utilities and maintenance costs, van expenses, and field trip costs. The cost per student participating in the thirty-three-week school-year tutoring program was approximately $1,200, excluding Junior Staff salary costs. For the summer day camp, CYCLE charged each kid $25 for the six weeks, discounted the rate for a second child from the same family to $15, and any imposed no charge for any other kids from the family. This fee included all learning materials and field trips. Also, the federal government's summer lunch program provided food at no cost to the participants or the program. The one exception was the $5 charge to go to Great America at the end of the summer, assuming near-perfect attendance. But since the amusement park admission at the time was around $20, this served as a great attendance incentive for the day camp.

Scholarship programs cost about $1,500 a year per participant, which covered a coordinator's salary and benefits and program expenses. The I Have A Dream and College Opportunity Scholarship Program: Class of 1995 coordinators also asked the scholarships' sponsors to underwrite special activities, such as overnight camping trips or visits to local museums or events.

The program paid Junior Staff minimum wage with federal JTPA funds. Those in supervisory roles, whose responsibilities were greater, received a 25 cent to $2 raise above minimum wage, and this was paid out of CYCLE general funds. During the school year, each Junior Staffer worked 12 hours a week for 35 weeks; during the summer they worked 25 hours a week for 6 weeks. Junior Staffers employed during both the school year and summer earned $1,140 (1979) to $2,180 (1993) a year, significant money in the Cabrini-Green context.

Essential CYCLE assets were its vans. The program had six fifteen-passenger vans (which, as administrators remembered, were usually stuffed with thirty kids, something that could not happen today). The vans proved critical to CYCLE's effective functioning in more than one way. They were indispensable to protecting kids from violence by driving each participant home from tutoring and other activities, even if just a block or two, and thereby ensuring safe passage through Cabrini-Green. Greg recalled the vans doing a U-turn in front of 515 West Oak to get youth safely across the street to 500 and 502 West Oak, a no-man's land for the three controlling gangs. Senior staff drove youth home and waited until they saw a wave from a mom or other adult before letting their charges leave the vehicle to enter their buildings. If no wave appeared from a window, staff would escort youth up the stairs to their apartment doors. Tamiko Jones recalled, "I lived on the fourth floor, and my mom or sister would meet me half-way down. [Gang members] used to turn out the lightbulbs. [Senior staff] wouldn't leave until we were up those stairs." Greg remembered taking a six-year-old home several times to her apartment in the Reds because her grandmother had forgotten to come out or was delayed somewhere: "It's like, oh my God! A six-year-old kid going into that. Not only navigating those stairwells, but who knows what she's going to see." He said that times like that were the most terrifying of his nearly fifteen years of working in Cabrini-Green.

The vans provided more than safety. They also transported participants all over Chicago and around the country to see the sites and to visit colleges. Scholarship coordinators recalled driving youth to college visits at Spelman and Morehouse in Atlanta and to Fisk in Nashville and Tuskegee in Alabama. "We drove those CYCLE vans everywhere," Bernard McCune said. "We had kids in public and Catholic schools; they had two different spring breaks," when high school students visited colleges. "We would drive from, say, Chicago to New Orleans and every place in between for the kids in public schools. We'd get back Saturday night, have a rest, and leave Sunday night to do the Catholic school tour—Virginia, Washington, DC. It would be like three thousand miles in two weeks—but that's what you can do when you're young!"

Because the scholarship coordinators also took turns driving each other's charges to school, home, or tutoring, they got to know youth involved in other programs and developed a collective understanding of the kids' strengths and challenges. As Craig Nash said, "We had vans going all over the place. We did all of those things together. Who's going to the South Side? Who's going north? We came up with a van schedule for our kids going to private schools so we could all take our turns getting up early in the morning." And because CYCLE still served young people who had moved away from the immediate Cabrini-Green neighborhood to other parts of Chicago, it took a couple hours to take everybody home. "You have to go from the far north suburb, you gotta take somebody home to Waukegan, you have to take somebody to the far South Side. The CYCLE kids in the neighborhood would say, 'We wanna ride.' They know you gotta bring the van back to the neighborhood to park, and they wanted to go along. That builds relationships." And, Bernard noted, "when you're talking about students and families living in poverty, they're very transient. Families would move, always looking for a better situation. Some would move within the neighborhood, some would move out. But once we made the commitment to a kid, we were still with them."

And so a less quantifiable, but very important, role the vans—and CYCLE—played was in lending the youth of Cabrini-Green a feeling of privilege. As alum Ken Dunkin remembered it, "A van coming to pick us up—I mean, somebody's looking for us, somebody's blowing the horn for us. It was special."

CHAPTER 3

Tutoring
Opportunities for Growth

CYCLE's tutoring program started in 1978 as a small enterprise with 30 youth and a few church volunteers. By 1992 it had grown to involve more than 300 kids each week, with most scheduled for two sessions per week. This included around 130 youth who were tutored as part of their scholarship program and 30 high schoolers who tutored younger kids as Junior Staffers and then participated themselves in evening tutoring sessions. At the peak of the program, most of the tutoring was done by the 250 or so primarily white volunteers from surrounding colleges and communities.

Tutoring was work for the tutors as well as the kids. Academic interests, skills, school work, and homework assignments varied greatly, defying the effective use of standardized grade-level protocol and requiring kid-by-kid attention from tutors and senior staff. Most of the tutors were initially thrown by what the students didn't know about school or life outside Cabrini-Green.

Few youngsters came through the door with any idea about how to "do school," or why, and most struggled with the daily life disruptions of Cabrini-Green and dysfunction of their neighborhood public schools. Volunteers had to deal with all they didn't know about black kids growing up in this high-poverty community and figure out how to manage the racial and economic differences between them and their charges.

Despite volumes of research on the outcomes of tutoring programs initiated in communities like Cabrini-Green, which show that poor kids and their middle-class tutors quickly abandon the endeavor, CYCLE facilities regularly were packed with young people involved with tutoring after school and in the evenings. The promise of snacks and the possibility of a trip out of the neighborhood enticed many young people to come to tutoring to see what it was all about. Others came because their friends or siblings attended; still others because their mothers insisted. The staff also visited nearby elementary schools to talk about the program with students and teachers. According to Greg Darnieder, they never did much by way of recruitment; word of mouth brought kids to their door. "We'd fill up soon right after the school year began," he said, "because all available tutors and junior staff had been assigned."

Sessions were intended to support students' academic work, but they also aimed to inspire meaningful connections between tutors and their tutees. The stated goals of positive development and futures for each participant depended on establishing and maintaining strong mentoring. Tutoring created close and, in many instances, long-term relationships between tutees and the senior staff, volunteers, and Junior Staff. Exemplifying this, more than twenty-five years after her involvement in CYCLE tutoring sessions, an alum posted this appreciation on Facebook: "A shout out to my tutor from CYCLE, Michelle McConnell—Thank you for caring enough to be part of my life. I was not the easiest to deal with some days. I love and appreciate it all. SAVED MY LIFE! Thanks Michelle, Greg, Craig and countless others—trailblazers for life." Jessica Nash, who participated in CYCLE from kindergarten through grade school, also recently thanked her Junior Staff tutor on Facebook: "She has been a constant in my life since I was 7. She tutored me and evolved into a mentor to me. She inspired me to be a teacher and leader striving to fulfill my passion. 25 years later, Nicole is one of the stones in my foundation, someone who still gives me confidence that I will be supported no matter what I do or where I go. I'm thrilled that CYCLE was the thread that bound us together."

William Gates recalled his tutor's "tough love" and the difference it made in his life: "She began to make me be accountable to CYCLE in addition to getting my grades up. She's like, 'Okay, William, if I'm going to tutor you, you're going to tutor somebody else.' So Saturday mornings she would make me come in and tutor kids . . . It was Saturday, I was in eighth grade, worked my butt all week long, but I'm grateful that she did that, because she taught me responsibility and really helped me take life more seriously."

THE TUTORING SESSIONS

At 3:30 every afternoon, kids burst through the doors, grabbed their snacks, and met with their senior staff or Junior Staff tutors. Even as the size of the program grew, the eagerness of the children as they poured out of the vans and buses and into the building remained.

Both tutees and tutors knew not to be late, as time was the program's most precious commodity. Whether in the LSC basement or at the other sites acquired over time, the limited number of tables filled up first, then the floor space, including corridors, was claimed. And once the number of sessions outgrew the limited LSC basement space, the church opened its sanctuary to CYCLE (which was gratefully received, even in the dead of winter when the heat shut off at 5:30). Despite the inconveniences, complaints from youth or tutors were few.

Tutoring sessions were the core of CYCLE's commitment to the individual. Since the sessions involved personalized work, not group or standardized academic lessons, senior staff created a folder for each student. On the inside front cover of each folder was a running record, with a column for the work covered in each session on math, vocabulary, writing, reading, homework, or special school projects (such as history or science fair projects) and another column for notes on concepts, vocabulary words, or other skills to cover in the next session, based on previous sessions, grade-level standards, teacher feedback on homework and tests, and tutor observations. By the end of the year, some students had ten pages stapled to the front cover, providing a summary of their progress. This tracking strategy allowed tutors to review work from the previous session, expand on vocabulary words, push forward math concepts, and talk with students about books they were reading, as noted in the folder. It provided some consistency for the tutee, since any student could have two or more different tutors each week.

Michelle McConnell, the volunteer coordinator, read through these records every week, flagged any comments or issues that needed attention, such as an upcoming math test or issues with homework completion, and gave those folders to Pat Ford, who, as academic director, touched base with tutors about needed supports. Staff knew the kids well and often recommended things for a tutor to work on with their tutee. Some of them also knew about home situations or other personal circumstances that could make it hard for youth to focus on academics and that called for a sympathetic ear—an incarcerated sibling, a death, a mom having problems.

A member of the first Junior Staff cohort, Pat Ford became CYCLE's academic director and, later, the executive director of the Steans Family Foundation.

Programming in CYCLE's early years started with middle grade students (grades 5–7) and then added the elementary grades (grades K–4) before creating distinct sessions for grades 4–6, separating that intermediate age from those in grades 7 and 8.[1] Each age group participated in an outing once a month during the school year—roller rinks, museums, parks—and during the summer the three hundred or so youth in the day camp went on outings every day. On these excursions, each Junior Staffer had responsibility for supervising at least three youth, making sure they got their food, took bathroom stops, got on and off the van, and had fun. Greg wanted these relationships to go beyond mere babysitting: "Junior Staff knew what taking those kids meant in terms of boundaries on behavior and interaction—that they weren't supposed to be just a silent overseer. No silent reading. There should be continual verbal interaction. Interaction, interaction, interaction!" Every outing was to be a learning experience for both tutee and tutor. And, indeed, Junior Staff jumped in the swimming pool, played games at the park, jumped rope, guided participants through Brookfield and Lincoln Park zoos.

Youth in the program committed to consistent attendance; three unexcused absences during the school year and they were out. This reflected CYCLE's core principle of "minimal rules, maximum impact" and was strictly enforced. But it was a rare student who got to that third absence and was dropped. "If it happened," Greg said, "it typically occurred in the fall with a student new to us as they tested what CYCLE was all about." In 1985, in an effort to promote responsibility and academic achievement, CYCLE began an incentive program for students in grades 2 through 8 enrolled in the afternoon and Saturday morning tutoring sessions. Games, books, toys, radios, and other prized items could be acquired in exchange for points earned for attendance and academic performance. Senior staff felt the incentive program made a big difference in kids' promptness and lesson completion: "The students pursued the points they needed to obtain the game, toy, or book of their choice in the incentive box."

Since all age groups met at least twice a week, one of the two-hour sessions ended after about seventy-five minutes for Club, a time when the youth performed skits and played silly games. Club opened with five or six boisterous, interactive songs and then moved on to a skit, a silly game, or a puppet theater performance, usually on a biblical theme. Packing eighty to a hundred people into one of the classrooms became a logistical challenge embraced by all; younger kids typically sat on tutors' and Junior Staffers' laps. The kids, young and old, loved it and looked forward to it each week. Thirty years later, CYCLE alum fondly recalled Club antics in great detail, remembering the fun anticipating which unsuspecting victim would be embarrassed or what silliness would ensue. According to Greg, "Club time became a wonderful way to have a shared experience, a cementing of the relationships among peers and the entire group. It also stretched Junior Staffers' responsibilities while at the same time developed their leadership skills in designing and implementing a forty-five-minute session."

A YOUTH-CENTERED APPROACH

Tutoring at CYCLE revolved around engaging and supporting youth with developmentally appropriate activities and challenges. Many of the youth attended tutoring sessions on a regular basis from elementary through high school, and some returned from college, especially during the summer months, to work as tutors. This consistent engagement contrasts with the indifferent attendance typical to academic support programs in urban centers. Youth vote with their feet, and that's why programs struggle to retain youth over age twelve. CYCLE's developmental approach formed the foundation of the program's ability to attract and engage Cabrini-Green youth.

Tutoring sessions did not focus on fixing or addressing academic deficits but instead took young people where they were, encouraged them to set positive goals, and buoyed their efforts to reach higher. Pat Ford underscored how staff and tutors took a developmental approach when they reviewed youths' school work, pointing out opportunities for doing better rather than dwelling on shortfalls.

Further, senior staff and Junior Staff understood young people's family situations, and this knowledge supported a flexible case management approach to the youth and informed the focus of tutoring sessions. Pat Ford commented, "You get to know the kids and families over time, and that's the whole point. You're not going to have the same conversation with a kid who just became homeless as you are with a kid not struggling with those issues." Richard Blackmon, who supported CYCLE kids attending Providence–St. Mel's high school through the Bright Knights program, also saw close attention to life circumstances as essential to an effective relationship. In terms of expectations of and support for the young person, he said, "sometimes you would just recognize situations where you had to make allowances for that family. When you work in these capacities, you have to be consciously awake to everything that's going on with these families. You can't be insensitive to anything. If you don't have that . . . you'll likely lose the kid."

The individualized tutoring sessions relied on volunteers' and Junior Staffers' judgment about what a young person needed and the kind of activities that would be most beneficial in any given session. No tutoring manual existed; no best practices protocol or scripted curricula defined the sessions. CYCLE's youth-centered approach to tutoring contrasts with the tight structures in many youth programs, where top-down implementation directives and packaged programs can obstruct development of meaningful relationships between adults and youth.[2]

For CYCLE, tutoring was mentoring. Gloria Purifoy, stressing how important personal relationships were, noted how "the college students would provide tutorial support in our academics, homework. They [also] would just connect with us in what was going on in our lives and form relationships with us." At times the conversations focused little on academics but instead on the life issues confronting a young person—an incarcerated sibling, homelessness, domestic upheaval, abuse, gangs. David Gates also pointed to the many important lessons beyond academics that he learned: "Not only did we learn book things, but we learned life lessons. CYCLE taught us how to be proud of ourselves, be proud of our family, be proud of our surroundings." Emphasizing the critical function the tutoring program played in giving Cabrini-Green youth like him the motivation to stick with school, Ken Dunkin said, "CYCLE tutoring played the pivotal role for me. If we didn't get [support for school] at home—some of us did, but a lot of us didn't—you at least knew . . . that somebody had your back . . . and was counting on you to deliver in school, [and held] levels of expectations [for you] on so many levels."

To inspire younger kids and bring cachet to the tutoring program, CYCLE relied on a near-peer strategy. Near-peers, youth who are just a bit older and from a similar background, can inspire because their accomplishments seem possible, relevant, and their circumstances are familiar—If they can do it, I can do it![3] Younger kids' desire to imitate makes older peers powerful influencing agents, for better or worse. Especially for adolescents, near-peers often provide more compelling role models than do adults, because adults represent "them" whereas near-peers are "us."

The near-peers for kids attending CYCLE's tutoring sessions were the Junior Staffers, who tutored elementary and middle school youth. Many alums commented on the many ways Junior Staff tutors buttressed their efforts to stay in high school, encouraged them think about going to college, and counseled them away from gang involvement or early pregnancy. CYCLE alums stressed how the near-peer model and the constant presence of Junior Staff sustained their involvement in tutoring and their subscription to CYCLE's goals. Margie Davis, an alum who works for Chicago Public Schools' GEAR UP program, said, "I think the peer tutor was really important. When you have the peer, there's someone you can look up to, someone older, a little bit."

TUTORING FOR ADULTS

In keeping with the comprehensive nature of CYCLE's approach, the tutoring program was extended to adult family members of Cabrini-Green youth. Moms started showing up for tutoring when they found they were welcomed and treated politely by CYCLE staff. Pat

Ford recalled that staff were courteous to the kids' parents "no matter the situation... We had moms with developmental delays, moms with drug or alcohol issues. We always were respectful."

Senior staff looked for ways to recognize parents, involve them in activities, or lend them a hand (such as using CYCLE vans to drive them to the shopping mall) with the hope of drawing them into the tutoring program. Greg recalled the mom who earned her GED high school equivalency degree with the support of CYCLE tutors: "She started [coming] when she almost killed one of her kids because she couldn't read the label on a bottle." This mother eventually earned an associate degree.

Juanita White was the power behind the adult program. Greg remembered how "every time Juanita saw a mother dropping off or picking up her child, she would gently but authoritatively ask, 'What are you doing for yourself? Why not come to CYCLE's GED classes?'" He described her as a relentless advocate for the well-being of Cabrini-Green parents. Among her initiatives, she started a program recognizing Mother's Day and Father's Day with special luncheons held at St. Matthews Methodist Church or at CYCLE. She also established a resale shop in the LSC basement to provide gently used clothing and household goods to the families.

When the adult education aspects of CYCLE began to emerge in 1984, the need for government funds became apparent. "The private sector had absolutely no interest in funding adult programs," Greg said. "I guess their rationale was that it was a better investment to make with the children than all of the complicating factors facing parents and adults." CYCLE's adult programs grew out of Chicago City Colleges' community outreach programs, which provided support for the pre-GED and GED classes; it then got contracts from the Archdiocese of Chicago for teaching "soft skills" and targeted skill development for clerical jobs. Many of the programmatic adult-focused components were similar to those used with elementary, middle, and high school students: career exposure and building social and professional networks. Adult programming eventually expanded to include job readiness and word processing classes and a job placement program. Senior staff served nearly seventy adults weekly in various programs.

But the most important of all the CYCLE parent activities were the daily GED classes attended by many Cabrini-Green moms (but no dads, despite Juanita's outreach efforts). As parents achieved success, earned their GED, they were hired onto the GED staff and eventually the CYCLE staff. Gloria Purifoy's mom, Sharon Williams, earned the program's first GED. She became Greg's administrative assistant and then worked in a similar position at LSC. Having dropped out of high school because of pregnancy, she saw education as a priority and CYCLE as the opportunity she needed: "I knew I needed to have some kind of education, as I had a responsibility to take care of my family, and that education held the key for my three children's success." Other moms also moved ahead because of CYCLE's adult program. Peggy Burnett, mother of CPS administrator and CYCLE alum Julie Burnett, earned her GED and went on to earn a BA, becoming the first parent to receive a CYCLE college scholarship. Though it didn't produce a large number of parent GED graduates, the program stood as testimony to CYCLE's commitment to the entire Cabrini-Green community.

AN ARMY OF VOLUNTEERS

CYCLE's personalized tutoring program depended on the consistent, committed involvement of hundreds of volunteers. In the beginning, volunteer recruitment and support was largely ad hoc. Greg talked up the opportunity as he traveled around Chicago and was opportunistic in recruiting volunteers from his extensive personal and professional networks. For his part, Pastor Leslie encouraged members of the LaSalle Street Church to see volunteering at CYCLE as an opportunity to help fulfill the church's mission. And CYCLE staff persuaded their friends and relatives to become tutors. At a time when youth agencies in Chicago (and across the nation) labored to find and keep reliable volunteers, CYCLE experienced remarkable success in attracting and retaining them.

Also, through long-standing relationships with several area colleges and graduate programs, Greg channeled the idealism and energy of young adults into CYCLE's core tutoring program. Volunteers included college students from Wheaton College, Moody Bible Institute, Trinity College, Kellogg School of Business, Northwestern Law School, LSC parishioners, and Chicago professionals who wanted to work with kids in Cabrini-Green. In time, volunteer recruitment became institutionalized at Wheaton and Trinity. Volunteer coordinators on each campus provided information about CYCLE and coordinated recruitment. (Wheaton and Trinity students were also prized as tutors because the relationship typically meant one or two overnight stays in a tutor's dorm.)

Each evening, tutors from Wheaton came to CYCLE on college-sponsored buses loaded with thirty to forty students. Vans from Trinity also arrived for most sessions, with Northwestern Law students jumping on at stops along Chicago Avenue. Volunteers from the professional community, LSC, and Moody Bible Institute also rode the vans or drove themselves. The large number of volunteers meant that every CYCLE participant got personal, one-on-one tutoring attention. But as the program grew to involve "an army of volunteers," the program directors struggled to make sure volunteers had the supports and information they needed and were appropriately matched with a student.

In 1988, Michelle McConnell, a former CYCLE intern from Wheaton College, came on board as the volunteer coordinator and was charged with tending to logistics, supporting the volunteers, and being the point person for each session. She said it was the best job she'd ever had but admitted that it was hard at first. Having grown up in a small, majority-white Michigan town, she found Cabrini-Green to be a challenge when she became a CYCLE staffer: "There was a little bit of a gang civil war going on when I started—lots of violence right nearby. But I realized I didn't understand all of the layers of poverty and different issues I'd have to address . . . It was a process of unlearning . . . I just didn't realize the complexities of the problem. I didn't realize how much I didn't know about poverty." Developing an introduction to Cabrini-Green for the volunteers figured among Michelle's first tasks. Despite efforts to recruit a diverse group of tutors, almost all of the volunteer tutors were white and primarily middle class. The directors worried that volunteers would come into the housing project and walk away with reinforced negative stereotypes about black inner-city youth; they saw a thoughtful introduction to the Cabrini-Green community as essential to the tutoring program's success.

When they started, volunteers attended orientation sessions focused on the language and culture of the black community. Michelle saw herself as a bridge between the white tutors and the youth they would be working with and created a manual containing resources to assist them in working with the kids:

> I would say, "I know you might be coming into this with some ideas of what you think this community is. I'm here to help you experience what this community is really like." I tried to provide a lot of education materials, things to talk about, such as white privilege; . . . learning about urban slang and speech and how it developed; about how to be a mentor to the kids, to be a real role model for them but also learn from them. I had this great article, "Whose Language Is It Anyway?" To understand that they have valid things that they can teach you. I tried to help them think a little broader about their role.

She relied on Junior Staffers' participation in the volunteer training sessions, asking them to talk about things like "this is what it is like here," "this is who I am." She said, "I felt like I really couldn't tell their story. They needed to tell it."

Greg said that he and Michelle tried without much success to recruit African American volunteers from professional organizations, but "we never got the racial diversity we wanted. It felt like some of the stereotypes and barriers that were blocking white people from coming into the community were there for black professionals too. It was just really hard to break that barrier."

Volunteers made a firm commitment to tutor one night a week for thirty-three weeks. The senior staff intentionally addressed what many nonprofit leaders call "the Lady Bountiful problem," where individuals from different racial, social, or economic settings come to "do good" for the locals but, too often, end up alienating the intended beneficiaries and reinforcing the negative do-gooder stereotype. Greg asked potential volunteers to consider their reasons for coming to CYCLE: "We said to them, 'If you're here on a mission to help poor black kids, feeling sorry for them growing up in public housing, please don't come back next week.' I wanted folks who wanted to learn from the kids and junior staff as much as they wanted to give of themselves for that year."

As academic director and volunteer coordinator, Pat and Michelle worked together to pair tutors with tutees for a year-long relationship, and for many a relationship that would stretch over several years. For instance, some youth in the I Have A Dream Scholarship and the College Opportunity Scholarship: Class of 1995 programs had the same volunteer tutor for the six-year duration of these initiatives. Matching white suburban volunteers with CYCLE youth wasn't always easy, especially when the match proved different from volunteers' expectations, or discomfiting. One volunteer told McConnell, "I thought you were gonna put me with this cute little girl and we'd have this fun little relationship. And then you matched me with this boy who was pretty rough around the edges and difficult." But that relationship flourished; the young woman continued to tutor the young man for several years, and they remain close through Facebook.

Michelle made it clear that tutors needed to be there every week as scheduled, and they were to let her know in advance if conflicts arose so she could make sure students had someone there to tutor them. She and the volunteers came up with some creative solutions to address inevitable, and understandable, absences. For instance, two busy Chicago lawyers shared the tutoring of a scholarship student; if one couldn't make it, the other showed up. They stuck with the young man for six years and saw him off to, and then graduate from, one of their alma maters, Lawrence University.

Consistent attendance was expected of the tutees, as well. It not only benefited them, but it was also vital to retaining tutors' commitment and engagement. Senior staff chided youth and told them they would lose their tutor if they were late. Tami Doig remembered the effort she and the other scholarship coordinators made to get kids there on time: "We worked our tails off to get all those kids there, because you can't have volunteers come and their kid's not there . . . We'd get in vans and go to two different spots and get the kids to the Olivet building by 6:45 so that when the tutors arrived, they were there to tutor. Kids really needed to come so we wouldn't be embarrassed and lose our tutor relationships."

BUILDING RELATIONSHIPS

Youth came to tutoring faithfully in large part because of the bonds they formed with staff, volunteers, and other youth. Tutors became friends who cared about their tutees' lives, circumstances, and general well-being and who supported their healthy development in many ways. Those relationships were what kept kids coming back week after week and year after year. Greg stressed that CYCLE never was a "stick"—"We never, at any time, had students mandated to come." He described the deeply interpersonal quality of the tutoring program: "I would never claim we had a sophisticated tutoring strategy. It was largely left up to the 225-plus annual college and adult volunteers to figure out that day's lessons with their tutees. I was counting on their thirty-three-week commitment and the depth of the relationships developed to deliver academic gains and provide needed support . . . I was betting as much on the value of the relationships, on widening horizons, on multiple-year involvement by each participant as I was on the academics."

Both tutees and tutors benefited from their "gift relationship."[4] Junior Staff tutors served as essential role models to younger youth, and in carrying out this role they learned important leadership and social skills and gained feelings of self-worth and pride. Greg said that if he had it to do over again, he would increase the number of Junior Staffers, because "the benefits of their serving as tutors and mentors to younger kids in the community are evidenced now in the power of that experience in their adult lives."

And the volunteers who came to CYCLE every week became, as one youth put it, "our experienced friends"—individuals who could introduce them to the world of work and the skills they would need, help them navigate school, and encourage them think about future options. In turn, the volunteers learned important lessons about the many social and economic obstacles these poor, urban, black youth confronted daily and the resources they needed to meet those challenges successfully. They learned that the racial stereotypes associated with the youth growing up in Cabrini-Green generally ignored the complex and cumulative conditions associated with concentrated poverty. As a result of their experience with CYCLE youth, many of these volunteers have become effective advocates for making neighborhood-based opportunities more broadly available and been powerful voices in pushing against negative stereotypes.

In addition to the steady engagement and encouragement they provided, volunteers introduced youth to new ideas and experiences. Senior staff recalled the constant requests from tutors to take kids to events, such as to Chicago Bulls games or Wrigley Field, on restaurant excursions for birthday celebrations, to swimming lessons at their clubs. Many invited their tutees to family events or arranged visits to their workplace. Some tutors took youth on college tours and wrote reference letters in support of their admission. And the volunteers, as well as several parents of the college student tutors, often connected kids to Chicago companies and helped them find jobs.

In time, volunteers were integrated into other CYCLE activities, such as fund raising, coordinating outreach, helping with newsletters, and reporting to funders. They helped grow the CYCLE program. Volunteers' whiteness, initially a concern, proved an asset. As Bernard McCune put it, "The tutoring and mentoring program connected students with another person who cared about them and also helped them academically—folks who didn't look like them but who cared about them. So it was tremendously important for black students to know that, 'Hey, we kinda like all God's children,' so the whole race thing, at least for that hour or two, didn't matter."

The kind of relationships CYCLE established across racial and economic lines can be difficult to achieve and sustain. Psychologist Barton Hirsch points to the problems experienced between white tutors and inner-city black youth in the Chicago Boys and Girls Clubs he studied. He and other researchers who have looked at mentoring activities of the kind assumed by CYCLE's tutoring program have found that the process of matching youth and volunteers often is challenging and that relationships often fall apart after the introductory phase. Hirsch sees a critical explanation for these shortfalls in adult mentors' and youths' "extremely different worlds," nothing that "a white, college-educated, middle-class, suburban adult has just so much in common with a black or Latino inner-city youth."[5] Different worlds bring different assumptions, norms, language and expectations.

As volunteer coordinator, Michelle, and CYCLE generally, avoided such problems by carefully explaining responsibilities and expectations, directly involving Junior Staff as Cabrini-Green emissaries, and ensuring careful senior staff attention to matching and relationship building. Decades later, volunteers still talked about all they learned about the complexities of poverty and the false assumptions many hold about the abilities and motivation of poor, black, inner-city kids. Volunteering at CYCLE changed many volunteers' lives. There they earned the right to be heard.

CHAPTER 4

Junior Staff
Opportunities for Leadership

If tutoring formed CYCLE's foundation, the Junior Staff program supplied its inspirational energy and leadership opportunities. Every year, high school and college students from Cabrini-Green became members of the Junior Staff, the core of CYCLE's education and recreational programming. During the school year, thirty high school Junior Staffers planned and carried out activities, tutored, supervised, and mentored the younger kids, and in the summer around seventy high school and college students were responsible for running the day camp. The Junior Staff program involved youth as agents in the enrichment of their own lives, the development of their own abilities, and the advancement of the community as a whole. CYCLE saw Junior Staffers as Cabrini-Green's and Chicago's future leaders and as models for their peers and the younger children.

CYCLE youth became Junior Staffers as early as age fourteen, when they first became eligible for the federal funds that supported their work.[1] Pat Ford, one of the first Junior Staffers, took on the role even before she could be paid, volunteering at age thirteen. A CYCLE Junior Staff position held status and was coveted among Cabrini-Green youth. Kids couldn't wait for the chance to wear the green Junior Staff T-shirt.

Most of the six hundred youth who held that position took a path quite different from that of their Cabrini-Green peers. Every Junior Staffer graduated from high school, and while not all of went to

Former Junior Staffer Gloria Purifoy is the postsecondary specialist for the Chicago Public Schools' GEAR UP project.

college, according to the program's academic director, Pat Ford, "most of us had some," and "everyone is doing okay, and everybody has college for their kids."

Gloria Purifoy, who attended CYCLE all through her school years, said, "For Junior Staff, dropping out was not an option. We would graduate!" An outstanding student, she applied to multiple magnet schools and chose the Near North Vocational High School only blocks from her Larrabee Street apartment. Today a leading voice in postsecondary access and completion through her work as a college and career specialist with CPS's GEAR UP project, Purifoy says that she models her work on what she experienced at CYCLE as a Junior Staffer: "It helped me with my career decisions and developed by leadership skills. I always watched those older than me, so when leadership opportunities became available, I was ready to step up."

Brian and Carleta Alston were among CYCLE's first Junior Staff cohorts in the early 1980s. Both came from large families. Carleta's mom valued education and sacrificed greatly to send her and several of her siblings to private Catholic elementary schools while attending community college herself. Brian's path was filled with trials. In fifth grade, when his mom moved the family to Cabrini-Green, Brian found himself not only enduring corporal punishment at the hands of the Jenner school administrators and fighting classmates in an attempt to gain acceptance, but also battling to build his self-confidence. Placed in the "low" academic group, he struggled to find his place. The school band and basketball became his creative outlets starting in sixth grade, and as part of those groups he gained acceptance. And in high school he joined the UFOs and was among other guys who considered education something worth striving toward. Also, his involvement in CYCLE's tutoring component and his participation in Young Life further reinforced his view that "it's okay to be educated and cool."

Brian and Carleta met as Junior Staffers and "got hitched" right out of high school. To provide for his family, Brian worked four part-time minimum-wage jobs, always anticipating that something better was down the road. His curiosity with technology and strength of character proved to be a potent combination, and he went on to work at Cook County Hospital, keeping several thousand computers and related equipment fully operational. Carleta, always academically motivated, went to college as soon as she was able to, given family responsibilities. She earned her EdD in communication in 2015 and took an associate deanship at Malcolm X College. And later, for job promotion opportunities and also to be a role model for their youngest son, Brian enrolled in a bachelor's degree program. Carleta and Brian credit CYCLE and their Junior Staff involvement for expanding their horizons, laying the foundation for the leadership positions they have assumed, and reinforcing a strong set of family, work, and life values.

Brian and Carleta Alston, among CYCLE's first Junior Staffers, got married right after high school. Carleta serves as an associate dean of instruction at Malcolm X College, and Brian is a systems analyst for Cook County Hospital.

THE PAY

The Junior Staff program provided youth with opportunities to earn money and take on new roles and responsibilities. With federal funding, CYCLE paid the youth an hourly wage for twelve or fourteen hours a week during the school year and twenty hours a week during the summer. Greg saw this compensation as the "perfect carrot" to engage Cabrini-Green youth in constructive ways, provide benefits for them and their families, and expose them to the world of work. Jennifer Means remembered everyone eagerly awaiting their fourteenth birthday so they could become a Junior Staffer—"Everyone was all excited . . . They were going to get this job and be rich!" Even though the pay was only $2.25 an hour, she said, "to us it was a fortune." Former Junior Staffers recalled getting their first CYCLE check—how much it was for and what they did with it. Brian Alston remembered the exact amount, "$67.50!" and Lloyd Rogers said, "Just getting that first check was huge. I think I tried to frame it, but they said I had to cash it!" Lloyd, who is now a corrections officer, remembered heading out to a nearby cut-rate clothing store to buy shoes and underwear and then handing the remainder over to his mother. Because they were expected to help their mothers pay the bills, most Cabrini-Green adolescents could not have taken Junior Staff positions without compensation.

A graduated pay scale rewarded different levels of responsibility. CYCLE's general fund supplemented federal funds for Junior Staff placed in supervisory positions. Greg recalled that the raises ranged from twenty-five cents to a couple of dollars per hour. "It was probably illegal to give raises if you're taking federal funds," Greg said, "but I thought it was really important to do because it taught an invaluable lesson to all Junior Staff about the world of work, the rewards it contains, and the importance of showing initiative both at CYCLE and in the real world."

FEELING VALUED

Most young people growing up in Cabrini-Green struggled to feel that they counted for anything among the thousands of children packed into the housing project. Ambiguous signals from their schools about their capabilities left many feeling unimportant and discouraged about their futures. The Chicago Housing Authority's neglectful treatment of their homes reinforced feelings that they and their families were of little account. In contrast, being a CYCLE Junior Staffer conveyed a powerful message that they had something of value to contribute to the CYCLE community, that they would be missed if they did not show up as expected, and that they were talented, competent individuals with bright futures.

Junior Staffers knew they mattered. They saw themselves as part of a special group in their neighborhood context. As Pat Ford said, "It was a saving grace in Cabrini to affiliate with a good gang that had high expectations for you but also cared, exposed you to new situations . . . especially when I think of some of the guys and what they were dealing with." Ken Dunkin called Junior Staff "our gang of excellence, our gang of somebody covering our flank and expecting us to do better."

Jennifer Means, now a regulatory and startup lead for a contract research organization, put it this way: "I felt wanted, needed, valued. [My job] was not just to keep the young ones in line and get their ABCs, but I felt really that what I was contributing was valuable, special." She recalled how special her young charges made her feel: "I remember on various occasions when I'd be at the store, or just walking by, and the kids would yell our names and say, 'Hey, so and so,' and they'd go, 'That's my tutor!' It made me feel so good . . . It was incredible. It was so very incredible." She also felt that because she grew up in Cabrini-Green, she had a particular and unique contribution to make: "In Cabrini we all were poor, but there were a lot of folks who had nothing, who had no food, their clothes weren't the greatest, they probably hadn't bathed in a while, but we had to make them feel special and valued as well . . . And I think because we already had some connections to the kids in the neighborhood, it just made it that much more important that we didn't let them down."

DEVELOPING AND SCAFFOLDING RESPONSIBILITY

"Taking responsibility" is often cast as doing your duty, following through on obligations. Practitioners and researchers understand developing responsibility largely as a question of practicing responsible behaviors, or learning by doing: "We may become responsible by successfully and repeatedly carrying out our responsibilities."[2] The issue was not Cabrini-Green youth simply "taking" more responsibility but, rather, CYCLE growing that responsibility.[3]

Key to the program's leadership mission, the senior staff saw the growth of responsibility among Junior Staffers as essential to them securing a positive course out of Cabrini-Green—succeeding in school as well as gaining the self-confidence, knowledge, and skills critical to doing well in the unfamiliar mainstream world beyond the housing project. Excepting the many caring mothers and aunties who supported CYCLE kids as best they could, young people saw little in the way of individual responsibility exercised around them. Many adults focused on simply navigating the social and economic challenges they confronted daily and saw themselves as victims, with meager hope for a different course through life.

CYCLE's Junior Staff program represented a strategy to nurture success by increasing responsibilities and, in the process, changing their attitudes about what they could achieve. Senior staff did not teach these personal competencies in any direct sense; rather, they created experiences in which youth could understand for themselves what effective personal responsibility looks like. Not surprisingly, Junior Staffers seldom saw that intentionality as they progressed through the ranks. For instance, Greg recalled a conversation he had with David Gates about his accomplishments, the strong friendships that developed among peers and adults, and his joy at seeing his tutees do well. David responded, "I look back on the kids that I tutored and how successful they are and I'm like, 'Wow! This is just amazing to know that I did that.' So, like, I don't know if it was done intentionally." When Greg pointed out that it was CYCLE's leadership strategy, David responded, "Amazing. That was the start of my leadership skills . . . It was amazing, you know!"

David, tall, quiet, and handsome, is the fourth of six children born to Emma, who, as a teen, made the solo journey from Mississippi to Chicago in the early years of the civil rights movement. He and his siblings epitomize all Emma hoped for when she made that lonely trek. David and his siblings Peggy, Randy, and LaTanya have held down management jobs for as long as thirty years—at the Cook County Community and Economic Development Association, United Airlines, Federal Express, and Home Depot, respectively. His brothers William and Curtis (who is now deceased) were targeted as NBA material as early as the middle grades. After a career in professional basketball, William became an urban pastor. He was featured in the movie *Hoop Dreams*, which depicted the sports ambitions and careers of talented Cabrini-Green basketball players. Also a basketball player, David was the star of the Wells High School team; his commitment to CYCLE and the Junior Staff program found him rushing out of practice to get to 515 Oak to carry out his tutoring and program leadership responsibilities. Peggy and William also were Junior Staffers.

Former Junior Staffer David Gates is a manager at the Cook County Community and Economic Development Association.

The senior staff saw responsibility, personal accountability, and leadership as character traits to be learned from experience, unconditional support from more accomplished peers or staff, and challenging expectations—not assigned or taught. Greg has often said that "what we did at CYCLE isn't rocket science." It began with involving Junior Staffers in real work.

Paid work and positive messages about their capabilities and worth constituted powerful incentives for Cabrini-Green youth. But these attractors also played important roles in developing their sense of responsibility and obligation to fulfill commitments because they saw that their jobs involved "real work."

Researchers looking at adolescent development find that when teens are given authentic responsibilities, held accountable for them, and provided support to achieve them, they learn life skills such as punctuality and responsibility and develop positive ideas about their own economic competence.[4] In development of these life (noncognitive) skills, Junior Staffers received constant and consistent attention from the senior staff. For instance, from the outset Greg stressed being on time as an essential job skill. To bring home this point, he docked Junior Staff one hour's pay if they were even a minute late. Clear rules, clear consequences. No excuses for being late. "I loved walking into Monday Junior Staff meetings with a pocket full of quarters," Greg recalled. "And after some sort of admonishment to those who were late last week, I'd throw the equivalent of their docked hours onto the floor, sharing their 'generosity' with their fellow Junior Staffers. Needless to say, it only took losing one hour's pay once or twice to teach a valuable lesson."

Junior Staffers held consequential assignments as mentors, tutors, coaches, and program leaders. This delegation of responsibility for key elements of the CYCLE program taught them that the program depended on them and that it was work that mattered to the younger kids taking part in CYCLE as well as to their community. Unlike friends who worked minimum-wage jobs keeping floors and counters clean in local eateries, Junior Staffers felt their work had social and personal significance. Jennifer Means described her work as "a demanding occupation . . . It wasn't just babysitting." She said that the Junior Staffers worked hard "to get more out of people, even troublesome kids . . . But [it] had the added benefit of you seeing faces change when they learned something that they never thought they could. And I think because we already had some connections to the kids in the neighborhood, it just made it that much more important that we didn't let them down."

Youth engagement fueled youth development. Junior Staffers' involvement in tutoring and overseeing and planning activities provided grist for their roles, but CYCLE's scaffolded strategy enabled them to develop personal and collective responsibility. The program reflected a deep understanding of the social character of learning, the importance of providing opportunities for young people to experience meaningful challenges and succeed at them. Senior staff saw Junior Staffers as individuals. Tasks were not assigned in cookie-cutter fashion; rather, each reflected careful consideration of the young person's maturity, skills, and interests. Senior staff structured Junior Staff responsibilities to provide occasions for them to learn new skills, demonstrate competencies, and successfully take on greater responsibilities. And, as Greg said, they "weren't 'implementing' an existing CYCLE curriculum; they had to figure it out every day."

This approach also reflected Vygotskian notions that successfully carrying out harder and harder obligations expands and reinforces an individual's sense of being a responsible person.[5] Russian psychologist Lev Vygotsky's theories set out scaffolded learning approaches, in which a novice learns from a more advanced peer how to approach a challenging task successfully. He held that children learn best when pushed to undertake challenges that would be too difficult for them to complete on their own but ones that they could master with the support and guidance of a knowledgeable teacher or coach. All Junior Staffers recalled feeling stretched, stressed, and challenged, but they also remembered the feelings of accomplishment and gratification when they succeeded.

Greg based the Junior Staff strategy on his own experience volunteering in St. Louis: "Brother Tom gave high school students responsibilities that matched their maturity, interests and skills. High school students kept his buses repaired. We rehabbed a twenty-building youth camp over two years. Those experiences made a huge impression on me. So I thought, if giving high school kids real responsibilities based on what they cared about and could do could happen in St. Louis, why not in Cabrini Green?" Junior Staff responsibilities followed a near-peer pyramid design that involved young people helping other young people through positions, or tiers, of increased responsibility (see figure 4.1). Successful tutoring of two students led to supervising one new Junior Staff tutor while maintaining responsibility for two tutees. Success with one other Junior Staff tutor led to oversight of up to four Junior Staff tutors. Some of the most experienced Junior Staff tutors, typically those in college, were assigned up to twenty-five Junior Staff tutors and fifty participants to oversee for a six-week, eight-hour per day summer program

Tier 7: Assume full-time position on CYCLE senior staff

Tier 6: Take responsibility for entire age group during summer program, including overseeing academic tutoring, recreation, and cultural events (typically college students)

Tier 5: Supervise Tier 3-4 subgroups (small groups of Junior Staff in Tiers 3 and 4), setting expectations around behavior, homework completion, and instructional theme development (typically high school juniors, seniors, and college students)

Tier 4: Added to Tier 3 duties, tutor Junior Staff in Tier 3 and oversee their lesson planning: select appropriate materials, handle discipline and motivation issues, and manage expected interaction of tutors with tutees

Tier 3: Added to Tier 2 duties, supervise two or three new Junior Staff in the tutoring program (typically ages 15-16)

Tier 2: Tutor an additional two or three students

Tier 1: Tutor a younger student one-on-one (typically ages 14-16)

FIGURE 4.1 *CYCLE's near-peer pyramid design enabled Junior Staffers to advance upward and earn raises by taking on additional responsibilities over time.*

that included three hours of morning academic activities, lunch, and then three hours of recreational, cultural, and social activities in the afternoon. The summer program was all planned and carried out by Junior Staff, with older youth providing leadership. Greg said, "It was their program to make happen or not."

As the youth moved up the pyramid, more advanced Junior Staff learned supervisory skills that built self-confidence, encouraged leadership, and enabled them to interact effectively with less-skilled youth. As they took on increasingly challenging obligations, Junior Staffers experienced stress, worried about failure, and expressed doubts that they could meet expectations. CYCLE pushed every Junior Staffer to the edge of his or her comfort zone, yet alums agreed that they would not have learned as much or accomplished as much without the stress and escalating demands. Gloria Purifoy remarked on the importance of Junior Staff being "continuous learners": "We were constantly challenged to grow, to stay exposed to new things, to prepare ourselves for life. What was great was that you could not do the work without still learning." Lloyd Rogers recalled the sense of pride and leadership he felt as he took on greater responsibility: "I think my best years at CYCLE were the ones when I was actually in the leadership role. I was actually [in charge of] the preschool/kindergarten, that age bracket . . . I think I had ten to fifteen people in my group. It was great!"

CYCLE's approach to the Junior Staff assignments reflected another central component of Vygotsky's theory: the zone of proximal development. Junior Staffers' success in carrying out duties and meeting expectations built self-assurance and skills they could and would later use on their own. Jennifer Means recalled the sense of responsibility she felt: "I remember thinking 'how am I going to do this?' We'd have our Junior Staff meetings before, and I'm like, 'How am I going to figure out how to get them to do this or that?'" Like many others, she felt the high and boost of self-confidence that came when they saw that their choices were effective and that the activities they planned were successful.

Greg was confident that this near-peer, hierarchical approach was the right way to engage kids and build their capacity, but doing so turned out to be more challenging than he initially imagined:

> From the beginning, I had high expectations for Junior Staff members, but I quickly realized that it was going to take longer to fulfill those expectations than I had originally anticipated. This wasn't their issue; it was a matter of me dealing with the reality of skills that needed to be built and their being teenagers [growing up in Cabrini-Green]. The simple rules of engaging their tutees, for example, you had to be vocally engaged or never let your tutees out of your sight; on field trips you had to be in with your tutees the entire time; in art class you were to verbally encourage them, ask questions, motivate them, and you were not to be engaging with your fellow Junior Staff.
>
> I imagined Junior Staff assuming expanded responsibilities but saw that even leading a group game or speaking to an entire group was beyond their initial capabilities. But I also recognized that boundaries needed to be set on discipline, techniques inspiring motivation had to be instilled, and basic work norms had to be established, this being for many of them their first job. I kept Brother Tom's words in mind, that if a concept wasn't gaining traction in a kid's life, it was the responsibility of the adults to simplify the concept even further. That's what emerged as [a core principle for] Junior Staff and CYCLE.

Senior staff did not lower expectations or rescue youth from performance shortfalls; it set clearly articulated expectations and provided developmental supports for achieving them. For many Cabrini-Green kids, the capability question had to do with much more than learning how to lead a game or work with kids; it implicated larger questions of youths' everyday attitudes about personal responsibility and mattering. In Cabrini-Green, excuses like "things happen," "it wasn't my fault," or "just bad luck" often accompanied disappointing outcomes or failed responsibilities. And in many instances these mind-sets of "there's nothing I can do about it" had clear roots in their treatment in school, their personal family experiences, and the neglect and disregard of their housing project. For many Junior Staffers, the sense of responsibility and accountability CYCLE fostered involved a fundamentally new way of looking at themselves and considering their self-worth, something that had to be built from the ground up. It was, for many, a whole new identity. Junior Staffers took considerable pride in the assessment of senior staff "that they could be counted on" to do a good job, to achieve a goal.

Accordingly, in addition to considering a youth's interests, assignments also reflected Greg's and Pat's evaluations of a staffer's level of maturity. For instance, Greg judged Cyril Nichols at age fifteen not yet able to work with CYCLE's younger kids and assigned him to be the greeter, welcoming youth and others to the program, until he seemed ready to work with children. Once Cyril matured a bit, he successfully took on tutoring and other assignments with kids and eventually provided leadership. (Today, Cyril heads up athletics for the Chicago Community College system.)

Senior staff coaching also centered on individual improvement rather than comparative performance. Greg said, "We balanced high expectations with tailored supports to help youth succeed. It was not formulaic or standardized . . . It was pretty open-ended. The kids had to figure out how to achieve their goals and meet their responsibilities. We never put them in any danger, but we stretched them in terms of responsibility and expectations." Each new step up the pyramid asked Junior Staffers to take on new challenges and reinforced their personal growth. Careful scaffolding meant young people were not given responsibilities either in terms of tasks (design a summer activity) or roles (lead the summer team) until they were ready, and their assignments purposely provided occasion for growth. This approach meant that Junior Staffers were challenged by their jobs but confident they would be supported to succeed. Such an approach reflects learning theorist Etienne Wegner's view that "learning cannot be designed. Ultimately, it belongs to the realm of experience and practice . . . Learning happens, design or no."[6]

There are many accounts of program features that promote youth leadership and of why youth leadership matters to program outcomes, but less attention is paid to how leadership opportunities matter to youth development. Commenting on Greg's approach to the Junior Staff program, Gloria Purifoy said, "I don't know that he created the model, but he is one of very few people that understood distributive leadership and developmental leadership." She went on to say that he followed those design principles throughout the Junior Staff experience: "We were always given the opportunity to lead and to lead in our areas of interest. So I went from being a youth aide and tutor to being in charge of program activities and a Youth Leader for Club. I became a leader at CYCLE."

As much as possible, CYCLE embedded leadership opportunities in all Junior Staff routines. Most assignments required Junior Staffers to work together to achieve their goals, which taught them teamwork and leadership skills as they took on more and more responsibility. Carleta Alston said that her experience shaped how, as a college professor, she approaches teaching: "I was never really good at group work. I would rather work alone because I could get more done working alone. But we were forced to work with each other and engage with each other. It taught me how to take ownership of the situation, not just be a passive member of it but to be a part of making decisions and choosing and working with people—that group effort we had to learn how to do. I teach my students the same thing."

Senior staff saw the Junior Staff program as a deeply developmental and youth-centered experience rather than in more standardized, prescribed terms of "program implementation." The sense of personal responsibility that resulted from taking on increasingly challenging responsibilities enabled Junior Staffers to see themselves as adults.[7]

CLEAR RULES AND EXPECTATIONS

Also contributing to the program's effectiveness were the clear parameters defining roles and behavior. Nowhere did CYCLE's core principle of "minimum rules, maximum impact" operate more clearly than in the Junior Staff program. With scaffolded responsibility came explicit rules, expectations, and accountability.[8] Junior Staffers knew what was expected, what they had to do to be successful, what constituted a failure to meet expectations, and they had to figure out how to achieve goals and meet assigned responsibilities. While they had considerable autonomy in deciding how to interact with their tutee, or what might be fun in Club, they also had basic guidelines about expectations and norms of behavior as determined by the senior staff.[9]

Junior Staff tutors were to have continual verbal interaction with their tutees—no silent reading, no worksheet tasks, no look-up-ten-words-in-the-dictionary-and-write-definitions assignments. Play time at the park was structured, with half the time spent in organized games and the rest in supervised free time. Junior Staffers were to encourage and support kids' efforts, not give negative criticism or feedback. There was to be no corporal discipline, even when parents gave permission to do so. Junior Staffers also had to take care of business at school. To retain their status, they had to keep their grades up. If a report card showed more than two Ds, the staffer lost her job for ten weeks. The rules were simple, observable, few, and to the point. Senior staff could easily determine whether they were being followed and take appropriate action if needed.

While these rules were strictly applied, no Junior Staffer lost her job for more than one grading period, and all who did returned after the probationary period was over. Greg said, "The door was always open to coming back, and we'd provide tutoring, any needed supports for kids to get their grades back up." Jennifer Means noted that Junior Staffers were well aware of the rules under which they participated and that no one wanted to lose their place in the program: "That was the worst thing anybody wanted! 'I couldn't go to CYCLE? What?'... Because it was the camaraderie. You had the younger kids looking up to you. You had the leadership depending on you. It had so many ties to it that it had tremendous value, and no one wanted to lose that." Greg concurred with this assessment, acknowledging that "it wasn't just the paycheck; it was the camaraderie of working alongside friends, neighbors."

These basic guidelines offered daily lessons for both senior and junior CYCLE staff about motivation, appropriate discipline, and inclusion of socially and physically awkward kids into group activities. At the Monday night Junior Staff meetings, senior staff reviewed the past week's activities. Greg treated these sessions as teaching moments, using some things that happened as examples of what to do and what not to do as a Junior Staffer. "You could look at that as training, which it was. But it was about norming certain behaviors." Junior Staff also received formal feedback at least twice a year on such aspects of their performance as timeliness, initiative, interaction with tutees, control and discipline, attitude and teamwork—all key elements of the responsible attitudes and life skills the program aimed to cultivate. Junior Staffers also knew that they were accountable to parents if a child in their charge grumbled about something that happened at CYCLE—from perceived disrespectful treatment by a staffer to bullying by other youngsters to "going missing" from program activities. Greg told them, "If a parent shows up to complain, YOU are the one that parent will talk to!"

AGENCY AND CHOICE

Researchers find that leaders of programs with high ratings in development of youth responsibility have consistently "cultivated youth's experience of agency over their work" and "repeatedly referred to youth's 'ownership' and to the work being theirs."[10] Greg and others at CYCLE approached Junior Staff assignments as important contexts for development of initiative. "We tried to create a combination of structure and agency for the Junior Staff," Greg said. "Roles and tasks were unambiguously defined. They knew what to do when tutoring, when taking kids to the park, when taking them home at night. We had explicit expectations but allowed for agency, for the youth to figure it out—how to meet expectations and goals."

Junior Staff had a say in what roles they would plan and what they would be responsible for achieving. Senior staff established behavior boundaries and expectations but also, in keeping with their youth-centric principles, provided a lot of leeway for Junior Staff to make decisions and choices. Their involvement in the program carried clear rules and expectations about what they needed to do to successfully meet their obligations. How they chose to meet those obligations and expectations reflected their own interests, knowledge, and skills—what books to read with younger kids, what activities to do with summer campers, what Chicago excursions might be fun. Greg and Pat Ford tailored each youth's assignment to their interests. "Our commitment was to the individual," Greg said, "and if CYCLE's office or the computer lab or the art program was a better fit, that's where they went." Gloria Purifoy's memory of her time as a Junior Staffer confirmed this: "We were always given the opportunity to lead in areas of our talent."

Most youth got involved with CYCLE's academic tutoring programs, but some had no interest in tutoring and took on other roles. For instance, Margie Davis, who was interested in technology, helped run the computer lab, with five or six high school sophomores under her supervision. And Peggy Gates, who was not interested in tutoring, helped run the computer lab and also served as Greg's administrative assistant.

Junior Staffers' opinions about how things were going figured prominently in senior staff decisions about program activities. Greg used the Monday meetings to gather information from the ground-level Junior Staff about program operations.

> I wanted to get direct information as to the conditions which they were really facing . . . information unfiltered through the senior staff. This was particularly critical given the multiple programs occurring in multiple sites, six days a week over up to a fifteen-hour day. Such a

strategy required absolute confidentiality, hiding any clue that would identify the source. This information was invaluable in making decisions while maximizing strategies in the making of decisions. I also instituted complaint meetings with the Junior Staff, held about every six weeks . . . As teens, they had opinions on everything happening within the program and opinions as to what should programmatically be happening. I wanted to hear from them to have their voice in the mix. I couldn't care less whether we went roller-skating or to the zoo on an upcoming Saturday field trip, or which of five movies we should take them to, so these were easy ways to give them "power." For forty minutes every week they got to let off steam, make suggestions, file their grievances, etc. I saw this as quite constructive, since hidden inside of these conversations were significant clues as to improvements.

This ears-on-the-ground strategy not only provided a youth's-eye assessment of what was working or not, but it also helped Junior Staff develop a strong sense of ownership of the program. CYCLE's Junior Staff experience demonstrated that youth are most likely to develop responsibility when they are given responsibility for a task they care about and then see their views taken seriously.[11]

DEVELOPING COLLECTIVE RESPONSIBILITY

In addition to acquiring a strong sense of *personal* responsibility, CYCLE's goal for the Junior Staff program included fostering an influential sense of *collective* responsibility. Developmental psychologists stress how important it is for adolescents to have opportunities to interact with positively oriented peers and to be involved in roles where they can make a contribution to a group.[12] Strong social bonds provide the glue essential to sustaining commitment to a goal and to developing a sense of collective responsibility.

Junior Staffers' shared expectations, accountability, and clear value system created a powerful sense of "we" and a group identity. The senior staff pursued many strategies to build emotional attachments and commitment to peers and to CYCLE. These social and emotional bonds—interdependent norms of obligation and accountability, shared ownership, and collective agency—figured prominently in alumni's accounts of their experience. In addition to describing themselves in terms of "a good gang," Junior Staff also regarded themselves as "family." Older staffers were big brothers and big sisters, models to be emulated, sources of strength and protection. Familial norms of mutual obligation and care peppered accounts of how and why it mattered to be a Junior Staffer. Tamiko Jones commented, "We grew up together. They were my big sisters, and I was expected to behave a certain kind of way. I wanted to make everybody proud."

Van rides and trips played a significant role in creating strong connections among Junior Staff, and the residential camping experiences proved to be terrific places for many of the summer Junior Staff to get to know senior staff. Weeklong trips to New York, North Carolina, Minnesota, and Colorado in the fifteen-passenger vans established positive foundations for the next seven weeks, when Junior Staff would be together for eight or nine hours a day implementing summer programs for kindergarteners through sixth graders. Camping trips also provided opportunities for senior staff to observe each Junior Staffer and determine what leadership qualities needed to be further developed.

The summer of 1987 service trip to Mississippi was a standout CYCLE bonding experience, a shared ordeal. Greg took twenty-four Junior Staffers to a rural Mississippi town, one with dirt roads, sketchy electricity, and a depth of poverty that was shocking even in Cabrini-Green terms. "Public service" provided the ostensible purpose of the trip, but the real objective was to deepen Junior Staffers' relationships with each other and provide a common set of experiences before they assumed responsibility for running a six-week summer program for 250–300 kids.

The night after they arrived, however, local youth broke into the house where the Junior Staffers were staying and stole many of their possessions—including, to their great outrage, their new underwear. Greg remembered that "they were pissed. They demanded to go back to Chicago, because 'these people don't appreciate us.' It was a mutiny. I felt like I was dealing with a group of middle-class kids." Greg prevailed, and the Junior Staffers stayed to paint houses and sort donated clothing. Long after, this trip remained a touchstone for them, not just in terms of the shared bonds and interconnections they developed, but also their new recognition of relative disadvantage. Cyril Nichols said, "It was important because we didn't think anything was worse than Cabrini-Green. We couldn't fathom anything else out of Cabrini-Green being worse."

To maintain and grow the bonds they were forming, Junior Staffers gathered on Friday afternoons to talk about issues they confronted both at CYCLE and in their lives. Pat Ford recalled that this was also a space in which these young people could seek advice and comfort, since so many of those Friday discussions centered on grief: "All of us knew people who had been shot or killed or sent to jail. Just the impact of incarceration in your family is something. When a loved one goes away, to the rest of the world they may represent a drug dealer, or whatever; but for you, he may be your big brother or your cousin or your friend." In addition to the Friday gatherings, Pat conducted a support group for Junior Staff girls that focused primarily on relationships and avoiding early pregnancy. Bernard McCune ran a group for young men that took up the challenges facing young black men growing up in Cabrini-Green and society and, more generally, in late-twentieth-century America.

CYCLE used the power of these bonds among peers and with senior staff to reinforce this culture of social responsibility and personal accountability. Junior Staffers said that their motivation to meet expectations and fulfill obligations turned significantly on their sense of responsibility to the group. They felt a strong sense of mutual obligation and talked in terms of "being all in," "whatever it takes," "doing whatever needed to be done." This "good gang" didn't want to let the group down by doing an inadequate job or not following through. They felt they were doing important work and knew that if they didn't complete an assignment, it would not get done. Senior CYCLE staff did not bail them out. In addition to wanting to live up to commitments made to the group, Junior Staffers' commitment to follow through with their tutees or with the younger kids motivated their efforts. Their reputations as responsible people mattered to them.

The social investment Junior Staffers made in one another and their commitment to achieving CYCLE's goals went a long way toward explaining why they stuck with it over the years, even in the face of demanding responsibilities, performance and behavioral expectations, and long hours, as well as the lure of activities generally more appealing to an adolescent. As Gloria said, "We didn't want to let each other down, even if sometimes we felt it was just too much."

LESSONS FOR LIFE

Without exception, former Junior Staffers who participated in this follow-up study said that the experience made them who they are today. Many pointed to a number of ways in which the concepts and norms of personal responsibility they learned as Junior Staff at CYCLE played out in other life contexts. Many males—Brian Alston and Craig Nash, for instance—pointed to their long marriages, their stable jobs, and their active roles as fathers and husbands. Cyril Nichols proudly underscored the ways his cohort all became successful adults: "If you just think about my group of guys, we all live in homes right now. We all have families. We all have good jobs." These men hold these accomplishments as especially meaningful given the economic and social context they experienced growing up in Cabrini-Green, where both involved dads and meaningful jobs were few.

The careers Junior Staffers chose signal a compelling sense of personal responsibility that they carried forward. A great many chose careers that they described as "giving back"—coaches, social workers, law enforcement officers, youth work, doctors, philanthropists.

Many became educators with the goal of "giving other kids opportunities—reinvesting."[13] Gloria Purifoy said, "We came back and we gave back. It was the model I knew. Being involved. Being responsible. That's what I was comfortable with." Likewise, Ken Dunkin framed his political career in terms of the values he learned at CYCLE: "It's about really giving back, because the tone was set, folks like [Greg] and CYCLE really gave us the opportunity to believe in ourselves, so that we can be value-added at this point."

Many also indicated that the behaviors they learned from older staff mentors shaped their parenting. For instance, Brian Alston recalled that when his initial response to his young tutee's drawing was "it's ugly as heck," a senior staff member said, "You don't say that. Even though it doesn't look good to you, it was his best effort. You encourage him to keep going." He noted how "that revelation stayed with me all my life with my kids. In this household, we never call each other stupid, dumb, or ignorant. 'Oh, is that what you did? Okay, that's nice. But if you try a little bit this way or try it that way'—Keep moving it, keeping encouraged."

Decades later, Junior Staff alums still referenced the foundational values and norms of behavior they learned at CYCLE. To a person, they said that those norms and expectations have become part of who they are. As Gloria said, "All these years later, I still find myself asking in some situations, 'What would CYCLE consider the right thing to do? What would CYCLE say?'"

CHAPTER 5

Scholarships
Opportunities for Success

Most kids growing up in Cabrini-Green in the mid-1980s did not graduate from high school, and few entertained thoughts of college or other kinds of postsecondary education. As CYCLE began to succeed in getting its participants through high school, questions emerged about the next steps. Cabrini-Green families did not have the financial resources or the knowledge and skills to support college going or other postsecondary schooling, and there were few role models in the Cabrini-Green community to inform and motivate young people's educational hopes and plans. Though CYCLE consistently stressed the critical importance of education for productive futures and satisfying lives, the program needed to be able to make that message a reality for its young people. If its kids were going to diverge from the negative path traveled by most Cabrini-Green youth, CYCLE needed to make it happen.

Cabrini-Green youth required a strong practical and psychological direction to help them move confidently onto a positive life course. Alums acknowledged the essential role CYCLE played in moving them toward their future. Brian Alston said, "We knew they were trying to put us in better positions in life," and Cyril Nichols noted how the program introduced the youth "to an idea of a better life through education," adding that "it wouldn't have been possible for us [African American males] to navigate through school by ourselves. Look at the ones that tried, they're either dead or strung out."

In the early 1980s, Greg began to actively engage Chicago-area philanthropists with CYCLE's mission, enlisting them to support the kids' education through five distinct scholarship programs. While these different programs expressed the same general goals—providing educational opportunities for Cabrini-Green youth either in private schools and or college—each took a somewhat different approach. Three chiefly functioned as traditional scholarship programs awarding funds based primarily on students' aspirations—Schuessler, Bright Knights, and Education Assistance Limited. And two—I Have A Dream and College Opportunity Scholarship Program: Class of 1995—took a comprehensive youth development approach, supporting a cohort of students through middle school, high school, and on to college or a postsecondary program. Each scholarship program offered students a supportive peer community, helped them graduate from high school and college, and broadened their thinking about educational options and future careers. In 1992, the year Greg left the program, CYCLE administered sixty-eight scholarships ranging from $250 to $7,500 to support its students at thirty-one colleges and universities around the country and at six Chicago-area private elementary and high schools.

Commitment to education figured as the primary consideration in the more traditional scholarship awards. "We did not cream [select only the best students]," said Greg. "We responded as we could to kids' interests and motivation." Pat Ford, who oversaw the programs, explained CYCLE's scholarship philosophy:

> We're not just concerned about the kids who just do well in school, who get the A's and B's. We have kids who didn't do well in school... We'll give a scholarship to a kid who someone else might not... if a person has demonstrated that they want to go to school, and the can articulate why they want to go, and they have the desire, CYCLE has been able to give them money. And I like the fact that we're not just working with the bright kids... [Some might] say, "Oh, there aren't a whole lot of bright kids in Cabrini." But we look at our average kids

and say, "Yeah, they're bright and they have the potential." So we see to it that they have the money to go to school.[1]

Greg described much the same philosophy when he recounted his efforts to motivate a bright, underachieving young man:

> In eighth grade, he's being courted by St. Joe's, and probably a few other high schools, to come attend there because of his basketball skills. But he had failed every subject in the first semester. And he was short about $500 to go to St. Joe's. We knew he was really smart, but he was just not applying himself in school. And then there was that Illinois constitution test that you had to pass in order to graduate. So I basically said, "I've got this money for you to go to St. Joe's, but I'm not going to give it to you if you have straight Fs. You've got to get these grades up to above passing. Because when you decide you want to focus and such, you will focus and you will do it." So that was the deal. And he would come in every day for like half an hour for special tutoring before regular tutoring started. So he goes from straight Fs to at least straight Bs. And, if I remember correctly, he had the highest score in his class for the damn constitution test. And so he got a $500 scholarship from me to go to St. Joe's.

Effective supports for CYCLE participants, Greg knew, involved more than writing a check. Personal supports were just as important to a young person's ability to succeed academically and make choices different from those made by friends, family members, neighbors. The low expectations that many encountered in their neighborhood public schools presented a major challenge. Bernard McCune's recollection of an elementary school teacher telling him he was really smart and motivating him to excel in high school, college, and graduate school was not the usual experience for these kids.

Many of the expectations about what they could or would do in school were based on stereotypes about their Cabrini-Green address. Youth heard disparaging comments about them being "project kids" from teachers and fellow students in the city's competitive public or private high schools. Similarly, police regularly stopped kids in Cabrini-Green on the assumption that they must be up to something no-good. David Gates described such an encounter: "I start to walk toward my mom's house and these police jump out of the car and started rushing toward me. They say, 'We heard about you and you're selling drugs.' I say, 'You've got the wrong person' . . . They just jump to a conclusion about black males in Cabrini, you know."

Each scholarship program had a coordinator dedicated to providing the youth with whatever supports were needed, and all the recipients attended evening tutoring sessions. But beyond that, the programs looked quite different, depending on leaders' and students' interests and enthusiasms. For instance, one group gathered weekly to discuss films relating to the African American experience; another filled summer afternoons with tennis lessons, art projects, and visits to ethnic museums. Two groups created poems and short stories for CYCLE's literary magazine that expressed the experience, frustrations, joys, and fears of life in the project.

GETTING YOUTH INTO BETTER SCHOOLS

The Schuessler and Providence–St. Mel programs focused on getting CYCLE kids into more rigorous schools and supporting them while they were there.

Schuessler/CYCLE Scholarships

The generally poor quality of the CPS schools serving Cabrini-Green students and the limited educational options available to them prompted Greg to approach local businessman Walter Schuessler, who cofounded the Schuessler Knitting Mills located on the Near North Side close to Cabrini-Green, and tell him how several of CYCLE's earliest students were receiving college acceptances but needed financial assistance over and above tuition to attend. In 1985 Schuessler stepped in to provide discretionary funds to meet CYCLE students' basic needs in college. Pat Ford received the first scholarship of $500, half of which went directly to the college and the other half she kept to help with expenses. This amount did not cover the full tuition or all the expenses; students had to get jobs to supplement these scholarship awards.

The Schuessler general college scholarship fund quickly expanded to include high school students as CYCLE sought to place the most promising youth in more academically rigorous and supportive schools. Also, Greg felt that getting kids into better schools would provide better peer supports for them. One of the most consistent findings in education research is that poor kids do better in high-income schools. But, in Greg's view, the cards were stacked against qualified participants' ability to access the best high schools or universities. "There seemed to be a silent, accepted quota system in place," he said. "One graduate from each Cabrini-Green elementary school got into either Lane Tech or Whitney Young, the two most prestigious high schools north of the Eisenhower Expressway that students could possibly be admitted to. Yet, there were at least a dozen students at each of the five elementary schools with the same academic record."

In response to the limited seats open to Cabrini-Green youth at Whitney Young and Lane Tech, and the general lack of rigor at Wells and Lincoln Park High Schools, where they were assigned to matriculate, CYCLE moved to enroll kids in private high schools like Josephinum, Holy Trinity, and Providence-St. Mel and even some elite schools, such as Parker and Latin School.

In 1987–88, the Schuessler/CYCLE Scholarship fund allowed thirty-one students to attend nearby high schools or colleges of their choice. Greg and senior staff selected students for the scholarship based on the school or college at which they were accepted and the likelihood that they would be successful. Any student was eligible, but most awardees came from the Junior Staff program. Many elementary-aged students participating in the tutoring program also received scholarships to attend private high schools. In the 1989–90 school year, $40,000 of the Schuessler funding was allocated to meet the academic needs of nearly fifty students. In the early 1990s, some funding began to go to support students in private elementary or grammar schools and even to parents who expressed interest in getting a college degree.

Tamiko Jones's older cousins introduced her to CYCLE when she was in first grade, and she spent the next eight years faithfully taking part in the tutoring program. After elementary school, she attended Providence–St. Mel on a Schuessler scholarship and went on to graduate from Northern Illinois University Rockford and earn a master's degree from Roosevelt University and a doctorate in science education from Loyola University. The third of five children, Tamiko credited her mother, Liz Lowery, and CYCLE for keeping her focused on education. Sixteen-year-old, pregnant Liz came to Chicago from Florida in the 1970s and moved into the Town and Garden Apartments. A high school dropout, she wanted to give her first child the best start in life and believed that there were more opportunities in Chicago than in the South. She recounted the poverty in which she had grown up and stories of her slave-born grandmother to urge her children to make education their top priority. Liz was one of the first

Tamiko Jones with her mother, Liz Lowery, in 2017. Tamiko, who has an EdD in science education, holds an executive position with Pearson Education.

moms to receive her GED through CYCLE's adult program, and she went on to take a teacher assistant job in that program.

Tamiko recalled her mother talking to her and her siblings "about how everything was directly tied to your education . . . and watching her gracefully struggle as a single mom. She would say, 'If you want greater things, then you need to make sure that you get a high school degree, you get a college degree.'" And whenever Tamiko was tempted to give up on her education, she thought about "what my mother would say, and all that CYCLE had invested in me. I think I refused to be a statistic—I said, 'I will break a cycle.'" Today, Tamiko holds an executive position with the publishing company Pearson Education.

In August 1988, Anita Boyd joined CYCLE as the Schuessler scholarship coordinator. She was responsible for monitoring recipients' academic progress as well as the progress of the CYCLE alums attending college with support from Schuessler scholarships. Many times she teamed up with the other scholarship coordinators to devise recreational, social, and educational experiences for the scholarship kids. Greg said that although he knew that "the Schuessler students would not need support services to the extent that students in the other scholarship programs needed them," because they were selected based on academic promise, CYCLE still "needed someone specifically assigned to look after these young people."

All CYCLE youth who received Schuessler scholarships to attend a private high school graduated and went on to college. And, as Greg remembered it, most, if not all, of these youth, as well as all of the young people who received postsecondary financial support only, graduated from college or university—"There may have been a few who did not graduate from college, but I can't think of any."

Education Assistance Limited

Chicago businessman Swede Roskam founded the national Education Assistance Limited program in 1982 because he saw college as a "game changer" for young people. As a poor teen growing up in rural Iowa, he had little prospect of going to college. But when the son of a neighboring couple died unexpectedly, they gave all of the money from their son's college fund to Swede, and he was able to attend Knox College in Galesburg, Illinois. Swede subsequently made a fortune from his invention of kitty litter as a by-product of his Oil Dry company, though the money supporting EAL came from the sale and barter of excess inventory solicited from companies around the country.

Like the other CYCLE scholarship programs, EAL identified middle grade students as its first priority, although students in the high school grades were also eligible. It helped students who could not be supported financially through the highly competitive and limited number of Schuessler scholarships. The EAL program's challenge was that the scholarships were limited to about forty mostly private higher education institutions that agreed to EAL's unique bartering arrangement that generated the scholarship dollars. The bartering concept was fairly straightforward: EAL would sign agreements with colleges to place about 85 percent of the cost of needed products donated to a campus into a scholarship fund, and EAL would take the other 15 percent to cover its administrative costs.

Another challenge was matching the interests of CYCLE's EAL participants with the limited number of participating colleges. This was made even more complicated because one college or university might have $50,000 in scholarships to distribute and another might have only $5,000, which resulted in an uneven allocation of scholarship dollars as well as a struggle to place multiple students at the same school. Yet, despite these difficulties, EAL represented a way to expand the scholarship opportunities available to CYCLE youth.

Nate Thomas served as the initial project coordinator while working toward his PhD in clinical psychology at De Paul University. EAL was an open-application program that recruited students from all Cabrini-area schools. CYCLE staff asked teachers for recommendations, young people referred one another, and CYCLE staff visiting area schools let kids and teachers know about the program—"Hey, we have these opportunities. Are you interested? Can you recommend someone?"

The EAL group included middle grade and high school students from several Cabrini-area schools. Bernard McCune, who succeeded Nate Thomas as scholarship coordinator, recalled that there was at least a four-year age difference among participants. EAL participants met once a week in small groups and also took part in CYCLE activities—tutoring, mentoring, college trips, field trips, summer camps. Attendance at tutoring was mandatory but, as Bernard noted, for kids from that neighborhood, attendance wasn't an issue: "We didn't have to make them mandatory because the kids always wanted to be there . . . You look for something positive to do. If you're not doing something positive, there's a whole lot of negative you can do."

The EAL group took several big trips. For the alums of that program, the most memorable trip was to Washington, DC, which included a tour of Howard University, a meeting with Illinois senator Paul Simon, and a meeting with a sitting Supreme Court justice. "It was huge for our students to see the world outside," remembered Bernard. "Their world was probably a four-to-eight-block radius, because we don't normally go out of the community." CYCLE offered guidance and support to the EAL students, hiring several as Junior Staff, thereby providing them with additional mentoring and leadership opportunities. And the program continued to support its students even after they graduated from high school. Bernard remembered driving them to college to see that they navigated "the lines and the paperwork. I wanted them to have someone who cared."

EAL outcomes evidenced the support that CYCLE provided the young people: all twenty-two recipients graduated from high school. By Bernard's estimate, around 80 percent of them went to college, and about 65 percent of them earned a bachelor's degree.

Providence–St. Mel Scholarship

Providence–St. Mel, created in 1969 with the merger of Providence and St. Mel Catholic high schools, was saved from closing nearly a decade later through the leadership of its principal, Paul Adams, and his colleagues. The Archdiocese of Chicago sold the school to Adams for one dollar in 1978 for him to operate as an independent, college preparatory school serving African American students. Initially started as a high school program, the school eventually expanded to include grades 1–12. Since 1978, 100 percent of Providence–St. Mel students have graduated and been accepted to college.

In 1989, with funding from Tom Dittmer, CEO of Refco, a global commodities trading company, ten CYCLE middle grade students began attending Providence–St. Mel on full scholarship. The next year Heller Financial became a corporate sponsor, and the first individual sponsor, Brian Battle, agreed to sponsor two young men. In April 1991, McDonalds restaurants agreed to sponsor nine students. In June 1991, Providence–St. Mel assumed total responsibility for all aspects of the program and changed the name to the Bright Knight Corporate Scholarship Program, whose stated purpose was to provide academic, cultural, and social support to black students from Chicago's housing projects and low-income neighborhoods.

In 1990 Richard Blackmon became the CYCLE liaison for the Bright Knights program. Having grown up in Cabrini-Green, he understood the struggles a kid from the project confronts in a competitive, rigorous academic environment, as well as the challenges faced every day in the streets, stairwells, and elevators of their homes. And Richard excelled as a student at Lane Tech, the University of Illinois Carbondale, and Notre Dame Law School. He described his role as a "liaison" or "bridge" between Paul Adam's no-nonsense, no-excuses leadership style that demanded academic excellence and CYCLE's "never give up on a kid" philosophy. Richard said he could work across "two different cultures" because Paul admired his record of academic excellence and Greg trusted him to look out for the interests of CYCLE kids.

As Bright Knights coordinator, Richard supported his charges academically and socially. In 1991, the program numbered thirty-four students in grades 5–8; it cost $5,600 per student, which covered the $3,500 annual tuition and the $2,100 for the Bright Knights activities. The youth attended afterschool tutoring Monday through Thursday, but Fridays was "fun time designed to expose them to different parts of Chicago," Richard explained. "We went to sports events, the amusement parks, restaurants, music events. Once we had tickets to the ballet."

He also established Saturday Knight School, which provided youth with individually designed tutoring and academic supports. Publisher McDougal Littell provided a full set of K-12 math and reading books for all grade levels of Saturday Knight School.

"The Bright Knights went to school six days a week. We focused on essential skills—almost all of them fell short coming from Cabrini-Green elementary schools." Richard visited classrooms regularly, observed, talked with teachers, and kept tabs on what his kids needed to be doing to keep on track academically. Bright Knights were required to attend summer school as well, which focused on academics but also included cultural activities, such as trips to the Ravinia music festival, the planetarium, Marwen art lessons, and an African dance workshop, as well as fun enrichment activities like baseball games, movies, roller skating, and trips to a wave pool. Some older Knights attended Providence-St. Mel's Summer Opportunity of a Lifetime program and traveled to such places as the Taft School, Interlochen International Camp, American Youth Foundation's Camp Miniwanca, and Camp Highlands for Boys.

To support the young men in the program, Richard developed Rites of Passage, a program that focused on black male experiences and legacies and their opportunities at Providence-St, Mel and how to succeed in that rigorous academic climate. The group talked about mainstream norms and expectations. Richard remembered that "several of them initially would come to school with knives and guns because that's what they needed for safe passage through Cabrini. I told them to leave them, they were not needed at the school or on the bus that transported them. The school was just an entirely different culture for them."

The Bright Knights did well academically. The program established benchmarks of a 2.0 GPA for fifth graders and 2.75 for eighth graders. Richard recalled that all the students met or surpassed that standard, and, like other students at Providence-St. Mel, 100 percent graduated from high school and went on to a four-year college or university, and, by his estimate, around two-thirds of them graduated from college.

CHAPTER 6

The I Have A Dream Scholarship Program

Shree Green recalled being a seventh grader at Byrd Community Academy on October 16, 1987:

> It was just a big thing the day when they announced that we were being given scholarships by the I Have A Dream Foundation. We didn't have an auditorium; we had this foyer area which was just basically a hall and a lunchroom. So they told us to get down there and they just made this announcement. We're like, "Oh, my God!" And they told our parents to come to the school... The mayor was there and everyone was there, and the Kaplans. And they just were gonna pay for you all to go to college, whether you choose a four-year college, whether you choose vocational—whatever it is that you choose to do, they'd pay for it if you graduate from high school.

New York businessman Eugene M. Lang launched the I Have A Dream (IHAD) Foundation in 1981 during a speech he gave at a sixth-grade graduation ceremony at the Harlem elementary school he attended fifty years earlier. When the principal told him that three-quarters of the class would probably not finish high school, he made an impromptu promise to guarantee college tuition to every sixth grader who stayed in school and graduated. IHAD quickly spread to cities across the country, including Chicago, where twelve programs operated in the late 1980s.[1]

Burton Kaplan, former president of the Sealy Mattress Company of Illinois, agreed to sponsor the Byrd IHAD class of forty-two seventh graders in partnership with CYCLE.[2] CYCLE was tasked with providing the home base for the Byrd Dream Class, and Greg Darnieder was responsible for general program oversight and guidance. Of the three Cabrini-Green grammar schools, Byrd was selected to participate in the IHAD program because its sixth grade was smaller than Jenner's or Manierre's, and principal Janice Todd was known to be easy to work with.

For Shree Green, being part of the Byrd class selected for the IHAD program was life changing. She grew up with her mother and younger brother in Old Town Garden apartments, and every school day, for safety's sake, she headed to her aunt's row house home to join her cousins on the walk to Byrd Community Academy. She credited IHAD and CYCLE for exposing her to new things around Chicago and the country, enabling her to attend a rigorous high school program, manage in college as a single mom, and take confident steps as a finance professional and later an entrepreneur. But thinking back to October 1987, Shree recalled being skeptical about this unexpected support for her and her classmates' futures. She doubted whether she would really get a scholarship: "So I said to myself, 'I've gotta graduate high school to see if it is true . . . I've gotta do my end to make sure' . . . This person, a business professional, why would he come

A Byrd Dreamer, Shree Green graduated from DePaul University in 2002 with a BA and in 2007 with a MA in accounting. After more than ten years in banking and finance, Shree followed her interest in personal fitness and opened a fitness studio with her daughter.

into the ghetto to offer us something? You're kinda like, 'Okay, what's the gimmick? What do you want?'"

Burt Kaplan and each of the Byrd Dreamers signed a contract that outlined their respective obligations. As sponsor, Kaplan agreed to provide not only a scholarship of at least $1,200 a year for four years of college or attendance at an approved vocational program but also educational support and guidance through high school. Students agreed to attend classes regularly, complete assignments, participate in tutoring and counseling sessions, and attend cultural enrichment events when possible. They also agreed to respect the rights and property of others.

All IHAD programs across the country include tutoring, summer programming, college preparation, career awareness, counseling, parent involvement, and social and cultural enrichment. In Chicago, with CYCLE, the Kaplans also committed to hiring a project coordinator to encourage, mentor, and work with each of the Dreamers over the six years until high school graduation. In Chicago philanthropist Harrison Steans's opinion, the "genius" of the I Have A Dream program "was not the scholarship, which gets all the attention, but coming up with the concept of a full-time project coordinator to work with each of these kids and their families." The project coordinator's manual elaborated no fewer than fourteen discrete responsibilities, with the last clearly conveying the job's personal demands: "This is not a 9-5 job!! Individual must be able and willing to work days, evening and weekends in schools, homes, streets, social service agencies, wherever necessary to reach goals."

COORDINATOR CRAIG NASH

Craig Nash joined the program in 1988 when the Byrd Dreamers were in their second year, heading into eighth grade. "They chased off the first coordinator," he recounted. "They went on a camping trip, and all I heard about was that she was traumatized after that trip and quit. They were a tough group."

Craig was raised in the Cabrini-Green community, and his early years were difficult. He lived with his grandparents much of the time, sharing a pass-through bedroom with his only brother. His anger bubbled near the surface, ready to explode at the slightest provocation, and school suspensions too often followed. The arts and drawing offered him an escape, and then in high school a buddy introduced him to Young Life and CYCLE, enticing him with the possibility of a free Florida spring break trip. Despite doubting that his academic achievements would earn him a spot, he threw himself into both organizations and quickly found what he had been searching for—family, peers who wanted something better for themselves, "a community that cared about you," and opportunities to lead. CYCLE helped arrange his enrollment at Lane Tech, Chicago's preeminent North Side high school, and there he joined the football team. He was named captain of the junior varsity and then varsity teams. Craig was a natural-born leader, whether as a director of one of Young Life's few urban programs, supervisor of art sessions at CYCLE, overseer of forty-five I Have A Dream participants, or, later, a tank commander in the US Army.

He credits Greg and the Junior Staff program with putting him on the path to college. "Because of CYCLE I finally figured out that I needed to get serious about school and make it to college. So Greg started giving me some educational and leadership opportunities." He attended Monmouth College, and on graduation he was commissioned in the US Army as a second lieutenant, married his sweetheart Deborah, and moved to Fort Knox. He served in the military for three years and then relocated to Detroit with his young family to search for employment opportunities. He turned down Greg's 1987 invitation to apply for the new IHAD coordinator position, but when it became available again in 1988, Craig was ready to return to Chicago and CYCLE.

In many ways, Craig was uniquely qualified to support the Byrd Dreamers through high school and into college or careers. He had deep appreciation for CYCLE's mission and developmental perspective. He understood personally the many challenges Cabrini-Green youth faced in simply making it to high school graduation, let alone college. His own brother was a "wounded soldier" of Cabrini gang warfare who made decisions that landed him in the Illinois state penal system with a forty-year sentence. Greg said, "There is no one who better manifested Young Life's principle that as adults we must 'earn the right to be heard' by youth."

THE BYRD DREAMERS

When Craig began as coordinator, almost half of his charges were at risk of not graduating from Byrd with their class.

> We had to hit the ground running, because this was eighth grade, and probably about seventeen students in the class were at risk for not graduating from grammar school because they did not score proficient on the Iowa Test. So we had to start a special tutoring [program] to prepare them for getting all the basics, to get them ready for the tests. I told them, "We're going to do this reading program. We're going to do these practice tests. We're going to do all these different things to help you get ready so you'll pass that Iowa Test . . . We're gonna work all week, and let's see how you do on a practice test. We'll keep doing this." And out of seventeen, fourteen made it! That was an important success.

The remaining three students attended summer school, graduated, and retained their Dreamer status.

Craig faced other obstacles than academic ones in supporting the students. Family engagement, a foundational component of IHAD, proved difficult. He said that not all parents were supportive, "whether it's they had to work all the time or they were having problems finding work, whatever the situation . . . We tried to be there for families, but you can't be everything to everybody." He explained that some parents were involved, "but for other kids [IHAD] was the only stable thing in their lives. I had a group of parents that volunteered to do this or to do that and come and help with different things. And those parents, some of the kids looked up to them and were like, 'Man, I wish I had that.'"

And in contrast to academic support programs that selected students of demonstrated promise or serve motivated students who seek out the program, the Byrd Dreamers had different individual academic and personal needs and diverse capabilities, which tested everyone from the outset. They were an overage group, Craig said, some having failed a grade, or two. "So, imagine having a sixteen-year-old that's graduated from eighth grade, a fifteen-year-old that's graduated from eighth grade . . . And as the Dreamers started eighth grade, one was pregnant and another already a mom." He explained that for these older kids, "already the deck was stacked against them . . . They were already beat up by the system."

IHAD ACTIVITIES

Byrd Dreamer activities followed the IHAD template of tutoring, mentoring, enrichment, and personal support and provided myriad ways to engage the students in the program and mission. Craig knew the importance of providing lots of positive opportunities to offset the lure of the negative so readily available in Cabrini-Green:

> If you keep kids busy with a number of good activities, sooner or later something clicks. And we tried to have them involved with stuff and make sure they got to school. So some kids got rides. Made sure that after school there were some opportunities. Summertime, there's some opportunities. We tried to keep them connected and involved, and keep them busy. So, if I picked you up after school or you came to tutoring, say we started doing activities at 3:30. I might not get you home 'til 9:30. When is there time to gang-bang? When is there time to have kids, all those kind of things? We're trying to keep you connected to some positives, so when that negative stuff pulls at you, it

pulls at all of us. "Hey, come on, do this!" You build up that strength, build up that muscle to say, "No."

All Dreamers attended tutoring sessions two times a week. Craig picked kids up at their schools, brought them to CYCLE, and saw that they got home safely. He learned that the only way to move the Dreamers ahead as a group was to take each one as an individual and respond to his or her particular issues: "You've got to deal with your top students and make sure that they're exposed and they have opportunities. But you also have to deal with your kids in the neighborhood schools who are struggling. You've got to make adjustments." CYCLE volunteers and Junior Staff tutors worked with Craig to personalize each session.

Junior Staff and volunteer tutors typically established close relationships with their Dreamer tutees and offered guidance about personal issues. But Dreamers also had "buddy" mentors from the Kellogg School of Management at Northwestern University, many of whom, in addition to their mentoring roles, also tutored their Dreamer, and sometimes even took them to spend the day at Northwestern, visiting the recreation center, the library, just walking around campus. Shree Green credited her Kellogg "big sister" with keeping her connected to school when peer pressure pulled her in other ways.

Craig worked hard to provide engaging activities and new opportunities that exposed the students to life outside Cabrini-Green and kept them connected to the program when academics were a struggle and school was tough going—"We had so many activities—movies, roller skating . . . We'd hop in the CYCLE van and afterward I would take everybody home." Everyone had a birthday celebration in a Chicago restaurant of their choice, and these celebrations and local outings were open to everyone. But "when it came to some of the larger stuff," Craig said, "to go on trips you had to attend tutoring regularly. We had expectations and a whole lot of carrots."

One of the IHAD missions was to introduce the students to new-to-them places and activities, to take them "out of that Cabrini box."

Shree noted that "the Kaplans wanted us to experience so many different things that you may not have, given the neighborhood or the environment that you grew up in. They exposed you to *everything* that they could think of! We went on college tours, we went camping, canoeing." The Byrd Dreamers also made several big trips, one of which was to New York City so they could see that they were part of a larger I Have A Dream family. With primary support from the Kaplans, they met other Dreamers in Brooklyn and elsewhere in New York City and also appeared on an episode of *CBS Sunday Morning* about IHAD. Craig remembered that "Shree led a song."

On another trip, the eighth-grade Byrd Dream Class went to Washington, DC. Craig called this the "come to Jesus" trip because it was a turning point in his relationship with the students. The class designed the trip and devised fund raisers, including selling candy bars and organizing a big carnival held in CYCLE's basement. The Kaplans helped sponsor the trip, and the Kellogg mentors held a bake sale and raised enough money to charter a Greyhound bus to take the group to DC in style. About thirty kids went on the trip, with CYCLE interns from area colleges and Junior Staff accompanied them as chaperones.

Craig recalled that a day or so into the trip, "the kids got fussy. 'We're tired of walking!' 'We're not having any fun!' They were tired of doing educational things . . . I told all the chaperones, 'You all go over there; let me talk to them.'" He then told the students, "I'm not going anywhere. We're in a relationship and this relationship is gonna last for the next six, seven years. Now, it can be a good relationship, or we can fight and fuss all the time. It's up to you. But I'm not going anywhere. What is your problem?" When they started to complain—"We don't like this," "We don't like that"—he looked at them and responded, "Then why did you design it?" He reminded them that many people had contributed to the trip so that they could "do some educational things" and asked them to redesign the schedule so that for "every educational thing that we do, we'll do a fun day." And so they did. They went out and bought water guns and had a huge water fight; they designated days when they could sleep in; and they still managed to visit Capitol Hill and other important DC sites.

Craig's response to the Dreamers' rebellion followed a core CYCLE principle: recognize a teachable moment and turn it into a developmental opportunity. With this conversation, he allowed the Dreamers to take responsibility for aspects of their trip they didn't like and become active agents in its redesign. He guided them in developing a new plan but did not impose one on them, as another frustrated, tired trip leader might have done. The individual responsibility, trust, and respect this conversation conveyed established Craig's commitment to the group and the understanding that their behavior would not chase him away, as it had the previous project coordinator.

ACADEMIC PROGRESS

Every semester, when grades came out, Craig and Burt Kaplan scheduled meetings with each Dreamer. They reviewed progress, agreed on goals for the next semester, and talked about ways IHAD could support the student academically or personally. But as the Dreamers moved through high school, many of them stopped coming to these sessions. Craig said, "Early on, I would say probably 75–80 percent of the kids came to the check-ins. Then, as we moved on, it got closer to graduation, then we had some fall by the wayside, and fewer and fewer came. So, we got down to probably about 50 percent who would come by." He noted that "it would mostly be the kids that were C or better" who showed up. "Some of the other kids, they just—the embarrassment or whatever, they wouldn't come by."

CYCLE's February 1990 IHAD report, which covered the first half of the Dreamers' freshman year in high school, conveyed a general falling off in their connection to school and their adherence to their IHAD contract. School attendance continued to be a major concern, especially for those attending the troubled Lincoln Park and Wells. At the time, Burt Kaplan wrote the report that "many Dreamers are barely keeping their heads above water, we will have approximately

20 pupils who will need to attend summer school." In addition, the report noted that struggling students were "not showing up consistently for tutoring; they blame the teacher, or just settle for a low grade."[3] And the next year produced a similarly downbeat account of the Dreamers' sophomore year, noting especially that "pregnancies are dreadful and school progress is fair." Of the 22 girls in the class, 8 were pregnant or already had a child; 3 already had two babies. And 2 youth were in being held in the Department of Corrections or St. Charles Prison (one was subsequently dismissed from the program, but the other did go on to graduate from high school). Burt indicated that 17 Dreamers earned full or almost full junior status and were candidates for college and identified 12 who might benefit from an alternative school. He concluded the report with, "We keep plugging hard."

Craig and the Kaplans took kids where they were. But they sent a clear message that wherever they were they could do a little bit better. Ds and Fs could become Cs and Ds. As long as they were trying, Dreamers were not excluded from any activity because of poor grades. Craig had remembered his own experience being left out of things in high school because his grades were not up to par: "I didn't want kids to feel that way, didn't want them shut out because of grades. There were a lot of good things going on! We didn't cream; we [even] took struggling students on college tours." Greg remarked that "CYCLE's philosophy was to never give up on a kid, and it certainly played out in IHAD." For instance, when four Dreamers were eventually dismissed from Providence–St. Mel for minor behavioral infractions or for failing to meet the required GPA (before the Bright Knights scholarship program launched), Greg and Craig worked to find the next best private or public school option for them. And Craig helped three Dreamers who were off-track in their comprehensive high schools move to alternative schools and graduate on time.

Craig also went to extraordinary lengths to keep the single moms in the program. Craig found spots for two in a residential school for moms and their babies, and he and CYCLE developed afterschool opportunities "that expressed real love and support for the teen moms." Community norms about teen moms presented an obstacle to staying in school, and he worked with those girls' families to provide the emotional and practical support that would enable them to graduate from high school. "In our community, the norm is for the girl to give up on her own development when she has a baby. The father takes off and she is left alone," he said. "Another community norm is 'don't let anybody watch your baby; you're not leaving the baby to go to school.' I worked with them on child care and other issues involved in keeping these teen moms in school." Craig was in a position to speak to this, since he and his wife, Deborah, had been teen parents, and they had both made it through college. "I worked with all of those young ladies and encouraged them not to give up."

BURT AND ANNE KAPLAN

The Kaplans played an extraordinary and active role in Dreamers' lives, providing support that extended far beyond a scholarship promise. From taking them on trips, to supporting their educational goals, to helping out with difficult life challenges, they treated the Dreamers as family. Craig said that the Kaplans had the attitude that "whatever you'd do for your own family, you do for the kids." Their care ranged from attending to the Dreamers' basic needs to "making a call [to] a psychologist or a doctor or whatever specialist we'd need . . . Whatever we needed, they looked at their network and made their network available. They cared. They really cared."

The IHAD contract committed the Kaplans to $1,200 a year to underwrite college or other postsecondary education for each Dreamer. But, by all accounts, their financial support went above and beyond this. Shree Green shared, "When I graduated from grade school, they were willing to put me through the Latin school for high school . . . Though I decided not to go, they were willing to pay [the tuition]." And when she got pregnant, she recalled, "the Kaplans were just so amazing," helping her figure out how to have her baby and still go to college. They paid for her child to go to the top daycare facility in Chicago. "If you wanted [assistance] and it was in their power to do it, they did it with no strings attached," Shree said. "Passionate people. People with true love for others. And then instilling those values. I don't even know if Anne and Burt understood how much they contributed to changing lives."

The Kaplans took the Dreamers to many Chicago cultural events—the ballet, the opera, museums—and, as part of the experience, a meal at a restaurant ("No burgers," Anne decreed). The Kaplans were actively engaged in all of these activities. Shree noted that they didn't just send the Dreamers on excursions, but they went *"with* us . . . making sure we actually experienced it on the level they experienced it . . . They were consistent in being part of everything." For instance, Burt, an aficionado of contemporary art and trustee of the Chicago Art Institute, often took the students on tours of the Institute. And the Kaplans also paid active and supportive attention to how the Dreamers were in life. "They were consistently coming to you saying, 'Hey, how are you doing?' *All* of us, no matter how we were doing," Shree said. "A lot of times in classrooms, if you don't do well, you just kind of fall on the wayside. It wasn't like that; they were still consistently reaching out even to those of us who didn't want to be reached. For me, they arranged special tutors to work with me if I was struggling in a particular subject—in addition to the tutoring we had at CYCLE."

The Kaplans' annual Christmas party at their home was a highly anticipated event for the Dreamers, one that made them feel like they were part of Burt and Anne's family. Craig recalled: "Anne didn't just do a [low-key] Christmas party. It was a staged event! There were decorations that she and her partner in her decorating business would do with different themes." And there was always a gift for each Dreamer. (Shree remembered receiving her "first cashmere scarf," as well as books and the Sony Dream Machine alarm clock.)

They involved the Dreamers in other aspects of their family life, including weddings, and they used family connections to place them in summer jobs and internships. One student worked with the Jewish Council on Urban Affairs, a group Burt was actively involved in. Anne's brother owned two McDonalds franchises and hired many Dreamers for summer jobs, and their son-in-law, a stock trader, took two of the kids to work as runners on the exchange floor—"They were making really good money," Greg noted, "thirteen-, fourteen-year-olds making $500 to $600 a week!" Through the Kaplans and their large network, there were many opportunities for any Dreamer who wanted a summer job. And, like family, the Kaplans attended every Dreamer's high school and college graduation ceremonies, even when they required travel out of state.

The Kaplans' generosity extended to Craig and his family, as well. "We vacationed with Burt, Anne, and the family," he remembered. "They had a house in Taos, New Mexico. We would go and go skiing. My girls learned how to ski in Taos Ski Valley. And Burt would just say, 'Get here, you just get here.' One year, I was like, 'Burt, I don't think my car can make it.' 'Oh, okay. Go to my house, pick up my car, and drive that.'"

Even after the Kaplans' contractual commitment ended, they were always open to a request for funds for Dreamers to attend school or a training program. And when Craig left CYCLE in 1992 to take another position, they funded a portion of his position so that he could keep in touch with the Byrd Dreamers as they went through college and provide any assistance they needed.

Burt Kaplan died in 2011, having suffered with Parkinson's disease during the last years of his life. The Dreamers were invited to his funeral, and a couple dozen made the trip to the Highland Park home to join family and friends in remembering him. Burt's obituary featured his support of IHAD and "adoption of a class of Cabrini-Green Byrd Academy 7th graders" and noted that "the class remains an important part of the extended Kaplan family."[4] More than twenty years after the Dreamers' high school graduation, Anne Kaplan remained in touch with many of them by phone and social media and was involved in their lives. For instance, in 2015 she donated her frequent flier miles to support a Dreamer headed to the London School of Economics to pursue a master's degree.

"What got me was that Burt said he would do it if it just impacted one [kid]," Craig said. Confirming this, Harrison Steans, head of the Steans Family Foundation and leading promoter of IHAD initiatives in the Chicago area, reported a discussion among a group of Chicago philanthropists around the question of how to measure IHAD program success. While some thought that success meant that every one of the kids would graduate from college, Steans said, Burt Kaplan spoke up, saying, "Look, if we can get one kid to make it, we've done something pretty good here."

DREAMERS' OUTCOMES

Most of this challenging Dreamer group went to low-performing local high schools, Wells and Lincoln Park, and others were scattered across Chicago in private schools, competitive public schools, or alternative schools. Of the original class of 44, 29 Byrd Dreamers graduated from a comprehensive high school, 3 graduated from an alternative high school, and 3 earned their GEDs, making for a 78 percent graduation rate. (Two moved out of state during the course of the program, and 1 was dismissed.[5]) Craig estimated that about half of the Dreamers who graduated used IHAD funds to go to college or get technical training. Among those who went to college, 5 went on to earn a master's degree, including 3 of the teen moms who attended the high school program for pregnant and parenting young women.

Judged by Burt Kaplan's standard, the Dreamers succeeded beyond his highest hopes. Judged by the standard of CPS's 35 percent high school graduation rate for the class of 1993, the Dreamers distinguished themselves. Similarly, research has found that CYCLE's Dreamers also did better than those in Chicago's other IHAD programs.[6]

But "success" for Burt and Anne Kaplan and for CYCLE was not understood only in academic outcome terms. Craig recalls that Burt was happy to see that most of the Dreamers made productive and constructive decisions about their lives, even if they did not use IHAD funds to go on to college or some postsecondary institution. As Craig reported, "They are taking care of their families, they're working at steady jobs, they're raising their kids. I get calls from them about, 'How can I get my kid into this program? How can I get him into this school?' Because of IHAD, they knew what steps to take and how to meet those needs. IHAD made the difference."

These positive Dreamer outcomes are all the more impressive when considered in the context of the students' generally dismal public school academic records. Some Dreamers, like Shree Green, excelled in high school, but many, especially those who attended low-performing schools, did poorly in school, with their junior year transcripts awash with Ds and Fs. Their high school transcripts show that between grades 9 and 11, around 50 percent of the students in the class of 1993 at Wells and Lincoln Park dropped out, signs of a school culture unsupportive of student success. This begs the question, Why did the Dreamers persist in school in the face of such a negative experience?

The answer lies in the values, expectations, and lessons imparted by IHAD and the personal, unconditional support Craig, the Kaplans, and the CYCLE staff gave each Dreamer. Greg said a central CYCLE strategy was to "keep kids focused on the future, help them survive the dysfunction of the Chicago Public Schools." Even for struggling students, IHAD's promise of funds for postsecondary education continued to be an incentive. For his part, Craig continually stressed how important it was for them to get a high school diploma—"You're just not gonna make it without that high school diploma." He made sure there were fun activities to keep them connected to IHAD, exposed them to a different way of life, and engaged personally with the Dreamers.

Some Dreamers stayed in school and connected to CYCLE to keep away from "the life." Shree spoke for many Dreamers when she pointed to the importance of not dropping out of school: "You had to do it because you didn't want to turn into some things that you saw around you. When you look around and all you see is gangbanging or drug addicts, you don't wanna turn into that, so you gotta do what you gotta do." Greg recognized that it was Craig's dedication to these young people and his commitment to their successes that made the program work for so many of them, that netted such positive outcomes. "I think Craig is the most dynamic youth leader I've ever had the chance to work alongside. His dedication to the young people that came under his wings was relentless and unwavering." He noted that "whether leading activities with 100 high schoolers or driving one of them ten miles out of his way to their newly relocated family," Craig never wavered or complained but saw it as "an opportunity to deepen their relationship. Always available to lend an extra hand, he has a heart of gold." Craig has remained involved in many of the Dreamers' lives, and he has also maintained a deep commitment to working with young men struggling with gang life and unemployment in Chicago's distressed neighborhoods, working as a Community Change Leader with Chicago CRED (Create Your Economic Destiny) to provide job training and life skills to males between the ages of seventeen and twenty-four in Chicago's economically depressed areas.[7]

However, there were some defeats, from Craig's perspective. This IHAD cohort, a typical Cabrini-Green grammar school class, presented challenges on many fronts, and Craig worked tirelessly to support his kids as they struggled with school, the streets, and life. But even with all the supports IHAD and CYCLE offered, some in that Dream Class were not able to defy Cabrini-Green's adverse life course predictions. By 1993, the year when the cohort was to graduate, nine young people had left the scholarship program. Two young women dropped out of high school when they got pregnant, despite Craig's and CYCLE's best efforts. And gangs and "the life" figured prominently in the experiences and choices of most of the young men who dropped out, loyalties that connected them to the gangs and the street and, eventually, prison. Craig also counted among

IHAD losses two that occurred after the 1993 high school graduation. One youth graduated but was arrested at age seventeen for his involvement in a gang-related murder, and another young man made it through high school but was murdered in his early twenties shortly after he got out of prison for selling drugs.

Craig cited parents' support for the program and for his leadership as the major difference between the kids who made it and those who didn't. What made "all the difference," he said was "if the parents believed in the program enough to make the kids go and to trust me, and, if the kids had not been beaten up too much already by the school system, [that their kids] would still be given a chance." With that support at home, those Dreamers generally made it. But reflecting on these IHAD losses, and how hard he tried to stem them, Craig said, "We just could not overcome the enormity of issues some kids had."

CHAPTER 7

The College Opportunity Scholarship Program: Class of 1995

In 1988, a year after the Byrd I Have A Dream scholarship program got under way, CYCLE launched the College Opportunity Program: Class of 1995 (COP95) with support from the Weinberg Family Foundation. COP95 promised $1,500 annual college scholarships to seventh graders from Cabrini-Green grammar schools when they graduated high school and were accepted at a college. Similar to IHAD, COP95 was designed to be a comprehensive youth development program with the goal of supporting one cohort of youth from middle school through college.

The Weinbergs, who first heard about CYCLE from their North Shore neighbors and IHAD sponsors Anne and Burt Kaplan, were part of the Elliott Lehman family, which owned Fel-Pro, a Skokie-based company that produced gaskets mainly for the automobile industry. Given its investment in education and especially annual scholarships for employees, support for CYCLE's COP95 proved a natural philanthropic extension for the company. In addition to the scholarship, the Weinberg Family Foundation contributed $500,000 to support a coordinator position and travel and other outings for the cohort. Greg Darnieder described the relationship between the Weinbergs and CYCLE as "pretty casual," noting that staff "met with David Weinberg's family two or three times a year at lunch to talk about how the program was going." Son David Weinberg served as the family's liaison with CYCLE and also led COP95's entrepreneurial program for seventh, eighth, and ninth graders for several years.

COORDINATOR TAMI DOIG

Tami Doig joined CYCLE in November 1988 as the COP95 coordinator. Her first task involved assembling the student cohort, which she undertook by designing a program application and accompanying Greg to talk about the program with the grade 6 classes at Byrd, Jenner, and Manierre grammar schools. Unlike the IHAD strategy, which adopted an entire grade at one school to support through college, COP95 selected ten students from each of the three Cabrini-Green grammar schools to participate in the program. (The initial group of thirty expanded to thirty-four with the addition of four youth in the eighth grade.)

Considering its college-going focus, Tami aimed to put together a COP95 cohort comprised of students who expressed interest in doing well in school and going to college and who had the support of teachers and parents or guardians. Interested students filled out a four-page application that asked about their career interests and goals, favorite things to do, and most favorite and least favorite subjects in school. In her application, Brenda Taylor, who now teaches science in a Chicago-area high school, wrote on November 3, 1988:

> My name is Brenda Taylor. I am 11 years old. I attend Byrd Academy. I am in the 6th grade. My favorite subjects are spelling, math and science. My favorite things to do in my spare time are read and write books. I plan to go to college and become a doctor. I'd like to be part of the program because it gives me the opportunity to go to college. Without it I probably would not be able to attend because of the high price of $1500 a year. Another reason I would like to be part of the program is it also has many good activities with CYCLE such as taking trips to other states. I think it would be fun.

Tami interviewed each of the students and met with their parents to gauge their support for the program goals and their child's participation. She worked closely with CYCLE's academic director, Pat Ford, who knew the families, and also met with teachers and school counselors to discuss students who'd applied and then looked at Iowa Test scores, report cards, and, most importantly, school attendance and discipline records to select the COP95 scholarship recipients.

COP95 scholarship coordinator Tami Doig is the principal of the Daystar School, a Christian elementary school in the heart of Chicago. She opened a Daystar secondary school in the fall of 2017.

Some in Cabrini-Green criticized COP95 for creaming the best students from Byrd, Jenner, and Manierre, but the academic records of students selected for the program ran the gamut, from fair-to-middling to strong, and about half of them had participated in CYCLE tutoring programs since early elementary school. Tami recalled that as they reviewed the applications, "it became obvious that we were not going to have a pool of straight-A students." Participants also displayed a significant range of tested competencies; their fifth-grade Iowa Test math scores (which indicate grade-level proficiency) ranged from 3.8 (the eighth month of grade 3) to 8.3 (the third month of grade 8), and their reading scores ranged from 4.0 to 8.4.

From the beginning, Tami feared that even the most promising students would not make it through high school and college without a support, and an incentive, like COP95. As she explained later to a successful COP95 college graduate's question about the program's rationale, "The fact that you all were living in poverty, most likely in public housing, mostly from single-parent homes meant that it was actually not at all likely that even the strongest of you would be able to overcome all of those odds without some outside support and encouragement."[1]

To get the program off to a positive and fun start, Tami designed a kickoff event for the thirty seventh graders and their families. She felt "it was important to make it feel to students and their parents that they had been very carefully chosen for a very special group." She remembered feeling a bit overwhelmed by the responsibility: "We created this kickoff event, and then they were mine. They're eleven years old. And they're supposed to go to college. I'm twenty-three years old. Those literally were my whole marching orders. I said to Greg, 'I don't know what to do.' He said, 'Do whatever you think is right. If I didn't think you could do it, I wouldn't have hired you!' That was my whole instruction!" The very next day, the COP95 group set off on its first outing. Tami and a CYCLE intern piled the thirty kids they barely knew into two vans and set off on a trip to Chicago's DuSable Museum.

Greg's injunction to "do what you think is right" empowered Tami to draw on her own youth program experience. Growing up in a small Oregon town, she had been deeply embedded in the Young Life program, serving as a program leader during the school year and working in Young Life camps every summer. "The whole model of Young Life," she said, "is you just hang out with kids, you just start showing kids that you care about them, and so that's what I started doing."[2] And after she began attending nearby Wheaton College, she became a volunteer tutor with CYCLE.

The COP95 students took part in Tuesday-night tutoring sessions at CYCLE, and struggling students were required to attend additional afterschool tutoring. With the help of her husband, Dave, Tami used CYCLE vans to pick up kids in two different meeting spots to get them to the Olivet Center by 6:45 so they'd be there when the tutors arrived. And, working with CYCLE, she also tried to create better academic options for the six COP95 students who attended low-performing Lincoln Park High School (the others attended private schools or selective public schools). Schuessler/CYCLE dollars underwrote some COP95 students' tuition at Providence–St. Mel, Josephinum, Chicago Latin, or Trinity High, but Tami began actively fund raising to underwrite other COP95ers' academic opportunities. She sent out an appeal letter to her family and friends asking them to support one student for $500 a year for four years, explaining that the students had been accepted at excellent private schools and that money was the only obstacle to their attendance. She received more than twenty sponsorship commitments in response to her appeal.

Tami established clear program rules and held high expectations. Participants were required to maintain a C average in school and attend 60 percent of the activities. No gang involvement and no pregnancies. "My students needed to be somewhere six days a week ... to have positive things to do," she said. In the beginning, COP95 programming was "just pieced together." "Greg, Pat Ford, Michelle—everyone was hustling to find fun and engaging things for us to do." The students took part in Robert Boone's writing program, took tennis lessons (courtesy of a CYCLE volunteer's membership at the Lincoln Park Tennis Club), went bowling, and went to movies and museums. Medical students from Northwestern University provided a sex education program. (Tami remembered, "We learned how to put a condom on a banana.") They also explored different Chicago neighborhoods and ate at local ethnic restaurants. Tami even drove small groups to her sister's suburban condominium for a pool party: "We couldn't bring thirty kids from Cabrini, so we would just slide them in, four or five at a time, whatever would fit in my car. I wasn't trying to show them things that would make them frustrated with their lives. I was trying to show them things that would make them want to go to college."

All COP95ers participated in the twelve-week Saturday program provided by Marwen, a Chicago organization that offered free visual art classes for students in grades 7–12. Joanne Minyo, the lead Marwen artist, created ingenious projects that built on work being done in other COP95 program components. One of the first projects involved the creation of African altars. One student chose to make a huge altar to his idol, Michael Jordan. (Tami remembered, "I'm unsure if his mom was very excited to see that monstrosity make its way to her living room, but it was pretty awesome.") Joanne also led the kids in painting a mural on the side of LaSalle Street Church's intern house, fashioning portable murals to serve as backdrops for CYCLE events, and creating ethnic scenes on CYCLE's oldest, most rusted-out, doors-barely-closed blue van. The scenes represented various Chicago communities the COP95 group explored in-depth one summer. They remained on the van until its dying day.

COP95ers looked forward to the annual Christmas party and end-of-year festivities, events that celebrated the group and its journey. While Tami followed the Young Life model and focused on building relationships, she also made sure that each student also received special, individualized attention. For example, every COP95er had a birthday dinner date with Tami—at McDonalds, Margie's Ice Cream, or the Red Hot Beef Stand. She maintained that "birthdays were a big deal . . . I just started trying to build relationships with kids; it went back to the Young Life style of figuring out what matters to them and paying attention to those things." And she did many other things to show youth she cared for them, from attending a grandparent's funeral to creating a COP95 photo album every year: "The albums were always in my office, and the kids loved to pore over them. I knew that was valuable to them. I always made two copies of a photo, and they could have one. It's one of those parts of life you miss if you live in poverty—pictures of yourself, someone who can keep life organized at a level that you get a photo album." And she created incentives for such things as having perfect attendance at COP95 activities, being on time, or getting good grades. "It was a lot of incentivizing with dopey little things like an ice cream outing at Margie's, a sleepover at my house, taking part in a tennis class," she said. It was all about "trying to motivate kids to stay in school and eventually go to college."

The group took many trips out of state, to Disneyworld (though one girl was not allowed to go because she got in a fight with another girl) and to Nashville, among other places. Starting in the ninth grade, she took COP95ers to visit college campuses, many local ones and some out of state, such as the Historically Black Colleges and Universities in Atlanta. After each trip, COP95ers completed a journal about their trip, recording the states they'd traveled though, special places they'd visited, most and least enjoyable activities, and new things learned.

The COP95 kids also took part in CYCLE's summer day camp program. Morning activities focused on tutoring or other educational activities, and recreational activities filled the afternoons. Junior Staff and an intern helped Tami run the summer camp. The first year, when the students were too young to go to Young Life or other camps by themselves, Tami planned and ran a sleepover summer camp for the group: "I rented a camp in Michigan. My husband and I did all the programming, all the food. It was ridiculous. It was nuts. But it involved an overnight experience for the kids."

COP95 OUTCOMES

"It's not an option," Tami famously shot back at her students at any mention of dropping out of school or giving up. And the COP95 group did her proud. All of the 23 young people who stayed with the program graduated from high school in June 1995: 15 of them headed directly to colleges, some in Chicago and others as far away as Tennessee, Georgia, Alabama, Wisconsin, and Washington DC; 2 joined the Marines; and 3 took jobs and sought no further education, though 2 of them eventually went to college and earned bachelor degrees. Of the original middle school group of 34, 8 dropped out of the program; of this group, 4 graduated from high school and 3 did not, and the path of 1 student remains uncertain. Including *all* the youth who ever participated in the program, COP95 posts an 88 percent high school graduation rate. These outcomes far exceed the 1995 CPS high school graduation rate of 35 percent. As a *Chicago Tribune* article on COP95 headlined, "Poor Kids Struggle—and Succeed."[3]

While an impressive statistic, what that number doesn't reveal is the very real obstacles many of the youth in the program faced. For instance, one young man, who stayed with the program through eleventh grade, struggled not only with multiple academic challenges, including severe ADHD, but even greater personal challenges. With a drug-addicted mother who could not care for him, he managed on his own until finally the streets claimed him. He got pulled into a gang along with his cousins and spent time in jail. Another young man, the son of an alcoholic mom, was also very much on his own and struggled to make it in school. He did graduate, but he fathered a child right out of high school, got involved in drug dealing, and served jail time. His life turned around when he was released from jail to a Salvation Army halfway house and decided to make better choices. He now manages a big Salvation Army store in Chicago and receives regular commendations for the quality of his work. And for yet another COP95er, it was mental health issues that plagued him; he did not graduate from high school and got involved with drugs—using and selling—and has been homeless or in jail for various periods. And one bright and academically successful youth graduated from high school and was accepted to college but declined admission and his COP95 scholarship. This decision puzzled Tami at the time, but she later learned that two young women were pregnant with his children at graduation time, and he felt that getting a job rather than going to college "was the responsible thing to do."

And not all the COP95 youth who went to college graduated. Several of the young women became pregnant and returned home, something that upset Tami at the time. "I went to a pretty bad place of failure when I say 'they all got pregnant.' It felt like they all got pregnant to me. But it really was only four or five of them. And they got pregnant by a neighborhood boy, not even a college boy!" And she learned well after the fact that several of the young women did not go to college because they were pregnant at their high school graduation but did not tell her." Tami felt that she made a mistake in sending such an unconditional message about not getting pregnant:

> I hadn't created an atmosphere where they could tell me that . . . I could have been more support to if [they] had thought this relationship was still open to [them]. But I had sent such a strong message . . . that I ceased to be available to them, which is not what I, of course, intended to send. My motive was good, but the message was so powerful that people [felt] it was punitive. And it put people out of relationship with me for years. You know, I find out later, "Like, how could you have a six-year-old?" And not that she had her in high school, but that she had her at nineteen. Several did. And they should have told me. I would have brought them gifts. I would have been sad, but I would have supported that. I would have visited them in the hospital.

In fact, Tami did support one participant, Brenda Taylor, when she got pregnant. In her 2010 memoir *Beauty for Ashes*, about the challenges of her childhood and young adulthood, Brenda wrote, "From as far back as I can remember, there was physical, sexual, mental and emotional abuse and confusion all around me."[4] She said that CYCLE and the COP95 community were unable to protect her from sexual abuse during her childhood or from getting pregnant at age fourteen. Although Brenda was a popular member, Tami recalled the pushback from the group when she was allowed to continue with the program while pregnant. "It was against the rules to continue if

Brenda Taylor, a COP95 scholarship student, survived an abusive childhood and marriage to graduate from Southern Illinois University Carbondale, becoming a science teacher in Chicago. Photograph by Foster Garvin.

you were pregnant, but they didn't understand statutory rape. They were angry that I didn't kick her out." Not only did she allow Brenda to continue with the program and to keep her Providence–St. Mel scholarship, but Tami invited Brenda and her baby to live with her and her husband for a time as the high school sophomore struggled to manage her new reality as a mom. Tami helped her arrange child care and even, on occasion, did the babysitting.

The COP95 group made Tami a book of photographs and written tributes, much like the albums she'd been keeping, and they presented the gift to her at their 1995 graduation celebration. Each student's note spoke of the transformative role she played in their lives.

> "Tami, to hear you say 'it's not an option not to succeed in life and to better your education' are words I never thought I would want to hear again, but this famous quote has gotten me where I am."
>
> "Tami, if I were to write down all the caring things you've done for me the last six years, I would be writing forever . . . I remember you telling me I needed to start thinking of myself . . . and in all the years that I've known you, you made sure that I did so . . . you made sure I went on to our college tours, tutoring, all of our trips. I'm now a wiser, open-minded, well-rounded female."
>
> "I used to think I wasn't good enough for college. I'm going to college! I'm going to study education. I'm going to be somebody."
>
> "I know in my heart I would not have been a successful person without you. I thank you from the bottom of my heart."

Tami's support for her COP95 students did not end with high school graduation. She drove students to college and helped them settle in, supplying them with sheets and comforter sets, so they would not arrive at college and be "so obviously under resourced," and helping them decorate their dorm rooms. She sent them birthday gifts and care packages. One student sent her a thank-you note saying how much her package meant since it was the only birthday gift he received. She called each student regularly to check on grades and ask how they were doing. She picked them up at the airport when they returned home for vacations. She wrote tuition checks from Weinberg funds for students who earned an acceptable GPA and continued in college. She also wrote checks from the Doig family's personal account to supplement the scholarships or provide funds needed for books or living expenses. And when Brenda Taylor wanted to come back to Chicago after graduating in 2004 from Southern Illinois University Carbondale, she and her two young children stayed with the Doigs while she looked for a job and housing. And those relationships continue more than twenty years after their high school graduation. Tami remains in touch with many alums via social media, attends their family celebrations, receives updates, and hosts an occasional barbecue at her home. "I just got a note—'You moved. What's your new address? I want to send you her school picture.' I'm still involved with their lives to the level that they want me to have their baby's school picture, and they know it's on my refrigerator." Tami was—and still is—a mom to her COP95 students.

The youth spent a lot of time with Tami and her husband, Dave—trips, overnights at their home, celebrations. Brenda Taylor stressed how important those experiences with Tami and her husband were to her:

> I was exposed to a lot of negative and not age-appropriate situations (growing up). And then there was Tami, and she was always appropriate . . . And I think we were more receptive to Tami because she was different from us, completely different background and way of life. We were intrigued. The experience of seeing Tami and Dave together, and how positive they were . . . A lot of times people don't have the experience of people talking to you the right way, or dealing with things in a certain way. They're used to someone yelling at them. So just having them be like a standard, "This is how we talk to each other. This is how it looks." We had it modeled every day.

Years later, Tami was moved to learn that she and the program made a difference even to those kids who, as she put it, "did not fill my bucket," young people whom she felt had moved irretrievably away from COP95 values and goals. For instance, she was stunned to run into a former participant at a 2014 rally protesting police violence in Ferguson, Missouri. "He'd been to prison for dealing drugs in jail—on a job we helped get him!—he's missing half his teeth, and he sees us and starts to cry and says, 'You guys! You have no idea how much you meant to me.'" She said that it was so meaningful to hear that when she'd always felt she had failed him somehow.

Reflecting on the COP95 students' pathways through school, their participation in the program, and their ultimate outcomes, Tami concluded, as Craig Nash did, that what distinguished those who were successful in the scholarship program from those who were not were the active involvement and the encouragement of a mother or adult guardian. Family support made a critical difference in whether the young person stuck with the program, worked hard in school, and made the most of COP95 opportunities. Tami noted that "the students that were harder to reach were the ones where I could never develop a relationship with their parents." She said that even without parental involvement, "things were accomplished, but not as much as we had potential to do." She worked hard to establish and nurture relationships with parents. But the fact that she was a white woman from small-town Oregon posed problems of race, culture, and local knowledge. And the fact that she was twenty-three years old also presented a challenge in her interaction with Cabrini-Green parents, many of whom were only a couple of years older.

> So, with parents, I just tried to start just being present. CYCLE had some built-in systems that tried to create a place where parents would want to be... So, my parents, some of them were already part of CYCLE . . . in the GED classes, their kids had been coming to CYCLE tutoring since they were seven . . . Some of them weren't new to us, but they were new to me. But these were relationships that had been

fostered . . . and they were ready to move past whatever issues they had dealing with white people. So, those were easy. The ones that were hard, which was probably most of them, there were all kinds of things to overcome in terms of just getting by . . . I tried to just start to be present and available and helpful.

The many notes filed in her students' folders document all she did to be helpful to these anxious parents—calling Social Services about problems with food stamps, brokering rent with a stubborn landlord, making sure a mentally ill mom had her meds, researching quality but affordable child care programs, writing job recommendations. Midway through the cohort's eighth-grade year, Tami said, she was finally accepted by those parents who initially were uncertain about her. She acknowledged that the support and counsel of CYCLE staff provided critical resources as she worked to develop positive and personal relationships with her COP95ers and their families. Junior Staff knew what was happening in the neighborhood and which families were under particular economic or emotional duress. Pat Ford, whom Tami called her "cultural lifeline," coached her in the ways of the Cabrini-Green African American community.

Even though not all COP95 high school graduates made it to college or to college graduation, many of their children have. Tami said that for some, their environment was impossible to overcome, but "we see the fruits of our work in the next generation." She also noted that the norms seem to have shifted for many. For instance, she is proud to see that one young woman who struggled with the challenges of an unsupportive and drug-addicted mother and left college after a few months to have a baby sent her daughter to Providence-St. Mel—"That's something for a single mom to come up with that tuition. She learned about how important education was . . . She just couldn't do it for herself." Brenda Taylor agreed: "I was exposed to art classes and everything, so when my kids were young I made sure they went to art classes, swimming lessons, and they did all of those things. I remembered how it impacted me when I was younger and wanted them to have those same experiences and exposure. So I made sure I did it."

"Seeds were planted. They know what's important and what to do," Tami said, recognizing that the next generation has benefited from their parents' involvement in the program. She recounted running into the woman who, as a COP95er, was not allowed to join the Disneyworld trip because of fighting: "I said, 'Let's get on a plane and get you there now.' She said, 'I've already been . . . I took my daughter.'"

PART II

TURNING POINTS FOR CYCLE YOUTH

CYCLE'S PROGRAMS ENABLED MOST PARTICIPANTS TO TAKE A different path through high school and into adulthood than the one predicted by their Cabrini-Green address. The scholarship programs changed their odds. Financial support mattered absolutely; CYCLE youth could not have gone to private high schools or on to college without the scholarships. But the essential supports they received from CYCLE's programs involved more than money; they involved encouragement, exposure, sympathetic understanding, a constancy, and a belief in the students and their futures.

Alums said that CYCLE fundamentally altered their ideas about who and what they might become, setting their sights beyond the negative examples they saw around them. Psychologists use the notion of "possible selves" to make a similar distinction between "hoped-for" and "feared" future selves.[1] Youth growing up in Cabrini-Green could not miss the everyday representations of their feared futures—high school dropouts, "dead or in jail by twenty-one" realities, drug sellers and addicts, welfare-dependent single moms. Alums credited their CYCLE experiences with opening their eyes to unimagined opportunities, encouraging them to reach for their hoped-for selves, and enabling them to become the confident, productive adults they are today.

Social researchers examining questions of how and why individuals' lives are changed, for better or worse, use the concept of "turning point" to signify a permanent rather than transitory life change. Turning points, embedded in a life course, are of two kinds.[2] One involves events over which an individual has no control. Catastrophic environmental incidents or serious accidents, for instance, occur beyond individuals' influence but nonetheless can fundamentally change lives. Individual choices and actions represent the second sort of turning point. Whether or not to join a gang, enlist in military service, drop out of school, get married, or participate in programs such as CYCLE are examples of these choices. However, these turning points represent *potential* only, since an individual's action is required to make them actual. As sociologist Andrew Abbott puts it, "A major turning point has potential to open a system the way a key has potential to open a lock. In both cases, too, action is necessary to complete the turning."[3]

Time tells. An experience or event can be deemed a turning point only after sufficient time has passed to see whether or not the new trajectory endures. Without this long-term perspective, it is impossible to decide whether a life course has been transformed or only temporarily modified by an event or experience. Abbott writes that "what makes a turning point a turning point rather than a minor ripple is the passage of sufficient time 'on the new course' such that it becomes clear that direction has indeed been changed."[4] A turning point gives rise to enduring change in the content and structure of an individual's overall life course.

CYCLE examples illustrate the importance of a longitudinal assessment in considering whether or not an experience comprised a turning point in an individual's life. For instance, one young man, with support from the Education Assistance Limited scholarship program and its director, Bernard McCune, graduated from a respected midwestern university with a degree in accounting. His high school and college graduation could count as a success in many outcome tallies and evidence that his CYCLE participation constituted a turning point in his life. However, on returning to Cabrini-Green, he got caught up in gang life, eventually becoming a drug "CFO" and going to prison. In his life story, CYCLE did not serve as a turning point; to Bernard's great regret, he returned to the path predicted for young people from the project. Not all changes or opportunities are turning points that fundamentally redirect life course pathways.

A short-term look at a young person's trajectory could also mistakenly discount the positive significance of an experience. COP95 director Tami Doig felt a deep sense of personal failure when several of the young women who headed off to college with COP95 scholarships soon returned home pregnant. She concluded that their life courses had not been changed by their years of participation in the program and that they were back on the familiar path that would lead them to stressful lives as single mothers struggling in a low-income housing project. For them, she thought regretfully, COP95 had not been a turning point. However, some years later, most of these women returned to college and graduated, and at least one also went on to earn a graduate degree. The experience did in fact transform their futures; "life" intervened, and it took time for them to get back onto the course they embraced as part of the program, but, for them, COP95 participation was a turning point.

Most CYCLE participants were able to grab the opportunities presented them because someone cared, showed them what to do, coached them in how to succeed, walked with them to new challenges and experiences—senior staff, junior staff, volunteers. In a community context where less than half of African American females and less than a third of males graduated from high school, and where gang membership and early pregnancies were the norm, CYCLE participants' accomplishments stand as exceptional.

What was it about the CYCLE experience that attracted young people to the program, kept them engaged, and changed the ways in which they saw themselves and their futures? What made it possible for them to turn the key? Across CYCLE programs and cohorts, alums consistently pointed to three features that mattered most to making them who they are today: exposure, mentoring, and membership in a community of belonging

CHAPTER 8

Exposure
You Can't Be What You Can't See

What do you want to be when you grow up? Adults, parents, and friends regularly direct this question to young people. Researchers who study adolescents living in impoverished urban settings like Cabrini-Green find that these queries typically elicit an array of unrealistic career goals—major league baseball player, movie star, pilot, fashion designer—but that youth have little practical knowledge about how to achieve these, or even less-lofty, ambitions.

Developmental psychologists agree that young people need continuous exposure to new things, places, ideas, and options to develop their potential and make positive life choices.[1] Some youth are fortunate to live in families and neighborhoods in which they have this exposure through an array of afterschool and extracurricular activities, travel, encounters with successful adult role models, and enrollment in challenging schools. But youth growing up in conditions of concentrated poverty, such as those in Cabrini-Green, have little opportunity to see futures other than the delimited or destructive ones they encounter every day.[2] According to former EAL director Bernard McCune, an urban educator who understands that families and neighborhoods make up the primary influences on young people's expectations about what their futures might hold, adolescents routinely encounter motivational slogans such as "Be all you can be!" but in reality, he says, "You can't be what you can't see."

RESTRICTED IMAGES OF POSSIBLE FUTURES

Youth saw depressing patterns of failure all around them in Cabrini-Green's economically and racially segregated context. Few gainfully employed males lived in the project; only a handful women held jobs in the tax-paying economy, though many of them participated in the cash economy—cosmetology, child care, or housecleaning. Most were on some form of public assistance. Few adults in the community held a high school diploma; college experience was rare to nonexistent. Even mothers doing their best to provide a safe and positive environment for their children could offer little concrete guidance about how to achieve school or workplace success, let alone plan for postsecondary options. Girls had little encouragement to stay in school, get good grades, or consider post–high school opportunities. Norms of the community held that a pregnant teen must drop out of school to take care of her child. And girls who did graduate from high school were expected to pitch in to help out with child care and family expenses, rather than consider any kind of college or career opportunity. As Shree Green explained, "From high school you just work, and you take care of your family. That's what you do." Tamiko Jones underscored the narrow conceptions about future she and her peers had, saying, "I didn't know anything about college. I didn't even know there was a college! In my neighborhood people just talked about making it through high school—that was the task . . . CYCLE introduced us to ideas about a better life."

America's public schools too often do not structure or support students' knowledge about alternative futures; instead, they leave them to figure things out on their own. The Chicago Public Schools attended by most Cabrini-Green youth in the 1980s and early 1990s did little to expand students' notions of what they might do when (or if) they graduated from high school. For the most part, students encountered low expectations about their achievement and academic futures. So questionable were prospects of a young person's high school graduation during the mid-1980s that in Cabrini-Green an eighth-grade graduation prompted the big celebration—fancy dresses, limos, promlike parties—since most youth did not make it through the twelfth grade.

The housing project provided little inspiration to consider positive options for the future. Its four blocks, what Tamiko likened to a "concrete box," provided a barren, isolating setting. There were few recreational options, since the gang-controlled parks were off limits, and hardly any commercial enterprise could endure in the face of unending violence and crime. And travel outside Cabrini-Green required young people to cross gang boundaries and navigate public transit. As a result, few kids growing up in Cabrini-Green had much acquaintance with downtown Chicago, just a mile away. Greg Darnieder recalled a Junior Staffer asking him how to get to Water Tower Place for a job interview, a five-minute bus ride straight down Chicago Avenue: "She could see the building from her apartment. She seriously had no idea as to how to get there."

In constructing their ideas about what might lie ahead for them, most Cabrini-Green kids could only draw on up-close experiences. Shree Green stressed how constricting this limited vision was: "I have noticed that people in the black community who don't have a lot of exposure tend to place values on different things. So the value in a black community was sometimes placed on who is the baddest, the roughest, the toughest, that type of stuff, and not about who's the person who's actually gonna go out and do something, get out of this and change some things and then be able to pull everyone else out."

With this in mind, exposure to new experiences, cultures, ideas, and values figured prominently in all of CYCLE's activities and strategies. Craig Nash continually introduced his Byrd Dreamers to new things: "The exposure to a different way of life was critical—'Here are some options, here are some choices, and here are some things you can do.'" Pat Ford reflected, "Communities like Cabrini are very isolated. So when we're going through the experience as kids, that's all we know . . . when people who do have a job are just working to get by, like my mom, cleaning houses. Having opportunities to really be exposed to possibilities and having adults who really believe in you—that has power and potential to change things." For many Cabrini-Green kids, just getting by overshadowed ideas about getting ahead.

EXPANDING POSSIBILITIES

Exposure to different people began the moment youth walked through CYCLE's doors, and the program's alumni credited this exposure for giving them needed confidence. David Gates told Greg:

> You guys were really our first experience with dealing with Caucasians, with white people. You guys gave us a reality check that everybody is the same. When you guys came in, you didn't treat us different, and you didn't treat us as underprivileged little black kids . . . You treated us like family. When we went to CYCLE, you guys were there and in authoritative roles, but we looked forward to seeing you, and we had great times . . . The camps, the group settings that we had, all the discussions that we had. We talked about everything. We talked and learned about life.

Almost all of CYCLE's volunteer tutors were white and came from middle-class circumstances. As David noted, for many, if not most, CYCLE youth, relationships with them provided their first up-close and extended interaction with white people. One tutor recalled a youth teasing, "You dance like a white girl!" to which she replied, "I AM a white girl!" These relationships played an important role in building confidence and comfort across racial lines. And Bernard McCune said that because of his experience at CYCLE, he knew he could go to a predominately white college and be successful—"I didn't have all the misperceptions of different races that other folks had." Cyril Nichols expressed similar confidence about being black in a white environment as he went off to college in small-town Colby, Kansas, where, he said, "they had never seen a black before!" And many alums stressed how the comfort with whites they learned at CYCLE stuck with them through the years. For instance, Tamiko Jones, who holds a high-profile educational sales job, says that CYCLE helped build her self-confidence in settings where there are few African Americans: "I am one of two African Americans who are at that level [in my company], and I am able to sit there confidently and know I am supposed to be there."

Michelle McConnell, CYCLE's director of volunteers, made the point that the "unlearning" about race and social class went both ways. Just as the youth had unlearning to do as they got to know people of different cultures and races, be they staff, donors, or volunteers, she (and many of the volunteers) had to unlearn some of the things she thought she knew about inner-city black residents. Over time, Michelle recalled, ongoing exposure to each other made conversations about race easy for both her and the youth. She remembered one conversation in particular: "I was driving the kids along Lakefront and there were a bunch of people jogging in shorts on a very cold January day. One of the girls said, 'You know, white people—they don't get cold.' And I said, 'Excuse me. We get cold. That person is crazy!'" But some of the experiences that were new to Cabrini-Green kids did stun CYCLE staff and volunteers. For instance, the first arts and crafts coordinator planned for a program to engage youth with different levels of competence, but she had to revise her plans after the first session, "shocked to find that most of them had never been exposed to scissors, pipe cleaners, colored paper, glue. Most of them didn't even know how to manipulate anything. No need for levels!"

Interactions with tutors as well as individuals who came to CYCLE to make presentations about different career opportunities introduced youth to an array of career and postsecondary options. "It was all about that exposure to different people and not being locked in to just the people in my neighborhood," David Gates said. "I got to gradually realize that these are just regular people like you and me . . . They put their pants on one leg at a time, just like you and I do. And when they began to talk about how they achieved what they achieved, it was not just about [white privilege or luck], it was hard work. That taught us a lot."

And the program's many, and very popular, field trips were all about introducing kids to new experiences and possibilities. Youth who came for weekly tutoring had a least one field trip a month to explore parts of Chicago on Saturdays and sometimes Friday-night trips for the K–8 kids—roller skating, visits to the zoo and Chicago museums, picnics in the parks. Jennifer Means stressed how important these outings were to her and other Cabrini-Green youth: "CYCLE gave us exposure. We in Cabrini-Green were just one mile from the Gold Coast, one the wealthiest areas in the nation, but we wouldn't have known anything about that or really anything else without having experiences. We set a goal to go camping—I had never been camping in my life! Or a service project to Mississippi . . . We'd never get to those places [otherwise]." One volunteer recalled taking a group of fifth and sixth graders to Sears Tower: "One kid said, 'What's that?' I said, 'What do you mean what's that?' He pointed out the window and said, 'THAT . . . that water.' He was pointing at Lake Michigan, just a mile away. He didn't know it was there."

Youth participating in the scholarship and junior staff programs traveled around the country in CYCLE vans to visit places such as the nation's capital, New York City, and Disneyworld. For Cyril Nichols, who runs the athletic programs for Chicago's community colleges, the most important part of CYCLE was being exposed to something outside Cabrini-Green. "For us to go to West Virginia, Colorado, Philadelphia—it was huge. We got exposed to a different way of life. And now here we are, living a different life."

But it was the college tours, all the alums agreed, that significantly altered their thinking about what their futures could involve and how they could get there. Cyril said that before the college tours, he had never been exposed "even to the Chicago community college that was three blocks from us. I mean, we didn't think we could go to college. High school was it, [and] a chop shop. We had no guidance. We didn't understand. We didn't know that there was [any other] option for us." Tamiko Jones also counted the college tours as an especially "impactful" opportunity. She had never considered college or even knew much about it: "I'm like, do you mean kids go to live in dorms without their parents, and there's a room, and you get meals, and all you have to do is go to classes and study?" And when Jennifer Means made her first college visit to Wheaton College, the thirty-miles trip from her home in the high-rise Reds "may have been the furthest I'd ever gone from Cabrini. I basically thought we were in another state!"

Senior staff designed trips to teach life lessons as well as open kids' minds to the options they might consider. Particularly memorable for all who participated was the 1987 summer service trip to rural Mississippi, where the twenty-five Junior Staff encountered levels of poverty and human desperation shocking even to them. All of them said the experience changed them in many ways. David Gates learned many lessons from the CYCLE trips, but most especially from the Mississippi outing: "One thing I tell my own kids is that no matter how good you have it, no matter how bad you have it, there's always somebody on the other side. There's always somebody that has it better than you and somebody that has it worse. So just be thankful for what you have and the things you can accomplish in life." Greg said that this lesson "is exactly why I wanted to take them to Mississippi, so they'd see that the realities of our lives are always situational, there's always others worse off and you have something to offer them."

CYCLE's trips and outings always involved new experiences—going to an amusement park, spending the night on a college campus, meeting with a congressman, going to a play. In addition, tutors and program sponsors regularly took kids on excursions—the ballet, the Civic Center, tennis clubs, concerts, "exotic" Chicago restaurants—and these often prompted conversations about life styles, choices, and implications for their futures. For instance, Richard Blackmon regularly took his Providence-St. Mel scholarship kids to the Ravinia music festival: "To get to Ravinia, we had to drive by all of those beautiful homes on the North Shore. So we would have a conversation about whether or not any black people live there, why or why not."

Every summer, more than fifty CYCLE kids participated in weeklong sleepaway Young Life camps, where they canoed, swam, parasailed, and spent time in mountains and forests all around the Midwest. Shree Green recalled the powerful impact the camp experiences had on her: "Coming out of somewhere where you maybe just have a baseball field or something and to be able to go camping, canoeing—the things you see on television, but you've never been exposed to." There were also camping trips during the spring and fall. The University of Illinois Chicago loaned youth programs needed camping gear, including tents, sleeping bags, cookware, and canoes, and CYCLE took advantage of every Wisconsin, Michigan, and Indiana campsite so that every young person could participate in a weekend camping excursion every year. Many clearly remembered those weekends: "It was sooo dark!" "So many strange noises!" "It was the wilderness. We're supposed to be tough, but we didn't even want to go out to pee!"

Spending several nights in a tent with other people built relationships that strengthened the work both junior and senior staff were doing in the program. As Bernard McCune said, "The camping was about more than fishing... If you take people away and they have to spend a night or two together and it's away from their normal environment, the bonds and the trust that they will build is just tremendous." Greg underscored how the bonding that took place on these trips, especially between junior staff and CYCLE campers, translated back to academic sessions, Marwen art classes, and other activities: "There's nothing like sleeping, fixing your meals together and having fun for a couple of days and nights to create the trust and connections you need to work together."

These experiences during the 1980s shaped the lives of not only the CYCLE youth but of the next generation. "It's interesting to watch these alums from the 1980s, now in their forties and early fifties, running their own kids from one activity to the next," Greg mused. "Driving them on weekends all over the Midwest as members of travel teams, or horseback riding, or dance class. And now that some of their kids are in college, helping them take advantage of the seemingly endless study-abroad and internship opportunities." IHAD alum Shree Green shared how she was determined to take her daughter to New York City on her eighteenth birthday and to instill in her daughter the importance of "exposure":

> Getting out, going places, and experiencing other things, experiencing other cultures, getting the understanding so that you'll be able to have a better way of living life. I wanted my daughter so much to be able to experience things that I had . . . New York! And when I couldn't afford airline tickets, I got in my car and drove her for her eighteenth birthday . . . I had to let her know that she needs to experience some stuff. I took her to see *Wicked* and told her, "We're gonna not eat anything, but we're gonna see a play and the city."

Similarly, Brenda Taylor, who struggled as a young single mother, made sure her two kids had art classes and swimming lessons, "because I remember how much it impacted me when I was younger."

UNDERSTANDING MAINSTREAM NORMS AND VALUES: AN EMBEDDED CURRICULUM

Exposure to mainstream norms and values was part of CYCLE's embedded curriculum. Sometimes that exposure served as an activity's explicit goal. For instance, staff arranged opportunities for youth to spend an entire day with a banking or insurance professional, shadowing him or her, eating in the corporate dining room, going on sales calls, being introduced to the folks an executive interacts with every day. CYCLE's Professional Partnership Program (PPP) matched youth with someone in the business world so they could learn about a job in the business world and to get an in-depth look at how professionals interact with colleagues both inside and outside a corporation. In preparation for the day, CYCLE staff instructed youth about how to build a resume, what to wear (which often meant borrowing the lone tie Greg kept in his office), and how to present themselves (eye contact, firm handshake)—all invaluable life skills. David Gates remembered wondering, "Why do I have to find clothes to dress up to go to fake an interview?" and questioning why he had to do "something [he] would never have to deal with." But years later he understood: "Believe it or not, in all those fake interviews I learned so much. Now, me being in a position where I'm interviewing people . . . when somebody comes in and they don't have on the right shirt and the right shoes, I'm like, 'When I was ten years old and I was taught how to go to an interview . . .' And then it makes me think, 'What sort of experiences did this person have? Did they have the opportunities that I had'"? PPP also aimed to introduce youth to the range of positions associated with a particular job sector. For instance, employment at a bank meant more than being a teller; there is the entire back office support system that relies on accountants, technology experts, and an array of other professional positions.

CYCLE kids learned much about mainstream norms and values by simply paying close attention to what happened around them in the program, by observing how senior staff treated one another and interacted with family members. Several alums mentioned the impression Greg and his family made on them—seeing what parenting looked like in the Darnieder household, how a husband and wife related to one another. Carleta Alston told Greg how much she and her husband, Brian, learned about parenting by watching him and his family disciplining their children: "You talked to your children. You explained to your children. And that was different, that was not how it was in our homes. And we used that with our children, communicating."

CYCLE staff intentionally used their own values, beliefs, interests, and understandings as resources for shaping how youth saw themselves in terms of their potential and possible futures. Greg purposely modeled the values of hard work, persistence, and commitment he sought to instill in the youth; he was the first to show up in the morning, usually the last to leave, and consistently went on outings. Senior staff threaded attention to life skills and mainstream norms throughout the programs, debriefings with Junior Staff, and daily interactions with participants—how to get along in society, how to behave in social settings, how to politely stand up for yourself. They modeled everything from table and restaurant manners to interview norms, and respect for cultural differences. They even showed youth how to navigate Chicago's transit system and airports. A longtime observer of Cabrini-Green's history of negative youth outcomes asked, rhetorically, "Where else would they have learned this stuff but for CYCLE? They saw none of this around them." The aim of the staff was to provide images of a successful adult, an involved parent, an engaged community member that were not abstractions, that weren't only "what you see on television" but, instead, were part of their lived experience.

CHAPTER 9

Mentors
Someone to Walk With

While CYCLE's strategies of exposing kids to new people and places expanded their ideas about their "might-be" selves, acquiring concrete understanding about *how* to achieve those adult futures and gain the confidence to pursue them turned on the mentoring they experienced at CYCLE. Mentoring was at the heart of all of CYCLE's interactions with youth. Caring adults—volunteers, senior staff, Junior Staff, sponsors—in varying configurations mentored all the youth every day. Alums consistently pointed to their mentors as fundamental to their being able to deviate from the expected outcomes for Cabrini-Green youth.

Researchers distinguish between mentor relationships that arise naturally in the course of a young person's life and those formed through formal volunteer activities associated with a youth program. Natural mentors can provide important, up-close, and authentic emotional support and concrete guidance and play a crucial role-modeling function. They might be neighbors, older siblings and friends, aunts and uncles, teachers, or faith leaders. Volunteer mentors are usually adults who are recruited to support youth engaged in a specific program or activity, often serving a coaching function. They can take an active role in expanding youth's horizons about their futures.

The mentoring concept took off in the late 1990s partially in response to the positive evaluation of the country's largest mentoring effort, the Big Brothers and Big Sisters program.[1] Mentoring appealed to the hearts and minds of policy makers and practitioners and was seen as a low-cost, volunteer approach to supporting young people through the personal challenges they encountered in schools, neighborhoods, and families. By 2011, more than three million youth were participating in five thousand mentoring programs around the country.

However, researchers Jean Rhodes and David DuBois worry that notions of mentoring have been broadened to include any relationship a young person has with an adult—service learning, out-of-school activities, tutoring—regardless of its motivating purpose.[2] Because a mentoring relationship involves complex and sustained relationships, they argue, activities that connect adults with youth do not necessarily represent a meaningful mentoring relationship. For instance, a basketball coach may serve as a role model and supporter of the young people on the team, but his interactions with them focus primarily on elements of the game and only secondarily, if at all, on life struggles and choices and strategies and supports for cultivating and achieving positive futures. Mentoring, argue Rhodes and Dubois, must be the intentional purpose of an interaction, not merely an aspect of a broad range of youth-focused activities. In their view, programs that have moved in the direction of bundling "mentoring" into an array of youth activities risk underestimating what research says sits at the very heart of a mentoring-based intervention: a caring adult-youth relationship.

Despite the warm glow that usually accompanies the idea of mentoring, little consistent evidence exists about the consequences of mentoring efforts. The inconclusive results ascribed to mentoring efforts express a degree of discrepancy that raises red flags about mentoring as a taken-for-granted beneficial youth development strategy. And Jean Rhodes, who has studied and written about mentoring efforts for many years, asserts forcefully that poor-quality mentoring is worse for many young people than no mentoring at all.[3] Negative consequences of participation in poorly designed and supported mentoring programs include lowered self-esteem, disconnectedness from social institutions, and little hope for a positive future, especially for youth from economically and racially segregated communities like Cabrini-Green. Yet, Rhodes and other scholars also find that mentoring, when effective, has greatest impact for youth navigating conditions of "environmental risk." Rhodes and DuBois conclude that "mentoring relationships are more likely to promote positive outcomes and avoid harm when they are close, consistent and enduring."[4] They contend that effective mentoring programs provide extended periods of exposure to the same staff and a culture supportive of mentoring but that few programs have been able to create and keep up such relationships.

CYCLE was an exception in that regard.

MENTORING IN CYCLE

As natural mentors, Junior Staff played essential support and motivation roles in CYCLE. Alums from different cohorts used similar terms to describe what these older youth meant to them—"big brother," "big sister," "someone who had my back." Ken Dunkin said that the Junior Staffers "were pivotal in getting us through Cabrini-Green because they were these two-to-three-years-older folk, like Craig Nash. They lived in our community—sort of big brother, big sister scenario. Somebody covering your flank and expecting you to do better, counting on you to deliver in school, your comportment, expectations on so many different levels."

As tutors, Junior Staffers modeled school success for younger kids and provided them with understanding counsel as they found their way amid the pressures and pitfalls of school, family, and neighborhood. They were proof positive that a young person from Cabrini-Green could aspire to and attain encouraging futures, stable jobs, and, later, stable families. And as admired youth from the community, they could steer youth away from everyday negative influences and options.

Many echoed Cyril Nichols's assertion that "black guys could not have navigated through Cabrini by themselves . . . Most of those guys not involved with CYCLE like we were are dead or strung out. The UFOs [the first Junior Staffers] were surrogate big brothers; they looked out for the shorties, would not let them be in a gang." Gloria Purifoy underscored how important Junior Staffers were to their sense of what they might become. "We saw them going to high school, we saw them go to college," she said, "but then they were back in the summer" to work with CYCLE kids and tell them about college. Of his mentor, Brian Alston, David Gates said:

> He was just a huge inspiration to me. I just looked forward to coming to CYCLE and being able to spend time with him. He genuinely cared about me, how I felt. He wanted me to learn. Back then, when you were in CYCLE, the junior staff might have been two or three years older than you, but it seemed like they were ten or twenty years older than you. You know, they just seemed so mature. And I look back to them and think, "Really? You were just two or three years older than me?" You had so much respect for your junior staffer, and you really looked up to him. That inspired me. When I got the opportunity to be junior staff, I modeled everything I did after Brian. I watched him. I learned from him.

The 250 volunteers who came every week to tutor at CYCLE were college and graduate school students, local professionals, or members of the LaSalle Street Church. In addition to working on academics, they also lent an ear (or a shoulder) to the young people as they discussed their personal issues and aspirations. Volunteers brought bridging resources to CYCLE, introducing youth to new possibilities, connecting them to opportunities, and advocating for them. I Have A Dream scholarship sponsor Burt Kaplan was a mentor extraordinaire. He connected kids to jobs, met regularly with them to encourage them to try hard in school and think broadly about their futures, made the IHAD youth members of the Kaplan family. As Shree Green put it, "Burt Kaplan was passionate and had a true love for us." CYCLE kids saw mentors' invitations into their homes and attendance at events as profound expressions of genuine commitment, "knowing you mattered to people who were not kin to you." Shree said, "I don't know if they understood how much they contributed to changing our lives."

CYCLE youth relied on the unconditional support and commitment of senior staff—founder and director Greg Darnieder, volunteer coordinator Michelle McConnell, academic director Pat Ford, scholarship coordinators Tami Doig, Craig Nash, Bernard McCune, and Anita Boyd. Tami and Greg, both of them white outsiders to the community, played an essential advocacy role, bringing resources to CYCLE and linking CYCLE with mainstream Chicago. And because she was from the community, Pat had personal experience with the everyday challenges youth confronted in their homes and schools and on the streets and could actively respond to young people's needs and tough situations and keep volunteer tutors informed about issues facing their protégés. In many ways, Pat was CYCLE's heart and soul—a natural mentor always available to kids and scholarship coordinators, always a sympathetic listener and trusted source of support.

Everyone at CYCLE mentored every day. Ken Dunkin spoke of the strong mentoring presence:

> People like Craig, people like Anita Boyd, Pat Ford—I could go on and on—Greg, as the leader, set parameters up for us to work within, really set the tone for us in terms of how we should proceed in life, even if it was just academically, but socially as well, just sort of a human consciousness . . . There was just sort of a good seed phenomenon . . . a sense of motivation, encouragement and security, a sense of belonging that really set the tone for a lot of us. And we just sort of gravitated toward it. And it was sort of a [constant reminder] that "you know better, you know better than to do that."

MENTORING OUTCOMES

CYCLE alums unanimously attributed their many positive outcomes to the mentoring relationships. High school graduation topped everyone's list. All Junior Staff tutors during the school year graduated from high school thanks, they said, to the attention, guidance, and support of the program's senior staff.

Tamiko Jones also credited her mentor, Pat Ford, with teaching her self-regulation skills and strategies for succeeding at school. Still other former Junior Staffers pointed to lessons they learned about self-discipline and responsibility. Craig Nash recalled learning that "hard work pays off, and 'just bad luck' was not an acceptable excuse to being late or not doing what you were supposed to do. You had to be accountable for you." And youth involved in CYCLE's scholarship programs pointed to the 24/7 "whatever it takes" support consistently provided them over the years by the coordinators. Their mentors, many alums said, played a crucial role in setting and meeting the expectations they set for themselves.

CYCLE mentors consistently nurtured the close relationships established with mentees, and in many cases these connections have endured over many years. Several features indicate how the organization understood and supported mentoring and why it was so effective for Cabrini-Green youth.

A Developmental, Strength-Based Focus

Many activities took place at CYCLE, but at its core the organization was all about promoting positive youth development, enabling Cabrini-Green youth to feel good about themselves, their potential, and their futures. Everything else—tutoring, art, trips—functioned in service of that goal. CYCLE's approach to mentoring was youth centered; it focused on young people's developmental needs in contrast to mentoring initiatives driven primarily by mentor interests (e.g., technology, sports) or the stated goal of the program (e.g., academic improvement, literacy, parenting). In focus-driven programs, too often youth experience activities as prescriptive rather than developmental resources and feel that the sponsors and coordinators pay little attention to their interests and needs in service of "implementing the program."

In a youth-centered mentoring setting, youth and mentor *together* set goals and work toward them within a developmental framework. At CYCLE, mentors remained attuned to a young person's immediate needs or struggles and adjusted activities accordingly. Mentor-mentee interactions always centered on encouraging potential rather than addressing deficits. As Ken Dunkin recalled, "Mentors would send a message of 'here's how you could do better and here's how you can get there.'"

Focusing on the positive did not mean unconditional support from mentors but, rather, a combination of nudging, prompting, and supporting while holding clear expectations. As Richard Blackmon put it, "It was important that youth experience both structure and support. It wasn't enough to be friends, but the relationship had to be about something . . . a goal." Goals for CYCLE youth included being promoted to the next grade, graduating, postsecondary education, staying out of gangs, and not getting pregnant.

Consistent with that developmental, relationship-based stance, mentoring at CYCLE was not formulaic. Room existed for Junior Staff, senior staff, and volunteers to decide the best use of time on any given day. Mentoring was individualized in terms of participants' interests and life circumstances—effectively, a case management approach. Tami Doig counseled that to be effective, individuals working with youth should "figure out what matters to them and start paying attention to those things." Similarly, Richard Blackmon noted that "you've got to be in tune with what's going on in their lives. This is gangland. Many of these kids are just raising themselves."

A Consistent, Long-Term Commitment

CYCLE volunteers were advised to "be consistent if you're going to make this commitment to a person's life." Researchers agree that a mentoring effort will fall short when it consists of episodic, prescribed activities offered by a changing parade of adults. For youth such as those in CYCLE, inconsistent mentoring relationships risk more than disappointment. Disruption and pain can result from unreliable mentoring relationships because they touch the vulnerabilities of youth who anticipate being let down or put off by mainstream adults. A mentor who does not show up on time or at all, who does not follow through with promises, who does not try to make a connection batters a young person's sense of self-esteem and worth. Jennifer Means recollected the disappointment she felt at other local afterschool programs: "These were young professionals trying to help out . . . but it was a hit-or-miss kind of thing. It left us feeling empty."

But it wasn't enough for volunteer mentors to just show up on time; senior staff stressed the importance of developing a relationship with the youth. Over and above their tutoring, volunteer mentors invited young people to ballgames, concerts, restaurants, and other sites and events around Chicago. As natural mentors, Junior Staff also assumed an active role helping with camping trips and other excursions around and beyond Chicago. Many mentors remained involved with their CYCLE kids for more than one year, and a few saw their protégés through from seventh grade to high school and into college, jobs, and sometimes beyond.

The scholarship program coordinators were also proactive, committed mentors. Bernard McCune said that they all sent "little care packages" to their kids in college, "because that's what parents of more well-off kids do." They were in touch regularly about grades so that scholarship funds could be released, and they were always available to provide counsel and support as their youth dealt with academic challenges, social concerns, financial difficulties, or worries about family back in Cabrini-Green.

CYCLE alums considered the many mentoring opportunities woven into the program's social fabric as essential to their success as adults; it was not enough to see possible futures, they also needed a caring mentor dedicated to seeing them achieve that future. Echoing the importance of mentors' constancy and reliability, Tamiko Jones viewed CYCLE'S "the earlier the better" approach and long-term engagement as essential: "You almost have to marry the child—not like in programs where folks are in and out. You've gotta have long-term relationships. How do you build up people that are broken? You build them up by showing them 'I'm gonna walk with you. I'm gonna show you this commitment.' It's important that programs think about the long haul . . . Not just 'I am gonna touch your life and then I'm gonna go away.'"

Shared experiences, even shared ordeals, held the mentoring relationships together. Mentors had fun with their protégées and with each other. They looked forward to Club silliness each week, and together enjoyed excursions and trips. Richard Blackmon recalled the time his Bright Knights were given access to a box at Wrigley Field and found a menu from which they could order anything they wanted—and they did. Carts of food—predominately sweets—appeared at the box door. The sugar high lasted for hours.

Support for Volunteers

Coordinator Michelle McConnell offered volunteers a preliminary introduction to CYCLE and Cabrini-Green, and she had the youth on hand to report on their lives and their community. Beyond this initial session, however, there was no formal training. Nor was there a manual. Instead, volunteers got ongoing, hands-on support from CYCLE senior staff that included everything from keeping running records of a youth's activities and achievements, personal check-ins if a volunteer needed to be aware of a situation in their mentee's life, thoughtful academic oversight by Pat Ford, and the active involvement of scholarship coordinators. This direct, personal relationship between CYCLE senior staff and volunteers contrasts with interactions found in many youth programs, then and now. Typically, volunteers have little communication with staff once their orientation session ends. Researchers examining mentoring activities of school-age children find that many volunteers "almost never" talk with staff.

CYCLE staff support focused on commitment, consistency, and caring relationships, supports directed toward personal growth and success. Mentors enabled hundreds of Cabrini-Green youth to hope for positive, productive adulthoods and then to achieve them. Tamara Laws wrote about the importance of these relationships in a poem she wrote during Robert Boone's 1992 summer writing program:

NO ONE THERE
"Study hard," a voice says.
But how can you when there's no one there?
No one to urge you to try harder
and no one there to tell you, "I believe in you. Now believe in yourself."
No one there to tell you, "Good job"
give you a pat on the head or some kind of reward.
To say that you studied hard.
If there's no one there
but that one voice who says,
"Study hard," then there is someone
and someone that cares.

CHAPTER 10

A Community of Belonging
A Good Gang

"We were a force." "We were a gang of excellence." "We were family." Expressions of "we-ness" dominate the stories CYCLE alums shared about their time in the program. It was clear that their experience as members of this community mattered to them as youth and, still, as adults.

The strength of that we-ness shows in the fact that more than thirty years later, strong relationships remain between CYCLE staff and the participants and among the "kids" themselves. Years after the COP95 program officially ended, for instance, coordinator Tami Doig continues to get notes, pictures of new grandbabies, and announcements of graduations, marriages, and births. IHAD coordinator Craig Nash remains in constant Facebook contact with program participants and regularly responds to requests to advise on a child's school options or lend a hand with finding employment. Greg Darnieder's connections with former CYCLE youth remain unbroken, and IHAD sponsor Anne Kaplan still hears from individuals who participated in the program decades ago.

The participants preserve the strong relationships they formed at CYCLE. Former Junior Staffers remain especially close. Many live in Chicago. They vacation together; they serve as godparents to one another's children; they sponsor an annual reunion barbeque; and a few are even married to each other. Junior Staffers living outside the area return for friends' important celebrations, such as a new graduate degree, a wedding, a promotion. Participants in CYCLE's scholarship programs also remain close. In December 2016, for instance, when a COP95 student completed her master's degree, two COP95 friends flew to Washington, DC, to attend her graduation and live-streamed the ceremony on Facebook for Tami Doig and other friends who could not be there. COP95 and IHAD participants stay in touch with program directors and each other through social media.

It is almost cliché to point out that as they grow up, young people profit from a strong network of relationships—peers and adults who encourage them, teach them, challenge them.[1] Youth workers, educators, researchers, and others concerned with positive youth development agree that few young people can alone achieve a healthy adulthood; positive youth development requires a structure of supports and social relationships consistent with constructive values and ambitions.[2] In his examination of many successful lives, Malcolm Gladwell writes that "no one—not rock stars, not professional athletes, not software billionaires, and not even geniuses—ever makes it alone."[3]

Connections feature prominently in the CYCLE alums' accounts, which highlight the number of strong relationships with peers and caring adults the program offered. However, the we-ness they describe is much more than multiple reliable connections; rather, it references the strong community that enveloped them at CYCLE. As Craig Nash put it, "We became a family, walking through life with each other." Or, as David Gates told Greg, "You guys became family immediately. I don't know how you did it. You loved the good kids just as much as you loved the bad kids. You wanted everyone to learn and grow the same way." In her book on mentoring emerging adults, Sharon Parks asserts that community finds its most powerful form in a "mentoring community," which "offers hospitality to the potential of the emerging adult self, poses challenging questions, and provides access to worthy dreams of self and world."[4] Certainly, mentoring animated all adult-youth interactions at CYCLE, as well as relationships between older and younger youth.

But the alums' *we* also signaled more: it meant belonging, security, unconditional support, trust, shared accountability among members of the community. The community of belonging at CYCLE provided the social support and learning environment that allowed young people to take risks, stretch themselves, and reach for worthy futures. Craig Nash asserted that what made CYCLE better than other youth programs was "that we really cared about each other." Another Junior Staffer echoed this thought: "It was a place where, outside of my home, where commitment and loyalty really mattered, it was the first time I experienced a place where people who weren't related to each other were committed to each other. It was one of those places I felt was a community in itself."

Arguably a community of belonging serves as a critical asset for all young people. However, in Cabrini-Green's complex context of concentrated poverty and social and institutional isolation, and with its negative stereotypes and predicted futures, CYCLE's strong community constituted essential support.

When alums said they "could not have made it through Cabrini without CYCLE," they pointed to the community they experienced there as the necessary resource. In their view, the mentoring and exposure they received would have fallen short absent the community that protected them, held them accountable, embraced their goals, and had their backs. CYCLE's community of belonging provided the context for effective action. Pat Ford dubbed it "our gang of excellence." David Gates used similar language to describe the CYCLE posse: "We were a group of positive people. Everyone tried to be positive. Instead of trying to be the baddest gang, we were trying to be the nicest, trying to help each other, and help other people . . . CYCLE molded a lot of positive young men who, without CYCLE, would not be where they are today." An IHAD scholarship alum said, "We were family. I felt like people really cared about me."

WHAT CYCLE PROVIDED

Simply wanting a better life was generally not enough to make it out of Cabrini-Green. Needed were the social, practical, and relational supports provided by CYCLE, a setting and community that offered youth freedom to grow and become, a secure place to imagine and achieve their hoped-for selves.

Safety

Physical and psychological safety presented ongoing, pressing concerns and demanded constant attention in Cabrini-Green. CYCLE staff went to great lengths to keep youth out of harm's way, to keep the bear at bay.[5] For instance, the absence of safe transportation—or any transportation—was a major consideration in kids' willingness to attend afterschool programs in or near the project, or in parents allowing them to do so. To ensure their safety, staff transported them home in vans, even if just down the block.

Belonging to CYCLE brought youth its own protection. Membership in this community shielded youth from targeted assaults or pressure to affiliate with one or another of the Cabrini-Green gangs. Although CYCLE kids, like anyone else living in the project, had to be vigilant about what route to take to school and aware of what was going on in recreational spaces, as well as avoid crossfire or snipers, gang members generally provided them safe passage. They were members of the CYCLE gang. More than one alum recounted instances of gang members warning them to "come back later" because shooting was about to start. As one said, "They knew what we were about and intentionally didn't bother us . . . even though they were right next door to 515 Oak."

But equally important to young people's survival and positive outcomes was their sense of emotional and psychological safety in the program.[6] The CYCLE community established clear rules about behavior, acted with consistency in upholding those expectations, and provided unconditional support for kids when things in their lives went wrong. Greg commented on the emotional repair work often required: "Some days it took us a couple of hours in the afternoon after school to undo the damage done to these kids. All they hear all day is how bad they are. We can't even begin our work until we can make them feel okay, feel good about themselves." Sometimes providing that personal support and encouragement took the entire tutoring session, regardless of the lesson planned.

The community afforded a secure, predictable space for youth navigating the unpredictable challenges of Cabrini-Green; it safeguarded both their emotional and physical well-being. As Craig Nash said, "If a person is hurting, if they don't feel safe, if they don't have enough to eat . . . if certain things aren't addressed, they will never hear the message. They're never available for the message because they need basic things first. We got our needs addressed at CYCLE. We felt safe. We felt loved." Pat Ford stressed the fundamental importance of safety and security: "It makes a world of difference for kids [like those growing up in Cabrini-Green] to have a safe place to go and some place to call their own. I always felt like CYCLE belonged to me, my home away from home." "Everyone knew my name," Tamiko Jones said. "I felt like I was part of a true family . . . It really made me feel like I was in a safe space."

Self-Confidence and Personal Efficacy

According to psychologist Albert Bandura, "Unless people believe that they can produce desired effects and forestall undesired ones by their actions, they have little incentive to act."[7] Likewise, sociologists Steven Hitlin and Glen Elder argue that effective use of personal agency requires general optimism about life outcomes.[8] Membership in the CYCLE community boosted kids' self-confidence and sense of personal efficacy.

Alums recalled often feeling isolated, inadequate, and "inappropriate" growing up, feelings related to their race and their Cabrini-Green address. One bright Junior Staffer declined a scholarship offer to a prestigious Chicago private high school, for example, because she "felt like a blackhead on a creamy complexion." Youth attending competitive CPS high schools or private schools regularly gave their address as "Near North" rather than mention Cabrini-Green. The adults and older youth in CYCLE pushed back against these negative feelings about themselves to feature positive options and show youth what they needed to do to achieve their dreams. Junior Staffer Jennifer Means recalled how, despite her misgivings about going to college, "I felt like, 'Okay, someone's in my corner. They're really serious about this, about me going to college, about me taking on a leadership role.' I came from a rough place, but being part of CYCLE just an opened my eyes to possible relationships, to relationships that are not what you see around you . . . to relationships that are totally unexpected." Another former Junior Staffer echoed this idea, saying, "We knew they had our backs—that they were committed to each of us. They were people who believed in you enough to stand with you and by you, to push you to ask tough questions about who you are and what you might become, what you needed to be successful." David Gates noted that CYCLE "taught us to be proud of ourselves. I found out I had some talents I didn't really know I had before."

In the scrapbook Tami Doig's COP95 students compiled for her in their final year of high school, one student wrote about feeling cared for and protected as part of the group: "You were always there to listen and help me out like a guardian angel. When I got stressed out from working so much, you were there to offer support. When my college advisor said I couldn't make it into U of I Champaign-Urbana, you were there to think things over, and congratulate me when I was accepted." Another offered, "Even through the tough times I have had to face in life, you have always been there for me to help me overcome these obstacles and set important goals . . . and become a successful person."

Being part of the CYCLE community insulated youth from the acts of discrimination they experienced daily in the low expectations expressed in the public schools, the civic disinvestment in their homes and neighborhoods, and the social stigma associated with a Cabrini-Green address. Youth felt recognized both for who they were and who they were becoming and were celebrated within the CYCLE community for their hard work and accomplishments.

Collective Efficacy

Participation in the CYCLE created a strong sense of collective efficacy that reinforced individual agency and strengthened the group's, and individuals', work. "We were a force!" Junior Staffers' shared belief in their power to produce effects through collective action heightened members' motivation to accomplish their individual and collective goals and strengthened their commitment in the face of challenges or setbacks.[9] Collective agency is more than the sum of individual efficacy beliefs; it's the product of shared knowledge, skills, and values of its different members. "It is an emergent group-level property."[10]

The group's strong sense of efficacy enabled them to create their own environments for action. One summer, for example, twenty-five to thirty Junior Staffers formed the Breakfast Club. The group gathered on Tuesday and Thursday mornings at 7:00 at the Atrium Village, just outside Cabrini-Green, to talk about their summer programs and share ideas and problems. Greg, who did not learn about these sessions until summer's end, saw the Breakfast Club as a sign of Junior Staffers' tight sense of ownership and collective agency. "They wanted time together—away from CYCLE staff. I was so proud of the culture and the personal bonds they created." Several dozen junior staffers similarly took initiative; they regularly arrived at 7:00 a.m., ninety minutes before their official reporting time, to collaborate on developing activities for the day.

Among the most significant consequence of the collective efficacy that characterized the CYCLE community was its effect on individuals' motivation, staying power, sense of responsibility, and accountability. David Gates pointed to the inspiration and positive energy the CYCLE community provided: "There were a lot of negative people in my life. And this was a group of young men and young women that were doing positive things. I was like, oh man! I want to do this! I started hanging out and it changed my life."

Alums also stressed how important it was to them not to let the group down, to fulfill commitments and meet expectations. Older Junior Staffers modeled expected behaviors for participating kids as well as for younger Junior Staffers. For instance, as a college student, Craig Nash oversaw afternoon art classes during summer day camps. He knew all eyes were on him, observing both how he conducted art lessons and, more importantly, himself—"They didn't miss a thing!"

OPPORTUNITIES FOR BONDING

Communities such as CYCLE are rare, fragile constructs that are vulnerable to such threats as disconnections among members, new participants, uneven subscription to group norms and values. They require constant nurturing. The strong CYCLE community resulted from intentional strategies and management choices. Relationships formed the cornerstone of program activities, and Greg's management style focused on developing strong relationships within the programs and between staff and youth—on building and nurturing a community of belonging.

Several strategies were key to building strong relationships within CYCLE because they provided opportunities for bonding between youth, staff, and volunteers.

Attendance. CYCLE's strict attendance rules (miss three tutoring sessions and you're out) aimed to promote strong relationships among youth, staff, and volunteer tutors and between youth. A drop-in program with episodic participation, in Greg's view, could neither foster nor sustain close relationships. Showing up and participating on a regular basis served to build relationships among youth, between adults and youth, and within the community. Long-term participation also mattered. Greg and senior staff endeavored to "get 'em early," at least by middle school, if possible; but many kids came to CYCLE as kindergarteners.

Social events. CYCLE hosted many social events during the school year and the summer program. They were intended to be fun and to provide occasions for Junior Staff to spend time together and with their tutees. During the summers, for instance, three or four picnics and barbecues in Lincoln Park brought Junior Staff together to kick back and enjoy each other's company. Many also attended Wednesday nights' Young Life Club meetings during the school year and week-long camps in the summer. Every Saturday and every afternoon during summer day camp included an outing with a different age group.

Shared experiences. Excursions to local campgrounds and camp sites around the Midwest fostered friendships, encouraged collaboration, and developed shared experiences—though some called them "shared ordeals" because they had to pitch tents, cook meals, and deal with darkness few had experienced before. The senior staff intended these camping expeditions as ways to introduce youth to new environments, but they also understood the significant bonding opportunities camping provided, both during the long van rides and in the unfamiliar rustic settings.

Ongoing attention to norms and expectations. A healthy community requires shared language, shared norms and expectations, and constant attention. Weekly half-hour Junior Staff meetings during the school year and daily during the summer provided the young leaders opportunities to hash things out, plan for the next day or week, and discuss shortfalls and the lessons they taught. Senior staff used these meetings to build social cohesion among programs and to protect the common understandings foundational to the organization's community. In their tributes to their COP95 leader Tami Doig, most all students wrote about the significance her oft-repeated dictum that failure was "not an option" to their perseverance and commitment to achieve stretch goals. "Constant attention," says Tami, "was just that: constant attention! I was one of the first to get a cell phone (the giant one in a bag) so students and parents would always be able to reach me."

Interdependence. CYCLE senior staff knew each other's kids, swapped van-driving responsibilities, and generally could pick up where another left off. They took each other's students to Young Life camps and went on college visits across program lines. They formed a tight community of practice. By design, Junior Staffers also functioned interdependently. The tiered structure of responsibility for tutoring and other activities moved certain people into increased leadership roles. They needed to listen, collaborate, and work with each other, whether in the office, computer lab, club, puppet group, construction group. They depended on each other for smooth implementation and successful outcomes, and this made for a supportive, cohesive community.

Near-peer relationships. CYCLE relied on near-peer relationships to enhance interactions between young tutors and their tutees around homework and other educational undertakings. This approach to engaging Cabrini-Green kids in their school work proved an effective one. But the near-peer strategy served more than academic purposes; it built relationships and community. Youth growing up in stressful contexts such as Cabrini-Green often feel they cannot make it in mainstream contexts and blame disappointments on their race or economic status. Being able to talk regularly with older youth from the community about their struggles and setbacks, as well as their successes in school or college, gave younger youth immeasurable reassurance and even inspiration to do better and pursue their dreams. Alums consistently spoke of the significance of the near-peer strategy in relational terms, as providing role models, serving as older brothers or sisters. Ken Dunkin put the power of the near-peer relationships he experienced at CYCLE this way: "If you look at folk like

Craig [Nash] and others who were ahead of us, there was just sort of a good seed phenomenon, just sort of humble, quiet, intelligent giants that really sort of penetrated down to younger folk. And I think, you know, with the leadership they provided, you're setting the tone and giving [younger kids] the space in which to operate, and giving them the motivation and encouragement and sense of security, sense of belonging." These relationships reinforced the norms and expectations expressed in CYCLE's community and have persisted through the years. Young adults returning from college checked in on their younger charges to see how they were doing, and reassure them that they could follow their college-going pathway. "It was tremendously encouraging," remembered one, especially in the context of worries about whether, as blacks, they would be overwhelmed in college by racial and academic expectations.[11]

Taking responsibility and ownership. Senior staff provided Junior Staff with opportunities to take meaningful responsibility for their work and regularly sought their input on what worked, what didn't, and how to improve programs. Responsible for designing and carrying out effective activities for younger kids in the program, Junior Staff approached this assignment as a team: "We'd sit around and brainstorm. [Greg] let us take responsibility for things. We weren't just carrying out directions." With this responsibility and accountability came a sense of ownership in the community. One alum put it this way: "There was this natural sense of empowerment and respect and gratitude that was there. We felt a sense of ownership . . . we weren't just employed . . . And there was such a level of accountability that we as peers had to each other. We held each other accountable . . . to make the right decisions . . . There was a sense in our hearts that we didn't want to let [the senior staff] down either." CYCLE's strong community of belonging mediated young people's often dysfunctional Cabrini-Green family, school, neighborhood, and peer contexts. It created substitute or supplemental family structures, relationships, and opportunities for kids who didn't have them otherwise. Its embrace of community kept young people safe, engaged in learning skills of leadership, and seeing futures different from those predicted for youth growing up in Cabrini-Green.

ACTIVATING TURNING POINTS: BRIDGING AND BONDING CAPITAL

Mentoring and exposure to new people and places fueled CYCLE youths' dreams and ambitions. Staff and mentors provided consistent and cumulative messaging about the young people's worth and potential and about their options. The CYCLE community fostered and reinforced identity changes linked to new social roles—being a member of a good gang, being a positive force in the community, being a high school graduate. It provided the supportive environment that enabled young people to reach for those different futures.

Alums highlighted three aspects of their CYCLE experience as essential to setting them on a positive course through and out of Cabrini-Green: exposure, mentoring, and strong community. Forms of social capital thread through each of them. As sociologist James Coleman defines it, "social capital inheres in the structure of relations between persons and among persons . . . [It facilitates] the achievement of goals that could not be achieved in its absence or could be achieved only at a higher cost . . . [It] is created when the relations among persons change in ways that facilitate action."[12] Social researchers and policy analysts have developed conceptual differences among forms of social capital that underscore their somewhat different functions. Distinctions between *bridging capital* and *bonding capital* suggest how and why participation in CYCLE enabled and empowered youth from Cabrini-Green to achieve their impressive life accounts.[13]

High-poverty, culturally and socially isolated communities such as Cabrini-Green generally lack the resources and networks needed to create productive connections, or bridges, to the broader community. "Old heads," a vital resource to youth growing up in poor, black communities, were few in Cabrini-Green.[14] Volunteer mentors and senior staff often provided youth that sage counsel and useful connections. And CYCLE afforded bridging capital through introductions to area businessmen, program sponsors, and volunteers and through connections to the larger Chicago community. Mentors from the Chicago area introduced Cabrini-Green youth to lives and cultures different from those encountered in their four blocks. Mentors inside and outside CYCLE offered consistent, long-term, personal support as young people imagined might-be futures, endeavored to reach them, and experienced disappointments and accomplishments along the way. Young people returning to Cabrini-Green and CYCLE from college also provided bridging capital—concrete, real-life examples of people just like them who could provide the advice about how to get there and the reassurance that they could be successful.

Greg tirelessly sought resources and opportunities for CYCLE youth. He brought in artists, writers, health educators, and other professionals. He negotiated spaces and places for CYCLE activities. He found philanthropists to sponsor scholarships and underwrite other opportunities for CYCLE kids. He cultivated relationships that would lead to summer jobs, internships, camping spots, and equipment. As Craig Nash said, "He went out there and found resources we needed to do the good work we were doing. I can't tell you the resources he brought in. He worked fourteen-, fifteen-hour days, going out there finding funders, introducing sponsors to the program. It was always about the kids."

But youth needed more than links outside their neighborhood to make it through and out of Cabrini-Green. By themselves, connections outside the Cabrini-Green community would have been insufficient to set the youth confidently on a positive path to their hoped-for selves. They needed strong supports within it. The deep bonds of trust and shared expectations young people found at CYCLE encouraged them to take risks, consider ambitious goals, and feel secure in the knowledge that their good gang, their "gang of excellence," would protect them if they fell short. They were not alone, they were a member of a team, a family. Young people's CYCLE experiences show how bonding capital can be foundational to effective use of bridging capital, how membership in a positive, coherent social group such as CYCLE actuates bridging capital and the potential of a turning point. Bonding capital—secure connections to a positive social group—galvanizes bridging capital.

Bridging and bonding capital work together to motivate and enable enduring, positive change in a marginalized young person's life. Neither by itself provides sufficient resource for kids growing up in poor communities such as Cabrini-Green. Many of the single moms struggling to raise their kids in Cabrini-Green profited from strong relationships with one another, and these bonds brought a sense of mutual care and dependability. Strong ties among moms, their parental monitoring, and vigilance about their kid's safety suggest a socially organized community. But without broader connections to mainstream institutions and opportunities, they and their children remained isolated and challenged to better their lives, to get ahead. It is the rare individual who can make it out of a context of concentrated poverty by themselves. As Greg has said, "There were few Lone Rangers riding out of Cabrini-Green."

More than one youth program supporter has puzzled over why, given resources, the benefits assumed for marginalized youth fail to materialize—*We gave them opportunities (tutors, special programs), what happened?* CYCLE's story shows how effective use of bridging opportunities or other such resources requires a reliable degree of within-program coherence, collective support, and security. For CYCLE youth, bonding capital, the positive peer culture and shared social identity that accompanied it created the foundation essential for making actual the turning points implicit in the opportunities and resources they received. Membership in a strong community of belonging enabled them to turn the key.

PART III
LEARNING FROM CYCLE

This book has three broad goals: to look inside the black box of program processes and principles to see what goes on in a successful youth program; to understand why and how positive outcomes were sustained over time (and a generation); and to consider how to move CYCLE's practices and outcomes from exceptional status to expected out-of-school time opportunities, most especially for high-poverty, inner-city youth.

The two chapters in Part III address these last two goals. Chapter 11 describes the community and culture in which senior staff worked—how they contributed fundamentally to the positive outcomes kids achieved and what happened when they were compromised by a change in leadership. Chapter 12 provides a synthesis of CYCLE's outcomes for kids, its core strategies, and the underlying design principles that created valuable opportunities for Cabrini-Green youth and then turns to the question of how to create more CYCLEs in the future and the implications for policy, practice, and research.

CHAPTER 11

A Community of Practice

CYCLE stands apart from most youth out-of-school time organizations not only in its comprehensive youth development mission but also in the consistency and coherence of the messages and goals expressed across its programs. Many, if not most, comprehensive OST youth programs (such as YMCA/YWCA, Boys and Girls Clubs) operate as loose confederations of different activities—sports, arts, academic supports. Although nominally part of the same organization, in practice they function relatively independent of one another and often reflect different activity cultures or goals. But at CYCLE, even though the tutoring, Junior Staff, and scholarship programs involved different activities, different people, different perspectives, and different talents, all expressed similar core values and practices regardless of the time of day, time of year, age group, program staffing, or venue.

For instance, each of CYCLE's five scholarship programs had its own identity depending on award guidelines, funder preferences, and coordinator background. Each employed different selection strategies. The IHAD group included everyone in the target class. COP95 selected a cohort of thirty students with interest in college and a supportive adult. EAL relied on word of mouth to bring motivated students to the program. The Providence–St. Mel scholarship supported thirty CYCLE middle grade students chosen for academic promise and a coordinator located at the school. The Schuessler/CYCLE scholarships went to students of promise who were already engaged with CYCLE and involved financial support only for attendance at private high schools or higher education institutions.

Despite these operational contrasts reflecting staffing or design differences, each CYCLE program achieved similar, positive outcomes: high school graduation and college-going rates that are impressive compared with those of the Chicago Public Schools and, even more so, other, non-CYCLE youth in the Cabrini-Green community. Being part of CYCLE brought an identity. Both staff and youth saw themselves first as a part of CYCLE and second as a participant in a particular program, like one of the scholarships. As Bernard McCune said, "The beauty of CYCLE was that all of us led different programs, and they might've had different names, but the kids got the same core set of support." CYCLE stood for something in terms of the expectations it held for the youth and staff and the supports it offered for achieving them.

What made CYCLE effective was its organizational culture as a *community of practice*—the values, mutual goals, and deep loyalty shared by all associated with the organization. Arguably, the power and synergy of this culture that characterized CYCLE's various programs provided the ingredient that enabled the consistent successes of its young people.

Not every group of individuals engaged in a common practice forms a community. University faculty, for example, function in a famously anomic organizational environment, one typically defined by competition not collaboration. And not every community revolves around practice. Communities defined by factors such as geography, ethnicity, or religion reflect individual attributes but not a common practice. A community of practice describes a group of people who share a concern and a deep commitment to what they do and who come together regularly to learn how to do it better.[1] Learning from each other's knowledge and experience animates and shapes everyone's work. In the course of routinely spending time together, members of a community of practice develop common language, shared understandings of goals and ways of doing things, ways of talking, and ways of solving problems of practice.

The concept of a community of practice is not a new one, but it provides a useful perspective for understanding how CYCLE's senior staff and Junior Staff worked together to develop the shared repertoire of resources, coherent messages, and shared supports that made such a significant difference in kids' lives. The strength of CYCLE's community of practice can be seen in the fact that after more than two decades, recollections of their work and time together remain fresh among members of the scholarship groups and Junior Staff. For instance, at a March 2014 reunion of all five scholarship coordinators, one had only to prompt colleagues to remember "that canoe trip," "the lady in the red dress," "the trip to the outlet stores," "when Greg's shoe fell through a hole in the van floor" to produce laughter and more than a few rolled eyes. And the Junior Staff trip to Mississippi still elicits friendly jabs at Greg for taking them there. Alums provided detailed accounts of the first summer camp session they led, or the first time Greg entrusted them to drive the van to pick up kids at Lincoln Park, or their boisterous trips. Senior staff, Junior Staff, and Greg recalled their shared triumphs and ordeals with continued mutual respect and with profound pride in what they accomplished together.

CYCLE's community of practice constituted an essential resource for the various programs. Senior staff and Junior Staff regularly made choices about what to do and how to proceed that reflected their own preferences and interests, or assessments of what a young person needed on any given day and how best to provide it. Kids came to tutoring, for instance, with different levels of skill and knowledge; even youth at the same grade level usually needed different supports. Careful notes of previous tutoring sessions enabled tutors to tailor a session to what a young person most needed. There were no curricula or scripted procedures to follow, just individual judgment. As Greg directed Tami Doig as she took on COP95, "Just do what you think is right." (Tami, who now heads an independent school, built her career on this "build it as you go" strategy: "I am famous for saying 'curriculum is crappy when you write it down.'")

An energized, coordinated community of practice proved indispensable because most every decision at CYCLE was context dependent. Both Junior Staff and senior staff needed to be attuned to what was going on in students' lives, in their schools, and in the neighborhood. Construction of practice in the dynamic and unpredictable Cabrini-Green environment required improvisation, interactive coordination, joint problem solving, and ongoing communication. Craig Nash said, "Day in and day out, when there was an issue with our schools, with our kids, we attacked it as a team."

A strong community of practice made possible consistent messaging and constant reinforcement for kids participating in the different programs, no matter which adult they were interacting with. Bernard McCune recounted the senior staff's steady messaging to youth: "We kept talking over and over again about what they could [accomplish] and why it mattered. Telling them that graduation and college was something they could do and it was attainable for them, we just kept at it." These coordinated practices developed as a product of an ongoing, dynamic decision-making process about what to do, when, and how. Staff met regularly to talk about their work. Junior Staffers met with Greg and Pat Ford every Monday evening to review the preceding week and plan for the upcoming one and also organized their own regular get-togethers. Scholarship coordinators came together as a group once a week to talk about issues that had arisen with their kids, parents, or schools and to explore resources for upcoming activities, share ideas, and map ways in which they could support one another. And, informally, senior staff and Junior Staff connected every day around tutoring sessions and the logistics of getting their kids to and from CYCLE. The strong community of practice provided both the content and the context for these exchanges and generated a powerful kind of social energy that forged coherence in values and program strategies.

Few youth OST programs operate as a community of practice. Many, if not most, function according to a more individualistic model that holds activity specialists responsible for their own practices but not for the collective outcome. CYCLE's organizational culture stands apart. What distinguished it from other youth programs? What made it work?

LEADERSHIP

A vital community of practice, whether operating in a youth program, a school, or a business office, cannot be commanded into existence. Leadership being attentive to an organization's culture of practice—"the way we do things here"—and making it coherent constitutes the nonnegotiable requirement of a vibrant community of practice. Greg Darnieder's leadership as CYCLE's executive director intentionally featured, nurtured, and sustained the program's core principles of practice and cultural norms. He put structures and routines in place that generated daily conversations among staff about programs, choices made, how they did or did not represent the mission and beliefs, and how to learn from experience. Senior staff integrated these core principles in their own roles, producing tightly choreographed relationships among all associated with CYCLE.

Every successful community of practice, like every successful collaboration, needs someone to nurture and tend it. Greg's steadfast leadership provided a clear vision for the program, an express belief in staff abilities, and concrete support for their work. And he walked the talk. Greg showed up at 6:00 a.m. every day to ensure that all was in order; he attended countless meetings to garner necessary supports for CYCLE youth and staff; he went along on summer camping trips; he ran Saturday movie and popcorn events.

Academic director Pat Ford provided senior staff and Junior Staff everyday support and nurturing: "I became a CYCLE convert at age thirteen. That became my life from that point on." Any of the programs that dealt directly with youth—the scholarship programs, tutoring,

Junior Staff, day camps—fell under Pat's caring purview. Although each of the coordinators reported to her, "it wasn't about hierarchy at all" for her but about working together as effectively as they could. She knew the young people associated with each of the scholarship programs, the activities they were involved in, and the obstacles they faced in their lives. She checked in regularly with the coordinators to see how things were going; she brokered opportunities and resources, such as the Marwen art program and influential volunteer tutors. Her insider knowledge and perspective allowed her to serve as Greg's "barometer," he said, as CYCLE's comprehensive mission emerged:

> She was a person who knew every CYCLE participant, had the administrative skills to supervise staff at every level, had the ability to develop program strategies and train staff while overseeing the implementation of multiple initiatives. She was the ultimate team player bringing the highest level of commitment, empathy, vision, someone whom everyone looked up to. She had the respect of her peers, respected boundaries, held information in confidence . . . There wasn't anyone who I depended on more. And she was from neighborhood and had credibility.

Each scholarship coordinator commented on the important guidance Pat provided, even while acknowledging that they were all about the same age. Craig thought that "Pat had a maturity beyond her years. The woman knows what she's doing. She can lead—I would go into battle with her, and it was battles sometimes when we were trying to figure out, how to make it happen for the kids." Tami Doig made similar points about Pat's capacity as academic director: "Pat was a profoundly competent twenty-two-year-old, and in this lovely, gracious way she kept us on track . . . I was not ever confused that she was totally my boss!"

Pat, like Greg, believed deeply in the importance of senior staff working as an orchestrated team rather than a loose confederation of similarly tasked individuals. She reflected, "I am not sure how much impact you can have as a lone fish swimming in an environment like this one. I'm just not sure." She also talked about how commitment to the program's mission and the kids outplayed the low wages and long hours: "The strong culture and environment that you create makes people stay, feel committed enough to stay. Because the pay is bad, and the hours can be a little, um, unwieldy!"

SHARED VALUES AND EXPERIENCES

Trusting relationships create the foundation for an effective community of practice. CYCLE scholarship coordinators functioned as a strong community from the outset because most of them had grown up in the Cabrini-Green community. Anita Boyd and Pat Ford were from the same neighborhood; Bernard McCune and Pat went to the same high school; Bernard knew Craig Nash from his Junior Staff days, and their older brothers were close friends; Pat was academic director at CYCLE when Craig was Junior Staff.

Each of them experienced firsthand the culture, norms, and dangers of Cabrini-Green. Craig and Bernard, whose brothers got caught up in gangs, painfully understood the challenges facing young boys growing up in the community. As Bernard said, "We weren't too far removed from the experience ourselves, so we could actually relate and emphasize with [kids'] struggles." Each was passionate about helping young people from *their* community find footing on a positive path, and they were in agreement about how to do that. And while Tami Doig shared neither race nor neighborhood with other scholarship coordinators, based on the deep connection forged when she interned at CYCLE as a Wheaton College student volunteer, she wholeheartedly matched the others' dedication to CYCLE's mission and goals for the Cabrini-Green kids. Pat Ford underscored the importance of this shared buy-in and commitment:

> Being committed for the long haul . . . being steadfast. There's nothing gimmicky about this work. It's all about the value and belief the

adult community has in the kids and the families they are charged with helping. The issues of poverty are way more complex than any of us can imagine . . . There was a philosophical glue that held us together . . .We're all in it together, and we all have something to learn and give . . . You really do feel like you can roll up your sleeves when you're all wanting the same thing [and] believe in the power and light of kids, not just collecting a paycheck.

The group's determination to provide the best possible experiences and supports for their young people allowed the candor essential for them to learn from each other and from their mistakes. As Greg said, "There had to be an openness to consider anything that would help the kids; it was totally kid-centric. That kind of norming across programs required everyone to buy in, and talk it through." Not everyone who joined the scholarship teams had that commitment, however. The first IHAD coordinator fled after a trying summer camp experience with the Dreamers, and the EAL program had more than one leader before Bernard came on board. Despite these two instances, Bernard underscored, the staff maintained a strong sense of teamwork: "It was a tremendous group of people who had a focus and who also cared more about others than they cared about themselves. And none of us was perfect, but in terms of working together as a team . . . it was something that we really, really believed in."

Senior staff and Junior Staff also shared a spiritual, faith-based approach to their work and lives. Tami, Craig, and Pat had been involved with Young Life and saw its relational approach to working with youth as critical for CYCLE. Since a Young Life ministry operated in the LaSalle Street Church basement, CYCLE's original home, many of CYCLE's young people were involved. Pat remembered, "The Gospels were presented in a way that was relevant to high school kids. It was a little fun and goofy . . . We did goofy skits, sang songs. It wasn't like indoctrination but more of a character message, although from a Bible verse . . . a kind of spiritual ruddering." Craig called it "'sneaky churchy,' because all the morals, values we were exposed to were in the context of good clean fun."

SHARED PRINCIPLES OF PRACTICE

Because CYCLE's approach was not an institutionalized, scripted one, a unity of message and supports across programs depended on commonly held principles of practice. And senior staff well understood the necessity of achieving a delicate balance of love and support with expectations and structure. Pat spoke of people involved with youth programs "who want to do all the loving on kids but without the structure—it doesn't work. On the other hand, if you're a hard ass, the kids will think you don't care, and that won't work either. Our whole approach was to balance high expectations with support and to get to know those kids and families well, so we would know what was needed . . . Pushing and supporting, and also being an adult in their lives."

To achieve this fragile equilibrium on a youth-by-youth basis, CYCLE depended on a related principle of practice: attend closely to a youth's life circumstances and adjust accordingly. They knew that several moms grappled with mental illness or substance abuse; some kids encountered abuse in their homes; some were homeless at one or another time; almost all struggled at some point with the death or incarceration of a family member; many students struggled academically or personally in their school settings. Another principle of practice was to find the right balance of support and expectation: never give up on a child. Kids always came first at CYCLE.

All staff subscribed to the view that if one method, resource, or style of interaction did not advance a goal for a young person, it was adults' responsibility to try another approach, and another, until something did. Many times this youth-centered stance demanded staff persistence and pedagogical creativity to ensure that a young person understood a concept. "We never blamed the young person for not getting something," Greg said. "We needed to simplify the explanation, come at it another way . . . It is the art of teaching to break things down into simpler and simpler concepts. It was always the adult's responsibility . . . The assumption was the kid was trying his or her best." Other times never giving up on a kid required thinking about ways in which a young person's environment could be altered to promote hoped-for outcomes. Might a different school provide needed supports? Might experience with a new activity or place spark interest and purpose? Might more one-on-one contact with a CYCLE staff or mentor make a difference? Senior staff made many of those adjustments.

COLLECTIVE RESPONSIBILITY AND ACCOUNTABILITY

Senior staff and Junior Staff operated on assumptions of collective responsibility and accountability, and all the former staffers spoke of the power of the team to problem solve, support one another, lend a hand, and send a consistent message to kids about the importance of education and a belief in their potential. A homogeneous group can find strength in numbers, but a distribution of perspectives and expertise expands the reach of a community of practice. Even though shared values and experiences shaped their approach to their work, the diversity of skills, backgrounds, and experiences each staffer brought made the collective effort more effective than any single individual's. And the absence of a codified program made CYCLE's collective perspective all the more important.

Problem-solving around kids' needs figured prominently in each staff team conversation—finding summer jobs, getting work permits, making sure youth completed necessary forms for school and college, supporting youth with widely varying academic interests and abilities, dealing with tragedies or failures, and, often, running interference for moms and kids with social service agencies. Tami pointed to the value of candid senior staff discussions about practice: "The freedom we were given was empowering but our thinking probably had lots of errors in it. We called each other on those." Greg agreed, saying, "They could learn from each other because someone was always a bit further down a particular road." Shared norms and understandings fostered shared responsibilities. Pat remembered having to miss a summer camp session for personal reasons and calling the site manager to let him know. When he questioned whether anyone would be in charge, she replied, "Absolutely! They all know what to do in my absence."

The scholarship coordinators brought diverse backgrounds to the conversation. Tami benefited immeasurably from the local knowledge and cultural perspective Pat, Anita, Craig, Richard, and Bernard contributed. Tami called Pat her "cultural lifeline" in terms of learning what was appropriate or not in the black community. Pat also helped Tami navigate nearby resources for her kids. And Pat said that Tami had "more social capital than we had coming from Cabrini-Green." Greg recalled when Tami used her social network to raise funds to supplement tuition scholarships so that her COP95ers in underperforming CPS schools could attend better private schools. Craig reflected on how the team's distributed expertise mattered to him:

> It was great to be part of a team with different skill sets. I needed to work on my writing and all those types of things, the team would tighten up my reports. And so, everybody helped everybody... We all leaned on each other. I'm high energy and I can deal with the boys, but then we also had our women that could deal with the girls. So I didn't have to be everything, but I could just be a real project coordinator, move you to where you needed to be, get somebody in front of you that could help you and find those resources. I think everybody that was a part of the team would say it was the most effective team that they had ever been a part of. And I judge every team against it.

The strong, personal relationships that developed among the Junior Staff, scholarship coordinators, and the senior staff out of these shared norms and understandings made CYCLE's community of practice a particularly sturdy one. Every young person had a least one adult and one Junior Staffer tied to them, and these relationships were crucial to youth feeling cared for and unconditionally supported. Youth in the Junior Staff and scholarship programs experienced an unusual degree of steadiness in their leaders. Pat said, "We were a group of consistent adults who were in their lives for a good period of time . . . Kids knew they could count on CYCLE and count on us."

Strong relationships also mattered significantly to the adults at CYCLE. Senior staff cared deeply not only about the youth in their care but about each other. "Those people, that was part of the staying power; genuine relationships where I was allowed into a culture," Tami said. "They were really life-giving to me, the friendships, not just my getting meaning out of helping twelve-year-olds. Those adult relationships were part of what you wouldn't want to walk away from."

CYCLE CLOSES ITS DOORS

With Greg at the helm, CYCLE functioned as a mission-driven, relationship-based community of practice. Senior staff's steadfast commitment to CYCLE had nothing to do with bureaucratic accountability or HR-type job perks; it reflected their deep collective allegiance to the program's goals, mission, and values and to each other.

Greg left CYCLE in 1992, recruited by the MacArthur Foundation to lead the Chicago Cluster Initiative, a community revitalization effort using four neighborhood high schools and their feeder elementary schools as the core foci. The initiative sounded exciting to Greg and seemed to be an opportunity to build on his CYCLE work. But city agencies failed to put up resources to support the initiative, so he left after a year to become executive director of Chicago's Steans Family Foundation and its first employee.

CYCLE lasted only a few years after Greg's departure. The board's choice to hire leaders from national youth organizations brought different mind-sets to the position, including an allegiance to a scripted curriculum, new reporting requirements, and more narrow expectations about use of staff time. In practice, the clash of these approaches with CYCLE's core principles and understandings quickly fractured its community of practice. As Tami put it, "They hired people who were not there for the mission." One by one, senior staff—Pat Ford, Anita Boyd, Tami Doig, Craig Nash—left as they found themselves unable to function in the new and, to them, incompatible organizational culture. Even though each of them said that their work at CYCLE represented the best job they ever had, in the new organizational environment they felt they could no longer do that job. Tami wrote in her August 1994 letter of resignation: "Limiting of the work I've enjoyed over the past six years is why I feel I can no longer work at CYCLE. After six years of running a successful program, I would like to have the freedom to implement the program without being questioned and challenged at every turn. I think my program's success speaks for itself."

New leadership also brought major modifications to the program's daily operations. Changed expectations about activities and supports offered young people distressed senior staff. Most troubling, they found themselves responsible for carrying out standardized curricula and meeting program schedules and expectations, rather than crafting activities and supports based on youths' needs and interests. Pat Ford explained, "At CYCLE, it didn't matter if we agreed on this or that curriculum. What really mattered was how we valued and respected the kids and what we thought about their potential. Sometimes we didn't get it right, but I think for the most part we got that right most of the time because the group norm was strong."

Strong communities of practice afford an effective way for organizations to respond to unstructured and unanticipated challenges, such as those inherent to the young people who lived in Cabrini-Green; they provide an environment in which to share knowledge outside of conventional boundaries of programs or roles. A move to a uniform program format meant that tutors' and staff members' individualized approaches to working with youth became unsustainable.

Staff also became bogged down in paperwork. Greg intentionally minimized staff reporting, trusting them to "do what you think is right" rather than asking them to submit detailed program accounts. CYCLE's new leaders required staff to submit weekly schedules for approval before carrying out any activities and focused on upping program numbers in line with the national expectations about cost per participant. As Craig said, "It became all about numbers, not about kids." These new bureaucratic demands frustrated senior staff. Emblematic of their concern was the new leadership's insistence that they "chart" activities and expected outcomes, a requirement they felt shelved the relational elements all held as foundational to CYCLE's success. The required charts built on input/output checklist associations between tutoring participation and school performance, for example, but did not include indicators of *how* program activities were carried out. Tami recalled being told by the executive director that what she was unable to chart about her program's operation was "magic" and so inadmissible as an element in CYCLE's theory of action. Yet, she said, "'magic' is really just the relationships I've built with students and their parents over six years of constant communication . . . No amount of explaining can transfer that knowledge to another. It comes from loving students. But because it could not be charted on a neat diagram, it was not considered essential to what we do."

The new leadership was hierarchical rather than supportive of a strong team, and it took an institutional position rather than the moral authority once so defining for this community of practice. In the view of senior staff, the new procedures and expectations reversed the core CYCLE principle of "minimum rules, maximum impact" to create one that emphasized protocol and attended less to youth outcomes and teamwork than to prescribed programming and schedules.

Communities of practice form around things that matter to people. The approaches and mind-set the new leaders brought to CYCLE also pushed against the community's foundational principle:

never give up on a kid. This core principle directed close attention to an individual's particular needs and circumstances and to figuring out what sorts of supports might be most meaningful to that young person. With Greg's departure, CYCLE lost its defining focus on relationships as the foundation of committed action. New leadership directed staff to respond instead to centrally defined expectations and outcomes.[2] Tami recalled a dispute she had with CYCLE's new executive director that highlighted this value difference. When, in her weekly time report, she included a trip to the airport to pick up a COP95er returning home from prep school, "memos passed between [us] at least three times, me having to explain why that was a valid use of my time. I was told that this, then, was a personal investment on my part. 'We can't afford this kind of treatment for everyone.' I strongly disagreed!"

Tami's resignation took effect in November 1994, about eight months before her COP95 group's high school graduation date. She sent copies of her resignation letter to the CYCLE board and to the Weinberg family, the scholarship program's sponsors. She recalled, "It was pretty devastating to feel like I could not remain working there through my students' high school graduation. [The new executive director] briefly tried to run the program after I left, but the students and their tutors didn't really go for it." The Weinbergs pulled their money from CYCLE and used Tami's church as the 501c3 to underwrite her efforts to cobble together supports and resources for her group of high school seniors. Since the program was homeless, a COP95 tutor who worked as a general counsel for Chicago's Park District arranged for the group to use Lincoln Park space for tutoring. All of the COP95 volunteers switched their tutoring from CYCLE to this new space. And without access to the CYCLE vans, tutors organized car pools to help her get the COP95 youth to and from tutoring and to local outings. "We sort of limped through the end, but we did it. It was quite a group effort! It was very strange to be running the program basically without the support of any staff/team/facilities but this group of students and volunteers had really become a powerful community unto itself. We had the graduation party at another park district facility. Definitely the 'glory days' were gone, but it was a joyful celebration."

Several board members and all senior staff concurred that the individuals selected to succeed Greg turned out not to be good fits with the organization and that the leadership style they brought to the job precipitated CYCLE's collapse. Research about communities of practice concludes that the best succession strategy for mission-driven organizations like CYCLE involves promoting leaders from within so as to retain and extend the culture. However, CYCLE's board elected to bring in outsiders, even though Greg and the other senior staff felt Pat was the natural successor. Greg said that he feels guilty that he did not push hard enough for Pat to become executive director on his departure, that he left no succession plan, and that little documentation of CYCLE's culture existed. And although he offered to meet with his replacement to discuss the program's organizational culture, the new executive director never reached out to him.

CYCLE's decline and demise represented a significant loss for senior staff who had invested so heavily in the organization. But the closing of CYCLE's doors signaled an even more significant loss for Cabrini-Green's young people. Nothing took its place as a positive developmental OST resource in the community. Alums recounted stories of their younger siblings' and relatives' struggles to find a positive course through the neighborhood and Chicago schools absent CYCLE.

CYCLE's productive years illustrate how a strong community of practice can bind disparate activities and approaches into a coherent whole. Its end underscores how fragile that culture is and how vulnerable a community of practice is to change in leaders' priorities, expectations, and mind-set.

CHAPTER 12

The Power of Opportunities to Change Lives

There is no doubt that CYCLE was an exceptionally successful youth program that transformed the lives of its Cabrini-Green participants. And the life stories of CYCLE alums show that the positive outcomes low-income inner-city youth attain though involvement with a quality out-of-school program can be sustained decades later. Though it closed in the mid-1990s, CYCLE offers three lessons for those seeking to make a difference in the futures of today's high-poverty kids.

A POVERTY OF OPPORTUNITIES KEEPS POOR YOUTH STUCK IN PLACE

One overarching lesson of CYCLE's experience is that it is not primarily a culture of poverty that keeps impoverished youth stuck in place but, rather, a poverty of opportunities. CYCLE's results present what social scientists call a "proof of concept" or what mathematicians name an "existence proof": the positive life outcomes experienced and sustained by most of the hundreds of Cabrini-Green youth involved with CYCLE over the years show that the damaging consequences of growing up in concentrated poverty need not be multigenerational.

Researchers looking at high-poverty communities generally portray concentrated poverty as an intergenerational phenomenon and argue that kids growing up in these environments are twice disadvantaged because their parents carry and pass on the marks of their own childhood experiences with instability, violence, drugs, low expectations.[1] In contrast to these discouraging projections, the vast majority of CYCLE participants are today productive adults, and their stories show that given effective opportunities and supports, youth raised in concentrated urban poverty can achieve and sustain satisfying, productive lives for themselves and their children.

"Being part of CYCLE changed my life." "I could not have made it through Cabrini without CYCLE." "I don't know where or what I would be without CYCLE." These claims reference the negative futures predicted for Cabrini-Green kids and alums' conviction that absent CYCLE their futures would have been bleak. When alums said that CYCLE positively transformed their lives, they pointed to how being part of CYCLE changed their sense of who they were, ideas about what they might become, and knowledge about how to get there. And their life stories demonstrate that these new identities were not only sustained into adulthood but shaped their children's lives as well. For instance, even if they did not attend college, most of their kids did. Regardless of their financial circumstances, CYCLE alums made sure their children had swimming or tennis lessons; took part in arts, sports, or other out-of-school programs; traveled to new places; visited museums and college campuses—just as they themselves did at CYCLE. CYCLE's experience teaches that the projected effects of concentrated poverty can be overturned for even the most vulnerable youth given quality out-of-school time opportunities.

This is a good place to recap CYCLE alums' achievements. All of the Junior Staffers, Providence–St. Mel Bright Knights, EAL participants, and Schuessler scholarship recipients hold high school diplomas, and most went on to college or university. Around 90 percent of the COP95ers and 80 percent of the IHAD scholarship cohort graduated from high school, and roughly one-third of them went on to college. Several CYCLE college graduates completed graduate programs: among the CYCLE alums there are 2 MDs, 11 doctorates, and many master's degrees, in areas such as business, education, accounting, communication, and urban architecture. Most youth who took part in CYCLE's scholarship and Junior Staff programs live middle-class lives; they are teachers, social workers, small business owners, administrators, coaches. These accomplishments would be impressive in any context, but they are stunning when contrasted with the overall Chicago Public School graduation rate for that time of about 35 percent and the college completion rate of around 5 percent.

Recall the Cabrini-Green setting in which CYCLE alums grew up—four city blocks jammed with thousands of kids and adults living in extreme poverty. The housing project's social and institutional structure disadvantaged kids and their families on most every dimension. Local schools were deemed the "worst of the worst." Job opportunities within the project were few to none. Because of downturns in Chicago's manufacturing sector, employment opportunities all around the city were limited. And where jobs did exist, the cost of travelling outside Cabrini-Green was high not only in terms of bus fare but also because of gang violence in the streets. Single moms headed most families. Few dads stayed with their "baby mommas," and Chicago Housing Authority's income limits for Cabrini-Green residence meant that employed dads could not live legally with their families even if they wanted to.

As was the case in most of the nation's high-poverty urban communities at the time, not many appealing out-of-school opportunities existed for Cabrini-Green adolescents. Even today, communities like Cabrini-Green afford adolescents few alternatives to the streets just at the time when they are making major choices about their lives and futures. Most males belonged to a gang for protection, a sense of belonging, excitement, or financial gain. Older brothers were expected to join a gang to protect the "shorties" in the family. Early pregnancy was a norm, along with expectations that a new mom would leave school to take care of her baby. Most youth dropped out of school, usually by the tenth grade, and so eighth-grade graduation occasioned the big celebration. Drugs and alcohol abuse plagued the project, leaving some youth to manage on their own and at high risk of becoming addicted themselves. Although many youth grew up in the loving embrace of moms, aunts, and grandmothers, there were few adults in Cabrini-Green who could model productive lives or offer guidance about how to plan for the future.

Early on, many Cabrini-Green youth dreamed that they would or could have lives different from those they saw around them. Most often, however, those hopes gave way to cynicism as they encountered low expectations in public schools, struggled to navigate gangland, and had scarce connections to mainstream jobs or positive role models to assist them in making better choices. Many of CYCLE participants' friends, siblings, and relatives had little confidence that they would or could experience a future other than incarceration, death, and welfare dependence and so saw little point in planning for a future. The often-heard slogan "dead or in jail by twenty-one" reflected the pessimistic expectations many young people held for themselves and their friends.

ADDRESSING THE OPPORTUNITIES GAP FOR IMPOVERISHED YOUTH REQUIRES ATTENDING TO BOTH CULTURAL AND STRUCTURAL ELEMENTS OF POVERTY

A second broad lesson of CYCLE's success is that attention to the character of the context available to high-poverty youth may be the single-most-important ingredient in transforming their sense of who they are and what they might become. CYCLE's experience counsels attending to changing young people's environment and the opportunities it provides, rather than zeroing in on changing the young people. And CYCLE teaches that simply wanting a better life is not enough to attain one if you are growing up in a community like Cabrini-Green; the structures, supports, and opportunities essential to doing so need to be available and accessible.[2]

CYCLE's impressive track record with Cabrini-Green kids speaks to the decades-old debate about the root causes of the negative attitudes and behaviors associated with extreme poverty. Are they cultural, part of lives lived isolated from mainstream America? Or are they structural, a result of such institutional disadvantages as poor schools, chronic unemployment, inadequate social supports? Accounts of life in Cabrini-Green provide compelling evidence that either/or explanations for multigenerational poverty miss the complexity of the multiple factors creating high-poverty communities and overlook the cumulative character of the capabilities, perspectives, and behaviors that result from living in such an environment. As William Julius Wilson argues, both social structure and culture matter to appreciating the tangible effects of life in high-poverty urban neighborhoods; addressing poverty's destructive consequences requires understanding the independent effects of each and how they intertwine to influence individuals' expectations, choices, and outcomes.[3]

Programs that fail to attract youth or lead to positive outcomes often fall short because they aim either at issues of culture (changing attitudes and behavior) or at structural shortfalls (providing a vocational program, supporting a gang-abatement effort). One way or another, programs targeting the problems associated with kids living in high poverty usually focus on "fixing" them—academic deficiencies, insufficient job skills, substance abuse, risks of pregnancy, involvement in the juvenile justice system—and they usually disappoint. Not surprisingly, teens don't attend them unless required to, and, once finished, they too often head back into the problem behaviors that landed them there in the first place. CYCLE succeeded with changing the life pathways of this at-risk population because it dealt with *both* the cultural and structural shortfalls present in the Cabrini-Green environment.[4]

CYCLE aggressively managed its program culture to promote kids' positive development and create constructive alternatives to the live-for-the-moment approach taken by many youth and adults around them. Staff closely monitored youths' adherence to the program's nonnegotiable rules of no fighting, no cussing, no gang signs, no disrespecting others to create a welcoming, drama-free, physically and emotionally safe and supportive environment. Attendance was voluntary but operated according to clear and strictly enforced rules about consistent participation in order to create community within the program. Senior staff recalled few kids who left the program because of spotty attendance.

CYCLE gave youth opportunities to plan, practice, and perform; failures were turned into learning opportunities. The program provided youth unqualified support for developing a positive sense of self and a hopeful future. Senior staff stuck with kids through crises and setbacks, and even when moves took youth out of the Cabrini-Green community to other Chicago neighborhoods.

Crucial to changing young people's expectations for themselves and their place in the larger world were the long-term, trusting relationships developed between senior staff and participating youth, Junior Staff and volunteer tutors, older and younger youth, and youth themselves. The strong CYCLE community reinforced shared values and goals, kept tabs on agreed-to responsibilities and commitments, cheered each other's accomplishments, sympathized with disappointments, and held one another in grief. In an environment where many young people experienced the adults in their lives as inconsistent, unsupportive, or unreliable, CYCLE ensured that every young person had a long-term, stable relationship with at least one mentor.[5] And the engaged and steady presence of CYCLE senior staff provided "anchor relationships" youth could count on to champion their healthy development.[6]

CYCLE staff directly addressed difficult racial issues. The kids daily encountered disparaging comments about black youths' attitudes, behaviors, and futures—racial putdowns from individuals both inside and outside their community. And they were all too aware of the racial stereotyping operating in society more generally. Volunteers and staff addressed these issues in every CYCLE program; they talked about what black kids could do and how they could do it.

Senior staff also knew that in addition to dealing with racial issues, kids from Cabrini-Green could encounter difficulty interacting in social or workplace settings because their socially isolated housing project provided little, if any, experience with conventional contexts. So CYCLE embedded a soft skills curriculum into all its activities to teach kids the skills necessary to succeed in traditional settings, things like how to present an opinion or disagree, the importance of persistence and keeping one's word, good academic habits, how to dress for and carry out a job interview, restaurant etiquette. Improvement of noncognitive, or soft, skills, CYCLE's experience suggests, can result from consistently embedding them in youths' everyday experiences and environment, making them part of "how we behave here."

CYCLE tackled Cabrini-Green's structural disadvantages in a number of ways. In treacherous environments like Cabrini-Green, youth need to be able to get to and from program activities without fear of violence, gang confrontation, or other threats. Close adult supervision and protected space ensured young participants' physical safety, and the vans played a key role in breaching the structural and social isolation that went along with living in the housing project. Never, while in CYCLE's care, was any young person the victim of the violence endemic to Cabrini-Green.

With CYCLE's help, many participants escaped the dysfunctions of their neighborhood schools. Senior staff assisted them in enrolling in competitive Chicago public high schools like Whitney Young or Lane Tech or secured scholarships for them to attend private schools, such as Providence–St. Mel or Josephinum. Also, the Junior Staff program employed several hundred teens over the years, an opportunity that put much-needed money in their pockets. But, as important, the program provided concrete experience with all that goes along with holding a job successfully—being dependable and on time, meeting expectations, acting as team player, being accountable for performance, effectively carrying out responsibilities. Junior Staff positions brought vital experience to teens who had few up-close role models to teach them about the attitudes and behaviors required to succeed in the workplace.

By its very existence, CYCLE responded to the lack of attractive, comprehensive out-of-school opportunities in the project. Chicago offered many afterschool or out-of-school programs for young people, but Cabrini-Green kids generally did not take part in them because it was unsafe to cross gang boundaries to get there, the costs of membership or transportation were prohibitively high, or the problem-focused content did not appeal to them. CYCLE provided fun, fellowship, and positive opportunities right in their neighborhood at no cost during the school year and with minimal fees for summer programs. And its approach to programming—open from morning to night, seven days a week, during the school year and summer—provided an accessible alternative to the negative options and pressures teens faced in their community. The program design and strategies kept kids engaged, attending consistently, and involved in their own personal growth and accomplishment from kindergarten through high school.

By attending to both the cultural and structural challenges of the Cabrini-Green environment, CYCLE exposed kids to opportunities usually associated with a middle-class lifestyle—such as participating in tutoring and mentoring to bolster academics, having a caring adult mentor and advocate, attending sporting and other local events, taking part in summer day camps and overnight camping adventures, visiting museums, traveling to colleges and sites around the country. Through the opportunities it provided, CYCLE changed its kids' context from one of social and institutional disadvantage to one that was similar to that of youth from more advantaged economic and social circumstances. As Bernard McCune put it, "We just tried to do for our kids what middle-class parents do for theirs." CYCLE operated on the principle "you can't be what you can't see, but you also can't be what you can't reach." Staff, volunteers, and program supporters provided participants with valuable connections beyond their economically isolated community and reinforced the idea that they had a place in the larger world.

Paul Tough, writing about how children succeed, most especially those growing up in difficult settings, sums up the significance of these supports and connections: "They did not get on that ladder [to success] alone. They are there only because someone helped them take the first step."[7]

A YOUTH-CENTERED, RELATIONSHIP-BASED PROGRAM

A third lesson from CYCLE has to do with its "secret sauce." Arguably, the CYCLE strategy most important to the positive outcomes participants achieved was its relationship-based, constantly adapting, youth-centered approach. CYCLE was not about implementing all-purpose, by-the-book programs created elsewhere. Nor did it carry out what some have called "herd programming," where groups of kids move from activity to activity on a strict schedule no matter what. CYCLE staffers were dedicated to providing resources and opportunities that built on each individual's strengths and potential; they focused on achieving hoped-for outcomes, rather than avoiding feared consequences, and they attended closely to each young person's needs.

This youth-centered philosophy assumed that the young people who came through its doors wanted to achieve and that they had preferences, talents, and skills to offer the program and society. And all staff functioned according to the core program principle: never give up on a kid. Each young person felt recognized for who they were and who they were becoming and felt supported in the face of life's inevitable trials and setbacks. Many alums contrasted CYCLE's developmentally attuned activities that stretched them to try harder to the dull assignments they encountered at their public schools, where little seemed to be expected of or for them. CYCLE offered authentic, meaningful learning experiences that exposed youth to real-life demands, real-life goals, balanced structure, and choices.

CREATING MORE CYCLES

CYCLE's ability to design a program that put most of its youth on a path to successful adulthood benefited significantly from its localness. Chicago-area philanthropists, business people, and community leaders eager to do something constructive for Cabrini-Green youth admired Greg Darnieder, bought into his vision, and trusted him to carry it out. This local support empowered CYCLE to work closely with the youth and community it served, to tailor activities, interactions, and experiences to kids' needs and interests.

This local advantage provided the program an essential appeal and credibility and attracted large numbers of committed local supporters over the years. But its fundamental localness raises some complicated policy questions for today. Some are concerned with program fidelity; others consider appropriate roles and responsibilities for different levels of the policy system; and still others relate to funding approaches. A continuing deliberation among policy makers and funders involves the extent to which a demonstrably successful program such as CYCLE can be carried out in new contexts. How, for example, could something like CYCLE be replicated today? At the heart of this debate sit questions of what it means to replicate a program, what is being reproduced.

Some advocate formulaic fidelity to the activities and strategies of the reputedly successful program, approaches that have been criticized as "cookie-cutter," "follow-the-dots" undertakings that typically fall short. Examples of this strategy exist in the disappointments associated with early attempts to duplicate the activities of reportedly successful reading programs like Success for All or in the assumptions that featured programs that initially motivated the federally supported *It Works* series published through ERIC (Educational Resources Information Center) would be faithfully replicated. Even current initiatives aiming to capitalize on reportedly successful practices but taking a less rigid approach to program fidelity run into problems when materials intended as guides are followed mechanically on the ground.

For example, Barton Hirsch documents the disappointing outcome of one Chicago Boys and Girls Club (BGC) chapter's by-the-book implementation of the Smart Girls curriculum that paid little attention to girls' interests. In contrast, other Chicago BGC chapters he and colleagues studied used Smart Girls materials as a guide and built on interactions with participating girls to carry out the program successfully.[8] Similarly, the very effective BGC and YMCA/YWCA programs described in *Urban Sanctuaries* grounded their success in their attention to what the kids needed and wanted to do and used materials from national offices to support them.

At the heart of debates about the meaning of implementation fidelity and implications for "going to scale" are issues of how much latitude to give front-line providers in making on-the-ground decisions—or where program implementation should sit on the tight-loose continuum advanced by education reformers.[9] What has to be "tight" and what has to be "loose" for an effective program to achieve similar outcomes in a new context?

CYCLE's experience counsels that an initiative aiming to create more CYCLEs must marry core design principles with local interests, opportunities, needs, and constraints. In this view, CYCLE-like youth programs would be comprehensive, relationship-based, and youth-centered undertakings that situate academics at the core but offer a variety of engaging activities, construct a strong community of belonging for youth, and provide a coherent community of practice for staff. Such a program operating in Pittsburgh would not look just like another in Dallas or in Bangor, but essential design principles and values would be identifiably the same. The fundamental approach would hold together in a consistent, coherent way across different settings.

Decisions about specific services and strategies need to be made by folks on the front line who know the community, know the kids, and know how to attract political and financial support to the undertaking. These decisions would be "loose," allowing for creativity and reflecting local knowledge, constraints, and resources.[10] Folks on the ground also are more likely to make staffing choices that fit program goals and the needs and interests of participating youth. Brenda Taylor talked about what made CYCLE and the COP95 program so effective for her: "CYCLE wasn't just a program. It was the people. You can't duplicate CYCLE unless you can duplicate the people—They really cared, stood by us, protected us from the negatives."

This position on loose local implementation choices does not advocate letting a thousand flowers bloom. Larry Cuban's history of the effective schools movement shows, for instance, how local autonomy that was too permissive compromised the movement, as "effective schools" came to have little in common.[11] Going to scale with CYCLE would entail constructing programs in diverse settings consistent with its core principles with the assumption that the activities associated with them would incorporate local resources, interests, needs, and constraints. And replicating CYCLE would also assume thoughtful attention to the culture and relationships that foster successful outcomes, not just the inputs. Recall CYCLE's demise when a new leader arrived on the scene, ignored mainstay principles about culture and relationships, and insisted on to-the-book implementation of prescribed guidelines and programs. Fidelity to principles with adaptation to local context and decentralized decision making make replication a possibility. But the tension between implementing a design and responding to local context is inevitable, and it calls for street-level staff to be able to make changes when needed consistent with program principles.

Managing the necessary tension between tight/loose program implementation requires leadership committed to, and clear about, essential principles and a motivating vision. It also requires leaders who promote the consistent, ongoing staff interaction that is necessary for practitioners to make adjustments based on their experience, conversations like those Greg fostered among CYCLE staff. As Michael Fullan advises, dealing effectively with the dynamic relationship between tight principles and loose responses to them requires a strong but a different kind of leader.[12]

This advice reflects the time-tested conclusions of implementation research. More than forty years ago, "mutual adaptation" entered the policy implementation conversation.[13] It signaled the need for system-level policies to accommodate local interests and capacities and for local choices to acknowledge policy goals and parameters. Researchers looking at efforts to improve education found that no single intervention or program worked the same way in different contexts. Implementing the same program in different contexts, researchers demonstrated, was never straightforward, mechanical, but instead created new problems (and opportunities) for front-line implementers to address.[14] Effective implementation of improvement efforts initiated by reformers at the system level (state, federal) involved mutual adaptation between policy and practice, or what Anthony Bryk and colleagues call "adaptive integration."[15]

CYCLE's success with local program construction and implementation suggests that sponsors and state and federal policy makers should co-construct activities with local educators and youth practitioners rather than insist on relatively standardized top-down program implementation. This view is consistent with other more recent findings showing that youth development initiatives which foster resourceful, site-level responses to system-supported reform efforts are more effective for youth than those that focus primarily on first making changes at the system level, with the expectation that they would trickle down to have a systematic impact on site-level practices.[16] Starting with a focused program initiative instead of with the whole system, experience teaches, can highlight changes needed at the top (or system) level to support site-level implementation and successful program outcomes—changes and supports that likely will differ across system contexts.

CYCLE and other efforts animated by grassroots actors suggest that successful out-of-school time opportunities take direction from those most involved, but that the system (public or nonprofit) responsible for site-level efforts enable productive work on the ground through the benefits of (relatively) stable funding, networks, cross-institutional connections, and political and regulatory supports. This approach to providing vulnerable youth productive out-of-school opportunities shifts public policy as well as national nonprofit youth organizations from a position of director to supporter of successful front-line work. Top-down support for bottom-up change.[17] Strong empirical support exists for improvement initiatives being user-centered in this way and seeing the problem from the perspective of the person actually experiencing it.

There are encouraging experiences of local, state, and federal efforts coordinating youth-focused funding streams and resources within and across policy systems. Thirty years ago, successful OST programs like CYCLE generally were the work of committed individuals like Greg Darnieder; little organized support existed to foster systems or networks dedicated to expanded youth development opportunities. The advice offered in *Urban Sanctuaries* about how to create effective youth OST programs was "go find a wizard." Today, however, many resources are available to promote and enable effective OST programs. Intermediary organizations (such as ExpandEDSchools in New York City, LA's Best, Chicago's After School Matters, Boston's After School and Beyond, the Providence After-School Alliance), and state-level groups (the 50 State Afterschool Network) work to develop political and interagency support for high-quality OST programs.[18] National organizations such as the National Institute for Out of School Time and the Forum for Youth Investment advocate for state and local investments in OST opportunities and assist in their development.[19] These local, state, and national organizations share promising practices, research quality program standards, convene policy makers and practitioners to assess OST needs and opportunities, and provide professional development support and technical assistance.

LESSONS FOR FUNDERS AND RESEARCHERS

Greg Darnieder secured funding from Chicago philanthropists and others basically employing a "trust me" model of assurance and accountability. Funders held him and CYCLE to no specific outcomes and required no program evaluation; they asked only for an annual program report and financial statement. Local funders could keep informal tabs on how the program was working for youth by stopping by or having lunch with Greg. This casual arrangement between funder and grantee worked well for CYCLE. Greg, a committed educator and advocate for high-poverty kids, had the experience, commitment, and passion necessary to create CYCLE and support its growth and success. *Urban Sanctuaries* deemed Greg a wizard in the youth development domain. The flexibility of a trust-me funding model was essential to CYCLE's effectiveness, Greg said. "I just could not have dealt with all of that paperwork stuff, and I didn't want my staff to have to deal with it either."

Today, the trust-me approach to philanthropy is admittedly unrealistic and impractical for most funders, especially for those operating at some distance from program activities and unable to experience programs directly. But CYCLE's experience shows the importance of empowering staff to quickly respond to unexpected situations, revise and reinvent program approaches, and rethink expectations about what kids could accomplish at what point in time without worrying about explaining or rationalizing their decisions or facing backlash if they deviate from a preset plan. Philanthropists often have more leeway in terms of grantee proposal and reporting arrangements than do public agency funders who frequently confront more intractable problems with mandated requirements. Nonetheless, youth development practitioners are of a voice in cautioning funders that inflexible planning, accountability, and funding requirements likely will impede necessary program responsiveness and innovation.

A funding or accountability approach tied to quarterly measurable outcomes, program checklists, and detailed protocol stands in blunt contrast to the open-endedness Greg enjoyed and ascribed to CYCLE's success. Grant management by tightly prescribed goals risks derailing youth-centered programs because, as CYCLE's demise illustrates, it frames accountability primarily in terms of participation numbers and easily quantified outcomes such as grades or test scores.[20] And for vulnerable kids like those growing up in Cabrini-Green, a standardized, checklist approach to program outcome expectations (such as achieving grade proficiency in a set period of time) ignores the cumulative effects of poverty and the uncertainties of daily life which make prescribed achievement yardsticks problematic.

Decades of research document the highly variable outcomes of OST and afterschool programs and demonstrate that not all youth programs result in developmentally powerful experiences, even when programs appear to have similar "inputs." CYCLE's experience directs attention to program operations as an explanation for these uneven outcomes. Many elements fundamental to CYCLE participants' personal transformation had less to do with program inputs and more to do with *how* activities were presented and carried out: the youth-centered, individualized approach to interacting with kids; the core belief about never giving up on a kid; the one-on-one relationship between tutor and tutee; careful attention to participants' physical and emotional safety; youth voice and near-peer relationships; staff and leadership committed to positive youth development principles.

CYCLE participants' life stories advise that unless these program elements are consistently present, the impressive outcomes they achieved are unlikely to occur in either the near or the long term. Yet many program planning, evaluation, or accountability strategies ignore such implementation features, giving them little consideration in program plans (or action models) or evaluation strategies. As a consequence, many youth program managers focus on inputs as traditionally conceived and featured in accountability requirements and pay little attention to process questions—Are the contexts provided youth developmentally powerful? Are there positive relationships between staff and youth? Do staff have the supports and resources necessary to work effectively with youth?—or the black box implementation elements now shown to be central to program quality.

OST funders, practitioners, and evaluators sometimes complain that these "process" features are too difficult to define and expensive to measure and, thus, not feasible to include in youth program plans or evaluations. Yet, significant progress has been made in defining program quality elements and making them operational. Several youth development organizations focus on identifying elements of program quality, determining how to "unpack" them in practice, and providing guidance on how to assess them. For example, the American Youth Policy Forum addresses practices and program settings associated with quality OST effective with older youth.[21] The Search Institute, based on the research-based conviction that quality out-of-school programs are "all about relationships," created an action-based developmental relationships framework to guide practice and research.[22] The David P. Weikart Center for Youth Program Quality (CYPQ), which works to introduce quality improvement practices associated with positive organizational climate and culture into afterschool programs and networks, carried out an intervention to examine the effects of continuous improvement practices on staff instructional practices and how continuous improvement can be implemented at policy and program levels.[23] Charles Smith and colleagues found that youth program managers can make significant improvements in elements of program quality with the availability of information to support continuous improvement. A 2016 CYPQ report details promising practices in social and emotional learning that are easily observable and relevant to most OST programs.[24] Other program elements key to CYCLE's success are easy to document—exposure to people, places, futures; financial supports for education; a close-by, no-cost out-of-school program that engages most of youth's discretionary time, either by itself or in partnership with other community agencies.

CYCLE alums' life stories carry other implications for researchers. While short-term, positive accomplishments such as high school graduation or postsecondary enrollment provide important markers of program effectiveness, they can say nothing about whether the positive developmental outcomes these benchmarks predict in fact occur or are sustained. Questions of sustainability require a life course perspective. The longitudinal accounts of CYCLE participants' lives over more than thirty years provide persuasive evidence of long-term effects of quality OST as well as a critical perspective on program features that mattered most to achieving them. Alums concurred about the program elements they found most significant in shaping their futures—exposure, mentoring, a community of belonging—and they could situate their explanatory narratives in the context of their adult lives. Even though they might have pointed to these same program elements one or three or five years after they left CYCLE, they would not yet have the life experience essential to explaining *why* they mattered and *how* they affected their life choices and outcomes. And the intergenerational consequences associated with CYCLE participation possibly provide the ultimate gauge of sustained effects.

Unfortunately, this type of longitudinal, narrative research is uncommon within the universe of youth programs, since, for many practical reasons, funders of research and programs generally opt for short-term assessments of program outcomes. But the life stories of CYCLE participants illustrate the distinctive contribution that life course research can make not only to questions of sustainability but also to discussions of essential program principles and design choices—most especially for initiatives aiming to support kids living in high-poverty communities.

A CALL TO ACTION

You Can't Be What You Can't See presents an optimistic account of the long-term, multigenerational benefits a youth-centered, relationship-based, out-of-school time program provided kids growing up in

Cabrini-Green. CYCLE demonstrates the power of out-of-school opportunities to be a turning point in the lives of high-poverty youth. The personal and professional successes achieved by CYCLE alums (and their children) need not be exceptions to outcomes forecast for inner-city, low-income youth. We know that quality OST programs can provide opportunities and resources that schools cannot. And we know what a quality OST looks like. Yet, comprehensive OST opportunities like CYCLE are few and far between, especially in urban communities of concentrated poverty.

The substantial gaps that exist in the availability of quality OST programs in high-poverty communities point to system (local, state, or federal) responsibilities for leadership, financial, and regulatory support, and attention to questions of equity. Nationally, elementary and middle school students' demand for afterschool opportunities of any kind exceeds supply.[25] And adolescents especially are underserved once school is out. The overall number of out-of-school offerings for adolescents has been inadequate and unchanged for more than two decades. More than twenty years ago, based on analyses of national data, researchers concluded that teens have a lot of discretionary time on their hands but that this time generally is not filled with skill building or other positive developmental activities.[26]

Teens from low-income families are least likely to take part in constructive extracurricular activities primarily because few attractive choices are available to them. But data show an even greater gap between demand and opportunity for youth living in contexts of concentrated poverty (defined as communities with 40 percent or more of their population falling under the federal poverty line).[27] Ironically, youth growing up in extreme poverty have even fewer out-of-school options than do teens who live in other settings, even though these kids arguably comprise the youth population most in need of positive things to do.[28]

Moreover, the number of young people living in severe poverty grows annually. The number of children living in areas of concentrated poverty increased between 2006–10 and 2011–15 by nearly 30 percent, from 7.9 million kids to 10.0 million kids. For African American youth, the percent living in concentrated poverty grew from 28 percent to 32 percent, or almost one-third of the nation's black youth.[29] It is no exaggeration to say that many of these young people move through an environment barren of feasible, attractive opportunities that contribute to and support their healthy development. Encouraging federal and state policy makers to weave together funding for afterschool programs and youth employment opportunities is one strategy to create more CYCLE-like programs in the nation's inner-city communities.

Another strategy builds on the "local advantage" and involves municipal leaders in framing the availability of high-quality OST opportunities as a community responsibility and bringing stand-alone youth programs into coordinated citywide networks to support children and youth.[30] But despite recent examples of how quality OST opportunities can make substantial and enduring difference in the lives of young people, investment in adolescents continues to hold less appeal to policy makers and funders than do programs for young children. Some see supports for teens as "too late" and so not a compelling move, all things considered. And pervasive, negative perceptions of high-poverty adolescents' antisocial attitudes and delinquent behaviors make it hard to generate persuasive advocacy for comprehensive OST programs like CYCLE at any level. Local leaders arguably stand at the forefront of the mind-set change needed to expand OST opportunities for the nation's most disconnected youth.

This policy shortfall signals a major youth development opportunity lost. The period of adolescence presents a singular occasion for developmental resources and opportunities to make significant and positive differences in young people's lives, for out-of-school programs to trigger movement toward a positive, fulfilling life purpose. The primary developmental task of adolescence is building a sense of self and place in the world, constructing an identity. "Never before in the human life cycle (and never again) is there the same developmental readiness for asking big questions and forming worthy dreams," writes Sharon Daloz Parks about mentoring opportunities.[31] CYCLE shows how that opportunity can be captured, embraced, and fulfilled to positively change the lives of poor youth and the lives of their children.

AFTERWORD

In early 2012, I began reflecting on the number of people from whom I was separated by one or two degrees since our time together in Cabrini-Green. Some of the relationships went back almost four decades. I thought about the power of many of those relationships in my life, the richness of them, my gratitude. I began mentally listing the career journeys of all these people and their professional successes as educators, businessmen and women, politicians, doctors, social workers, law enforcement officers, computer geniuses, etc. And I wondered how many of their children were pursuing higher education or were on track to do so.

I immediately thought that their individual stories should be captured and celebrated. Over the twenty-five years since I left CYCLE, it became clear that it was a unique place operating at a unique point in time and was led by an exceptional group of people. I knew that the story of CYCLE and its alums was an important one worthy of a book with lessons worth sharing. But it needed to be documented—rigorously—and I knew who would be up to that task.

Milbrey McLaughlin, a distinguished scholar at Stanford University, wrote about the promise of CYCLE with colleagues Merita A. Irby and Juliet Langman in their 1994 book *Urban Sanctuaries*. I approached her, hoping she'd be willing to revisit the CYCLE story, apply her researcher's lens, and make sense of what was accomplished within the context of what is known about effective youth development. Thankfully, she said yes.

The result, this book, far exceeds my expectations. It demonstrates that young people, and especially those living in difficult situations, can in fact rise to extraordinary heights when given the opportunity and can attain academic, professional, personal goals at the same levels as other socioeconomic groups. It also illustrates how high-quality afterschool programs can be structured at scale.

As I reflect on my forty-plus years of work with youth programs, it is clear that most of the government and private funding mechanisms focused on young people have not substantially changed. Grant funding rarely extends beyond three years and all too often is given for even shorter periods of time, such as for six-week summer jobs programs. Perhaps reading the stories of CYCLE alums will inspire and empower others to challenge the status quo and think outside the box, as I did when I took the helm of CYCLE.

In the early and mid-1980s I attended citywide Chicago meetings as the executive director of CYCLE and as a funder of youth programs in Chicago. City leaders were focused on keeping kids busy and off the streets, so they "wouldn't run rampant through the streets" or "burn parts of the city down." For as long as I could remember, youth had all too often been given meaningless work under the guise of skill building or leadership development. They were assigned fancy job titles like "'custodial engineer" but ended up pushing the same broom year after year. They were taught negative work attitudes and habits: come late but get paid for your scheduled time; work an hour and get paid for five; it doesn't matter how you dress, speak, or interact with others. All too often there were few consequences for inappropriate behavior. I found myself saying, "It doesn't need to be this way!"

I had been raised in the Christian faith to believe that each person is born with gifts and talents to be developed and utilized for the benefit of their families and society. As I matured, the Christian values of servant leadership and sacrificial love began to make sense to me in a real way. Organize thirty-mile walks at my college to raise funds for low-income communities throughout the world—why not?

Recruit thirty-five middle school, high school, and college students and buy an old school bus and drive it to Honduras to give to farmers to reduce their daily commute—why not?

Believe is my favorite word. Yes, it means something deeply spiritual to me. But it also carries the essential core meaning that powerful things are possible when we are called to work with young people. But, as I came to appreciate while working with colleagues from the Young Life youth program, as adults, "we must earn the right to be heard" when working with teenagers.

Certainly, youth programs today are inadequately funded, especially when it comes to those operating in low-income communities. But it is not, as President Barack Obama said in launching the My Brothers' Keeper initiative, that "we don't know what to do; it's a matter of whether we have the will to do so." *You Can't Be What You Can't See* documents what young people can achieve when the systems, resources, and adults around them are aligned over an extended period of time, and when they're given real responsibilities while at the same time chances to enhance their skills, expand their horizons, and empower and support themselves.

I hope this book serves as an encouragement to educators and youth workers in whatever challenges they face and honors them in ways they so richly deserve. And I hope this book contributes to community, city, state, and national conversations around our young people. As adults, it is our responsibility to get the organizational, school, and community structures in place so that the gifts, talents, and personal development of all our youth can be fully supported. The question is, are we willing?

Greg Darnieder
Senior Adviser to US Secretary of Education (2009–16)
CYCLE executive director (1978–93)

NOTES

INTRODUCTION

1. Milbrey W. McLaughlin, Merita A. Irby, and Juliet Langman, *Urban Sanctuaries: Neighborhood Organizations in the Lives and Futures of Inner-City Youth* (San Francisco: Jossey-Bass, 1994).
2. CYCLE was assigned the pseudonym "BEST" in *Urban Sanctuaries*.
3. Little longitudinal research exists on the long-term consequences of youth program participation. An important exception is the classic Perry Preschool study. Between 1962 and 1967, David Weikart and colleagues operated the High/Scope Perry Preschool program for young children in the Ypsilanti, Michigan, school district. The study tracked the lives of 123 children in the program born in poverty and at risk of school failure. At ages three and four, the children were randomly divided into two treatment groups: one received high-quality preschool and the other received no preschool. The most recent follow-up study interviewed 97 percent of the study participants at age forty and found strong evidence for the value of preschool as a social investment: those taking part in preschool were more likely to have held a job, graduated from high school, had higher earnings, and committed fewer crimes than were those in the control group. Lawrence J. Schweinhart, *Lifetime Effects: The High/Scope Perry Preschool Study Through Age 40*, 2005, https://highscope.org/perrypreschoolstudy. In another study, Joseph Mahoney and colleagues used data from the Carolina Longitudinal Study to examine relationships between extracurricular activities and various outcomes: long-term education success and interpersonal competence as well as development of antisocial behavior patterns. Participants were 695 boys and girls interviewed from childhood to the end of high school and again at ages twenty and twenty-four. See Joseph L. Mahoney, "School Extracurricular Activity Participation as a Moderator in the Development of Antisocial Patterns," *Child Development* 71, no. 2 (2000): 502–26; Joseph L. Mahoney, Beverly Cairns, and Thomas W. Farmer, "Promoting Interpersonal Competence and Educational Success Through

Extracurricular Activity Participation," *Journal of Educational Psychology* 95, no. 2 (2003): 409–18.
4. For a discussion of this project's research methods, see "A Note on Research" in this volume.
5. *Concentrated poverty* describes communities with 40 percent or more of its inhabitants falling under the federal poverty line.
6. Chicago Public Schools' graduation rates as found in district, University of Chicago, and newspaper sources. We could not locate disaggregated record data specific to Cabrini-Green. The Cabrini-Green graduation rates are based on the recollections of CYCLE senior staff and other knowledgeable observers of Cabrini-Green (former CYCLE board members, local political activists, clergy).
7. Researchers have begun to consider aspects of program implementation, or the "black box," that significantly affect program outcomes for youth. See especially Charles Smith et al., *Continuous Improvement in Afterschool Settings: Impact Findings from the Youth Program Quality Intervention* (Washington, DC: Forum for Youth Investment, 2012).
8. Important exceptions are Nancy L. Deutsch, *Pride in the Projects: Teens Building Identities in Urban Contexts* (New York: New York University Press, 2008); and Barton J. Hirsch, *A Place to Call Home: After-School Programs for Urban Youth* (Washington, DC: American Psychological Association; New York: Teachers College Press, 2005). Both books provide details on programs' daily activities, youth/staff interactions, and how these routines affected youth responses and outcomes.
9. Sociologist Glen Elder pioneered the life course analytic strategy in his 1974 Oakland study that followed youth into their adult lives to understand how events in their lives—centrally, the Great Depression and WWII—affected their developmental pathways. This point of view assumes that youth are not passively acted on by factors in their environment (e.g., neighborhood context, school rankings, metropolitan location) and that personal attributes (e.g., race, IQ, gender, family status) do not lead directly to either valued or feared life outcomes. A life course perspective departs from variable-based, causal explanations of individuals' attainments or shortfalls to consider life trajectories in terms of choices situated in changing, multi-layered environments. See Glen H. Elder Jr., *Children of the Great Depression: Social Change in Life Experience* (Chicago: University of Chicago Press, 1974).
10. Glen Elder and colleagues set out five "paradigmatic principles" in life course theory relevant to this book's narrative: Life-Span Development, Agency, Time and Place, Timing, and Linked Lives. See Glen H. Elder Jr., Monica Kirkpatrick Johnson, and Robert Crosnoe, "The Emergence and

Development of Life Course Theory," in *Handbook of Life Course*, ed. Jeylan T. Mortimer and Michael J. Shanahan (New York: Kluwer Academic, 2003), 10-14. Elder and colleagues join a life span focus with youth development theory to explore the ways in which changing lives and contexts affect developmental trajectories and how timing of events influences developmental impact.

11. For descriptions of these different life course models, see Mortimer and Shanahan, *Handbook of Life Course*.

12. See, for instance, American Youth Policy Forum, *Helping Youth Succeed Through Out-of-School Time Programs* (Washington, DC: American Youth Policy Forum, 2006); Joseph Mahoney et al., "Adolescent Out-of-School Activities," in *Handbook of Adolescent Psychology*, 3rd ed., ed. Richard M. Lerner and Lawrence Steinberg (New York: John Wiley, 2009), 228-69; Charles Smith et al., *Preparing Youth to Thrive: Promising Practices in Social Emotional Learning* (Washington, DC: Forum for Youth Investment, 2017); Helen Janc Malone and Tara Donahue, eds., *The Growing Out-of-School Time Field: Past, Present, and Future* (Charlotte, NC: Information Age, 2018). In addition, several centers provide current research and resources to OST programs, initiatives, and networks across the United States. The National Institute for Out-of-School Time (NIOST), an action-research institute located in Wellesley, Massachusetts, provides a national perspective on issues facing the OST field, documents promising policies and practices, and tracks research and evaluation. See https://www.niost.org/. The David P. Weikart Center for Youth Program Quality (CYPQ), launched in January 2008 as a joint venture of the Forum for Youth Investment and the HighScope Educational Research Foundation, supports the development and use of research-based quality indicators to support OST youth development programs. For tools and other OST quality resources, see http://cypq.org/.

13. Psychologist Asa Hilliard III distinguishes between an achievement gap and an opportunity gap to explain disparities between the academic performance of low-income African American students and mainstream white students. See Asa G. Hilliard III, "No Mystery: Closing the Achievement Gap Between Africans and Excellence," in *Young, Gifted and Black: Promoting High Achievement Among African-American Students*, ed. Teresa Perry, Claude Steele, and Asa G. Hilliard III (Boston: Beacon Press, 2003), 131-65.

CHAPTER 1

1. Harvey Zorbaugh's 1929 classic *The Gold Coast and the Slum* depicts the social and economic extremes on Chicago's Near North Side, which coexisted until the last Cabrini-Green high-rise fell. For example, in 1980 the median per-capita annual income in the city's mostly white Gold

Coast was $27,380; in all-black Cabrini-Green, just a few blocks away, it was $1,348. Cited in Gregory D. Squires, Larry Bennett, Kathleen McCourt, and Philip Nyden, "Is Growth Working for Chicago?" *Challenge* 4 (September–October 1987): 42–48.
2. Data shown are for 1981–82, the closest available to 1985–86, the years in which we carried out our original research at CYCLE. CHA data are either unavailable or nonexistent from the mid-1980s through the early 1990s.
3. CHA statistical report for 1983 cited in William J. Wilson, *The Truly Disadvantaged: The Inner-City, the Underclass, and Public Policy* (Chicago: University of Chicago Press, 1987), 26.
4. Ed Marciniak, *Reclaiming the Inner City: Chicago's Near North Revitalization Confronts Cabrini-Green* (Washington, DC: National Center for Urban Ethnic Affairs, 1986).
5. Merita A. Irby and Milbrey W. McLaughlin, "When Is a Gang Not a Gang? When It's a Tumbling Team," *Future Choices* 2, no. 2 (1990): 31–39; Laurent Belsie, "Children of the Projects: Will Cabrini-Green's Youth Start a Fire or Light a Candle?" *Christian Science Monitor*, April 29, 1982, https://www.csmonitor.com/1982/0429/042954.html.
6. Dominic A. Pacyga and Ellen Skerrett, *Chicago: City of Neighborhoods* (Chicago: Loyola University Press, 1986), 53.
7. David T. Whitaker, *Cabrini-Green in Words and Pictures* (Chicago: W3Chicago and LPC Group, 2000), 4.
8. Frank F. Furstenberg Jr., Thomas D. Cook, Jacquelynne Eccles, Glen H. Elder Jr., and Arnold Sameroff, *Managing to Make It: Urban Families and Adolescent Success* (Chicago: University of Chicago Press, 1999), 18.
9. For an extensive history of Cabrini-Green's evolution and demise, see Marciniak, *Reclaiming the Inner City*; Deirdre Pfeiffer, "Displacement Through Discourse: Implementing and Contesting Public Housing Redevelopment in Cabrini Green," *Urban Anthropology* 35, no. 1 (2006): 39–74.
10. "Schools in Chicago Are Called the Worst by Education Chief," *New York Times*, November 8, 1987, http://www.nytimes.com/1987/11/08/us/schools-in-chicago-are-called-the-worst-by-education-chief.html.
11. Brian D. Schultz, "Students as Activists: Stories from an Urban Classroom," *Schools: Studies in Education* 4, no.1 (2007): 97–124.
12. Marciniak, *Reclaiming the Inner City*, 80.
13. Whitaker, *Cabrini-Green*, 83.
14. Kathryn Edin and Maria Kefalas, *Promises I Can Keep: Why Poor Women Put Motherhood Before Marriage* (Berkeley: University of California Press, 2005), 204, 207.
15. Jody Raphael, *Saving Bernice: Battered Women, Welfare, and Poverty* (Boston: Northeastern University Press, 2000).

16. Kelley Farrell entry, *ChicagoNow* (blog), June 10, 2013, http://www.chicagonow.com/neighboring-the-neighborless/2013/06/growing-up-in-cabrini-green/.
17. Marciniak, *Reclaiming the Inner City*, 66.
18. Carolyn Rebecca Block and Richard L. Block, eds., "Questions and Answers in Lethal and Non-Lethal Violence: Proceedings of the Second Annual Workshop of the Homicide Research Working Group" (report, FBI Academy, Quantico, VA, June 13–17, 1993).
19. James Lockhart, "Living in Cabrini," *MAS Context* 4 (Winter 2009): 71–83, http://www.mascontext.com/issues/4-living-winter-09/living-in-cabrini/.
20. Lawrence J. Vale, *Reclaiming Public Housing: A Half Century of Struggle in Three Public Neighborhoods* (Cambridge, MA: Harvard University Press, 2002).
21. Michael B. Katz, *The Undeserving Poor: From the War on Poverty to the War on Welfare* (New York: Pantheon Books, 1989), 10.
22. Squires et al., "Is Growth Working for Chicago?"
23. Useni Eugene Perkins, *Explosion of Chicago's Black Street Gangs: 1900 to Present* (Chicago: Third World Press, 1987), 32.
24. Whitaker, *Cabrini-Green*, 162–63.
25. Wilson uses the term *concentration effects* to distinguish the experiences of poor families living in inner-city neighborhoods like Cabrini-Green from those who live in other areas of the central city. He defines social isolation as "the lack of contact or of sustained interaction with individuals and institutions that represent mainstream society." Wilson, *The Truly Disadvantaged*, 60.
26. See also Paul A. Jargowsky, *Poverty and Place: Ghettos, Barrios, and the American City* (New York: Russell Sage Foundation, 1997); Wilson, *The Truly Disadvantaged*.
27. Robert J. Samson, *Great American City: Chicago and the Enduring Neighborhood Effect* (Chicago: University of Chicago Press, 2012), 154.
28. Martha A. Gephart, "Neighborhoods and Communities as Contexts for Development," in *Neighborhood Poverty: Context and Consequences for Children*, vol. 1, ed. Jeanne Brooks-Gunn, Greg J. Duncan, and J. Lawrence Aber (New York: Russell Sage Foundation, 1997), 1–43.
29. See, for instance, Taylor Robbins, Shannon Stagman, and Sheila Smith, "Young Children at Risk: National and State Prevalence of Risk Factors" (report, National Center for Children in Poverty, Columbia University, New York, October 2012); Elizabeth P. Pungello et al., "Early Educational Intervention, Early Cumulative Risk, and the Early Home Environment as Predictors of Young Adult Outcomes Within a High-Risk Sample," *Child Development* 81, no. 1 (2010): 410–26.
30. See, for example, Brooks-Gunn et al., eds., *Neighborhood Poverty*.
31. See Sampson, *Great American City*.

PART I

1. For an overview of the tensions and controversies in the afterschool world, see Barton J. Hirsch, *A Place to Call Home: After-School Programs for Urban Youth* (Washington, DC: American Psychological Association; New York: Teachers College Press, 2005).
2. Robert Halpern, "Youth Programs into the Void," *Social Service Review* (March 2006): 180.
3. Amy F. Feldman and Jennifer L. Matjasko, "The Role of School-Based Extracurricular Activities in Adolescent Development: A Comprehensive Review and Future Directions," *Review of Educational Research* 75, no. 2 (2005): 193; see also David M. Hansen, Reed W. Larsen, and Jodi B. Dworkin, "What Adolescents Learn in Organized Youth Activities: A Survey of Self-Reported Developmental Experiences," *Journal of Research on Adolescence* 13, no. 1 (2009): 25-55; Amy M. Bohnert et al., "Young Urban African American Adolescents' Experience of Discretionary Time Activities," *Journal of Research on Adolescence* 18, no. 3 (2008): 517-39; Joseph L. Mahoney and Håkan Stattin, "Leisure Activities and Adolescent Antisocial Behavior: The Role of Structure and Social Context," *Journal of Adolescence* 23 (2000): 113-27, doi:10.1006/jado.2000.0302.

CHAPTER 3

1. Space constraints split the primary (K-3) kids into two groups: 4:00-5:30 p.m. on either Monday/Wednesday or Tuesday/Thursday. Monday/Wednesday evenings from 7:00-9:00 were reserved for students in grades 4-6 and Tuesday/Thursday evenings for those in grades 7 and 8. Junior Staff high school students attended tutoring sessions every Wednesday before the Young Life Club meeting. Tutoring sessions also took place on Saturday mornings for students needing additional support.
2. See, for example, Barton J. Hirsch, *A Place to Call Home: After-School Programs for Urban Youth* (Washington, DC: American Psychological Association; New York: Teachers College Press, 2005). He recounts the Boys and Girls Club Smart Girls program's largely shallow relationships as leaders dutifully followed the scripted curriculum. He concludes: "Comprehensive after-school programs are well aware of the importance of the relationship between staff and youth, but this awareness was not applied to Smart Girls. Absolutely nowhere in the (100+ page) manual is there reference to the relationship between the group leader and the girls" (107).
3. Developmental psychologists and social learning theorists stress the power of near peers, in particular race and social class. See Albert Bandura, *Social Foundations of Thought and Action: A Social Cognitive Theory* (Englewood Cliffs, NJ: Prentice-Hall, 1986).

4. British sociologist Richard Titmuss argued that pure altruism seldom motivates volunteers; their involvement is a gift, but benefits are expected to follow. Volunteers come to a youth organization for a purpose, often more than one—giving back, helping kids succeed, addressing a sense of moral or civic duty. Their commitment and engagement turns on the extent to which their experiences satisfy those purposes. Managing that "gift relationship" successfully requires close attention and support from an organization's senior staff. See Richard M. Titmuss, *The Gift Relationship* (New York: Pantheon Books, 1971).
5. Hirsch, *A Place to Call Home*, 57ff. On the difficulties and importance of achieving a successful match between an adult mentor and a young person, see Jean Rhodes, *Stand by Me: The Risks and Rewards of Mentoring Today's Youth* (Cambridge, MA: Harvard University Press, 2002).

CHAPTER 4

1. Junior Staff positions were supported initially under the Comprehensive Employment and Training Act (CETA) and then under JTPA, which was repealed during the Clinton administration by the Workforce Investment Act of 1998.
2. Dustin Wood, Reed W. Larson, and Jane R. Brown, "How Adolescents Come to See Themselves as More Responsible Through Participation in Youth Programs," *Child Development* 80, no. 1 (2009): 295–309.
3. In their important article on adolescents' responsibility development, Ida Salusky and her coauthors identify four aspects of a youth successfully learning to be responsible and integrating those behaviors and values into self-concepts: voluntarily taking on roles and obligations, experiencing challenge and strain, feeling motivated to fulfill those obligations, and internalizing changes in self and behavior associated with responsible behavior in other contexts. These steps correspond directly to those that made the Junior Staff program effective. Ida Salusky et al., "How Adolescents Develop Responsibility: What Can Be Learned from Youth Programs," *Journal of Research on Adolescence* 24, no. 3 (2014), doi: 10.1111/jora.12118. Their research is based on an interview study carried out in four programs pursuing the goal of fostering adolescents' development, including responsibility.
4. Glen H. Elder Jr., Monica Kirkpatrick Johnson, and Robert Crosnow, "The Emergence and Development of Life Course Theory," in *Handbook of the Life Course*, ed. Jeylan T. Mortimer and Michael J. Shanahan (New York: Kluwer Academic/Plenum, 2003), 3–19; Jeylan T. Mortimer, "The Evolution, Contributions, and Prospects of the Youth Development Study: An Investigation in Life Course Social Psychology," *Social Psychology Quarterly* 75, no. 1 (2012), doi: 10.1177/0190272511434911.

5. Vygotsky asserted that cognitive development stems from social interactions from guided learning within the zone of proximal development, which signals the individual's task of learning skills too difficult to master on their own but that can be achieved with the support and guidance of a knowledgeable person. See Lev Vygotsky, "Interaction Between Learning and Development," trans. Frances M. Lopez-Morillas, in *Mind in Society: The Development of Higher Psychological Processes*, ed. Michael Cole, Vera John-Steiner, Sylvia Scribner, and Ellen Souberman (Cambridge, MA: Harvard University Press, 1978), 79–91.
6. Etienne Wegner, *Communities of Practice: Learning, Meaning and Identity* (Cambridge, UK: Cambridge University Press, 1998), 225.
7. For example, see Dustin Wood, Reed W. Larson, and Jane R. Brown, "How Adolescents Come to See Themselves as More Responsible Through Participation in Youth Programs," *Child Development* 80, no. 1 (2009): 295–309; Salusky et al., "How Adolescents Develop Responsibility."
8. An analysis of the development of responsibility across eleven youth programs found that programs rated high in reported youth responsibility development had a clear a priori structure of rules and expectations. In contrast, programs rated low in youth responsibility operated in a more ad hoc fashion. There also were fewer structured roles for youth. Ironically, in some programs, low role structure resulted from a philosophy of youth leadership and desire to have youth create the structure for their work. In other low programs, adults exercised a high degree of control. See Wood et al., "How Adolescents Come to See Themselves."
9. Charles Smith and colleagues' investigation of promising practices for social and emotional learning shows how responsibility develops when young people have an opportunity to take on increasingly challenging obligations and staff provide clear structure and expectation but allow youth initiative and autonomy in fulfilling those duties. This structured but open-ended stance on youth roles and responsibilities results in ownership, pride in accomplishment, and confidence to take on even more challenging assignments. Charles Smith et al., *Preparing Youth to Thrive: Promising Practices for Social and Emotional Learning* (Washington, DC: Forum for Youth Investment, 2016), 82ff.
10. Wood et al., "How Adolescents Come to See Themselves," 303.
11. As Wood et al. conclude, "It should not be expected that leaders can simply impose demands on youth and expect positive outcomes when the demands are not linked to goals that are important for the youth" ("How Adolescents Come to See Themselves," 306).

12. Jeylan T. Mortimer, "The Evolution, Contributions, and Prospects of the Youth Development Study: An Investigation in Life Course Social Psychology," *Social Psychology Quarterly* 75, no.1 (2012): 5–27, doi: 10.1177/0190272511434911; Jacquelynne Eccles and Jennifer Appleton Gootman, eds., *Community Programs to Promote Youth Development* (Washington, DC: National Academy Press, 2002).
13. For instance, Julie Burnett had responsibility for the summer program, which involved developing and preparing the program, training around eighteen high schoolers to work in the program, and supervising their interactions with forty to fifty second and third graders. She became a lifelong educator, completing her PhD and then heading up CPS's literacy initiative for several years before returning to site administration. Julie's sister, Peggie, also a Junior Staffer, also holds a PhD, and she serves as a CPS principal, along with Nicole Monroe. Karoline Sharp, Altamese Purifoy, and Andre Stokes, are a few of the many Junior Staffers who went into teaching.

CHAPTER 5

1. Pat Ford, under the pseudonym "Renee," is quoted in Milbrey W. McLaughlin, Merita A. Irby, and Juliet Langman, *Urban Sanctuaries: Neighborhood Organizations in the Lives and Futures of Inner-City Youth* (San Francisco: Jossey-Bass, 1994), 92.

CHAPTER 6

1. For IHAD history and information, see https://www.ihaveadream foundation.org/.
2. Two Dreamers were added in eighth grade, a year later, bringing the IHAD class total to forty-four.
3. IHAD report, February 1990, Craig Nash's files.
4. Burton Kaplan obituary, *Chicago Sun-Times,* March 30, 2011, http://legacy.suntimes.com/obituaries/chicagosuntimes/obituary.aspx?pid=149789180.
5. Craig recalled the tough decision to take the Dreamer out of the program: "He was one of those kids who just kept pushing the envelope. We had a rule you had to go to tutoring before you could go to the gym. He just wouldn't do that . . . We couldn't continue. He was really bitter about everything. He was one of those kids that wanted to stand on the outside and [complain about his life], but he wanted to come to the program and act out. He wanted to do the same thing he was doing at school. As open as I want to be and try to give everybody a chance, I told him, 'I can't let

you come here and just let you disrupt everything we're doing.' So the military side of me kicked in and I was like, 'There's the door.' And one final time he walked out and never came back."
6. Researchers deemed the two Chicago IHAD programs they studied as "enormously successful" because their graduation rates of 71 percent and 69 percent were almost two times greater than their respective Chicago comparison groups. Joseph Kahne and Kim Bailey, "The Role of Social Capital in Youth Development: The Case of 'I Have a Dream' Programs," *Educational Evaluation and Policy Analysis* 21, no. 3 (1999): 321–43. There are few evaluations of IHAD, and of those, few consider high school graduation rates as an outcome measure. A 2006 Abt Associates review noted the many methodological issues associated with IHAD evaluations (small samples, validity threats) but concluded, based on them, that programs following the IHAD model generally improved students' lives and school experiences. No national evaluation of the IHAD program existed at the time of the Abt review, which concluded that "additional rigorous evaluation is required." William Rhodes, Linda Truitt, and Audrey Martinez, *A National Evaluation of the "I Have a Dream" Program* (Cambridge, MA: Abt Associates, 2006). In 2015 I attempted unsuccessfully to locate additional IHAD evaluations.
7. Chicago CRED was launched by former secretary of education Arne Duncan in 2015 and is related to the Emerson Collective, a group founded by Laurene Powell Jobs, the widow of Apple founder Steve Jobs, and dedicated to providing opportunities and supports that promote equality and enable people to "live to their full potential." See http://www.emerson collective.com/about-us.

CHAPTER 7
1. Letter to COP95 participant, August 13, 1997, Tami Doig files.
2. See https://www.younglife.org/About/Pages/MissionandVision.aspx.
3. Ellen Warren, "Poor Kids Struggle—and Succeed," *Chicago Tribune*, June 16, 1995.
4. Brenda D. Taylor, *Beauty for Ashes* (Chicago: Liberated Expression, 2010), 268.

PART II
1. For example, see Hazel Markus and Paula Nurius, "Possible Selves," *American Psychologist* 41, no. 9 (1986): 954–69; Susan Cross and Hazel Markus, "Possible Selves Across the Life Span," *Human Development* 34 (1991): 230–55.
2. Michael Rutter, "Transitions and Turning Points in Developmental Psychopathology: As Applied to the Age Span Between Childhood and

Mid-Adulthood," *International Journal of Behavioral Development* 19, no. 3 (1996): 603–26, doi: 10.1177/016502549601900309.
3. Andrew Abbott, "On the Concept of Turning Point," *Comparative Social Research* 16 (1997): 102.
4. Ibid., 89.

CHAPTER 8
1. Jacquelynne Eccles and Jennifer Appleton Gootman, eds., *Community Programs to Promote Youth Development* (Washington, DC: National Academy Press, 2002).
2. See Frank F. Furstenberg Jr., Thomas D. Cook, Jacquelynne Eccles, Glen H. Elder Jr., and Arnold Sameroff, *Managing to Make It: Urban Families and Adolescent Success* (Chicago: University of Chicago Press, 1999).

CHAPTER 9
1. Jean Baldwin Grossman and Joseph P. Tierney, "Does Mentoring Work? An Impact Study of the Big Brothers/Big Sisters," *Evaluation Review* 22, no. 3 (1998): 403–26.
2. Jean E. Rhodes and David L. DuBois, "Mentoring Relationships and Programs for Youth," *Current Directions in Psychological Science* 17, no. 14 (2008): 254–58.
3. Jean E. Rhodes, *Stand by Me: The Risks and Rewards of Mentoring Today's Youth* (Cambridge, MA: Harvard University Press, 2002).
4. Rhodes and DuBois, "Mentoring Relationships and Programs for Youth."

CHAPTER 10
1. Researchers focusing on adolescent development consistently highlight the importance of positive relationships and network of social support to positive youth development. See for example, Eugene Roehlkepartain, Kent Pekel, Amy Syverstten, Jenna Sethi, Theresa Sullivan, and Peter Scales, *Relationships First: Creating Connections That Help Young People Thrive* (Minneapolis: Search Institute, 2017), which concludes that "young people do better when they experience a strong web of relationships with many people" (8). See also William Damon, *The Path to Purpose: Helping Our Children Find Their Calling in Life* (New York: Free Press, 2008).
2. See, for example, the broad-based literature review contained in Jacquelynne Eccles and Jennifer Appleton Gootman, eds., *Community Programs to Promote Youth Development* (Washington, DC: National Academies Press, 2002).

3. Malcolm Gladwell, *Outliers: The Story of Success* (New York: Back Bay Books, 2008), 215.
4. Sharon Daloz Parks, *Big Questions Worthy Dreams: Mentoring Emerging Adults in Their Search of Meaning, Purpose, and Faith*, rev. ed. (San Francisco: Jossey-Bass, 2011), 120–21.
5. Paul Tough highlights the negative effects of stress, anxiety, and trauma for youth growing up in dangerous inner- city neighborhoods like Cabrini-Green. Paul Tough, *Helping Children Succeed: What Works and Why* (Boston: Houghton Mifflin Harcourt, 2016).
6. Charles Smith et al., *Preparing Youth to Thrive: Promising Practices for Social and Emotional Learning* (Washington, DC: Forum for Youth Investment, 2016).
7. Albert Bandura, "Exercise of Human Agency Through Collective Efficacy," *Current Directions in Psychological Science* 9, no. 3 (2000): 75.
8. Steven Hitlin and Glen H. Elder Jr., "Agency: An Empirical Model of an Abstract Concept," *Advances in Life Course Research* 11 (2007): 33–67.
9. Urban sociologist Robert Sampson introduced the concept of collective efficacy, defined as "social cohesion combined with shared expectations for social control," as a critical inhibitor of neighborhood crime and social disorder. He extends its importance to community-level cohesion and effective action but notes that it is largely lacking in poor, urban neighborhoods. Robert J. Sampson, *Great American City: Chicago and the Enduring Neighborhood Effect* (Chicago: University of Chicago Press, 2012), 27. Researchers examining collective efficacy in such diverse action contexts as adventure team racing and neighborhoods combating hate crime likewise find that collective efficacy fosters motivation, a sense of commitment, and staying power among group members. William A. Edmonds et al., "The Role of Collective Efficacy in Adventure Racing Teams," *Small Group Research* 40, no. 2 (2009); Carolyn Petrosino and James Pace, "Social Cohesion, Collective Efficacy, and the Response of a Cape Verdean Community to Hate Crime," *American Behavioral Scientist* 59, no. 13 (2015). Bandura concludes that diverse studies looking at the impact of collective efficacy on outcomes "show that the higher the perceived collective efficacy, the higher the groups' motivational investment in their undertakings, the stronger their staying power in the face of impediments and setbacks, and the greater their performance accomplishments" ("Exercise of Human Agency Through Collective Efficacy," 78).
10. Bandura, "Exercise of Human Agency Through Collective Efficacy," 75–76.
11. For notions of racial stereotyping, see Theresa Perry, Claude Steele, and Asa Hilliard III, *Young, Gifted and Black: Promoting High Achievement Among African-American Students,* (Boston: Beacon Press, 2003).

12. James S. Coleman, *Foundations of Social Theory* (Cambridge, MA: Harvard University Press, 1990), 302, 304. The concept of social capital arose from efforts to develop productive responses to poverty in urban and rural America.
13. See Susan Saegert, J. Phillip Thompson, and Mark R. Warren, eds., *Social Capital and Poor Communities* (New York: Russell Sage Foundation, 2001); and Deepa Narayan, "Bonds and Bridges: Social Capital and Poverty" (Policy Research Working Paper 2167, The World Bank, Washington, DC, August 1999), http://documents.worldbank.org/curated/en/989601468766526606/pdf/multi-page.pdf.
14. Elijah Anderson, *Streetwise: Race, Class and Change in an Urban Community* (Chicago: University of Chicago Press, 1992).

CHAPTER 11

1. Etienne Wenger, *Communities of Practice: Learning, Meaning and Identity* (Cambridge, UK: Cambridge University Press, 1998).
2. The importance of compatibility between organizational culture and program design finds consistent support in the broad implementation research literature. To this point, in *A Place to Call Home: After-School Programs for Urban Youth* (Washington, DC: American Psychological Association; New York: Teachers College Press, 2005), Barton J. Hirsch recounts his four years of research involving six Chicago Boys and Girls Clubs and highlights youth-staff relationships as the "heart and soul" of successful afterschool settings for urban youth. He documents the challenges experienced when the clubs, based on directives from headquarters, moved to implement the highly structured Smart Girls program. He found variable staff responses to the program and highly uneven implementation. These implementation shortfalls resulted, to a significant degree, from the lack of fit between this structured program and the culture of the successful clubs, which, like CYCLE, valued strong relationships as essential to effective programming: "Comprehensive after-school programs are well aware of the importance of the relationship between staff and youth, but this awareness was not applied to Smart Girls. Absolutely nowhere in the (100+ page) manual is there reference to the relationship between the group leader and the girls" (107).

CHAPTER 12

1. For example, sociologist Patrick Sharkey argues that the most challenging problem of urban poverty is that *"the same families have experienced the consequences of life in the most disadvantaged environments over multiple generations."* Patrick Sharkey, *Stuck in Place: Urban Neighborhoods and the End*

of Progress Toward Racial Equality (Chicago: University of Chicago Press, 2013), 26. Likewise, urban sociologist Mitchell Duneier maintains that the black ghetto is an "intergenerational expression of a series of vicious cycles within the realms of education, work, family life violence and local politics—all feed on each other in a spatial context." Mitchell Duneier, *Ghetto: The Invention of a Place, the History of an Idea* (New York: Farrar, Straus, & Giroux, 2016), 227.

2. This argument about the power of affirmative opportunity to change lives of youth growing up in concentrated poverty echoes Cloward and Ohlin's theory about the significance of "differential opportunity systems." Based on their examination of research and theory about delinquent gangs, the authors distinguish between legitimate and illegitimate routes to success, or the different opportunity structures available to low-income urban youth. They find that the gang is important to high-poverty youth because the group can hold promise of wages, jobs, and local status, an illegitimate opportunity structure: "Adolescents turn to violence in search of status . . . under conditions of relative detachment from all institutionalized systems of opportunity and social control." But with the involvement of a social worker and the presence of a legitimate route to goals of success, street gangs can turn from violence and delinquent behavior toward the norms of conventional society and legitimate practices. Richard A. Cloward and Lloyd E. Ohlin, *Delinquency and Opportunity: A Theory of Delinquent Gangs* (Glencoe, IL: The Free Press, 1960), 176.

3. William Julius Wilson, "Why Both Social Structure and Culture Matter in a Holistic Analysis of Inner-City Poverty," *ANNALS of the American Academy of Political and Social Science* 629 (2010): 200, doi: 10.1177/0002716209357403.

4. Geoffrey Canada's Harlem Children's Zone provides a well-developed example of a successful, comprehensive youth initiative that directly took on issues of poverty's culture and structural disadvantaged. See Paul Tough, *Whatever It Takes* (Boston: Houghton Mifflin, 2008).

5. Several accounts of effective youth development programs highlight the necessity of an effective social support structure for both adults and youth when programs aim at transformative change, new identities. See, for example, William Damon, *The Path to Purpose: Helping Our Children Find Their Calling in Life* (New York: Free Press, 2008); Nancy Deutsch, *Pride in the Projects: Teens Building Identities in Urban Contexts* (New York: New York University Press, 2008).

6. In *Relationships First: Creating Connections That Help Young People Thrive* (Minneapolis: Search Institute, 2017), authors Eugene Roehlkepartain et al. elaborate on the centrality of dependable "anchor" relationships to youth development; describe how a web of relationships enables young people to

thrive; and provide a developmental relationships framework comprised of five critical elements: express care, challenge growth, provide support, share power, and expand possibilities.
7. Paul Tough, *How Children Succeed: Grit, Curiosity, and the Hidden Power of Character* (New York: Mariner Books, 2012), 197.
8. Barton J. Hirsch, *A Place to Call Home: After-School Programs for Urban Youth* (Washington, DC: American Psychological Association; New York: Teachers College Press, 2005).
9. Influential advocates of school reform initiatives that are "tight" in terms of established parameters and boundaries but "loose" in regard to on-the-ground actors' ability to make choices that suit their particular contexts include Michael Fullan, *Leading in a Culture of Change* (San Francisco: Jossey Bass, 2001), and Richard Elmore, *School Reform from the Inside Out: Policy, Practice and Performance* (Cambridge, MA: Harvard Education Press, 2006).
10. For guidance, tools, and concrete case examples about building effective afterschool programs through strong municipal leadership, coordination reflecting local context, and successful stakeholder involvement in planning and program development, see Daniel Browne, *Growing Together, Learning Together: What Cities Have Discovered About Building After-School Systems* (New York: The Wallace Foundation, 2015).
11. Larry Cuban, "How Schools Change Reforms: Redefining Success and Failure," *Teachers College Record* 99, no. 3 (1998): 453–54.
12. For an extended discussion of how leaders can manage tight-loose dilemma, see Michael Fullan, *The Six Secrets of Change: What the Best Leaders Do to Help Their Organizations Survive and Thrive* (San Francisco: Jossey-Bass, 2011).
13. Paul Berman and Milbrey Wallin McLaughlin, "Implementation of Educational Innovation," *Educational Forum* 40, no. 3 (1976): 345–70.
14. See for example, Eleanor Farrar, John E. Desanctis, and David K. Cohen, "Views from Below: Implementation Research in Education," *Teachers College Record* 82, no. 1 (1980): 77–100; Milbrey Wallin McLaughlin, "Learning from Experience: Lessons from Policy Implementation," *Educational Evaluation and Policy Analysis* 9, no. 2 (1987): 171–78.
15. Anthony S. Bryk et al., *Learning to Improve: How America's Schools Can Get Better at Getting Better* (Cambridge, MA: Harvard Education Press, 2015). Related to the need for "adaptive integration," Bryk and colleagues argue that randomized control trials (RCTs) are seldom useful in advising schools how to improve because they can say little about the contexts that aid or frustrate implementation. While they are valuable in providing evidence about the worth of invariable "treatments" such as pharmaceuticals, RCTs cannot deal with the highly complex and variable conditions of schooling—key education (and youth program) implementation realities.

16. For instance, research compared the success of Beacons' initiatives, which link community-based and nonprofit organizations with schools to increase supports for youth and families, to the similarly motivated but differently designed New Futures program, launched to test the idea that strong political leadership, interagency collaboration, and other system-level innovations could promote better youth outcomes. Researchers contrasted Beacons' focus on grassroots actors to New Futures' efforts to foster "system change" in the local public and private institutions implicated by youth programs. Beacons sites generally succeeded in creating effective supports for youth through school-based community centers offering afterschool programs as well as extended programming for children, youth, and families in the evenings, on weekends, and during the summer. New Futures projects generally failed to achieve the expected local system level collaboration and so fell flat. And Beacons did result in system change because of its strong track record of success with youth and the positive, trusting relations created at Beacons sites and ultimately with various system leaders. Beacons' initiatives benefited from having the programmatic flexibility and decentralized management needed at the site level and the various supports needed from the system level. See Kathleen A. Dorgan and Ronald F. Ferguson, "Success Factors in Community-Wide Initiatives for Youth Development," in *The Youth Development Handbook: Coming of Age in American Communities*, ed. Stephen F. Hamilton and Mary Agnes Hamilton (Thousand Oaks, CA: Sage, 2004), 271–300.
17. Richard Elmore and others term this tactic "backward mapping." Richard F. Elmore, "Backward Mapping: Implementation Research and Policy Decisions," *Political Science Quarterly* 94, no. 4 (1979): 601.
18. For an account of OST intermediaries' activities, organization types and funding around the United States, see Collaborative for Building After-School Systems, *Making the Connections: A Report on the First National Survey of Out-of-School Time Intermediary Organizations* (New York: The After-School Corporation, 2012).
19. For example, the Forum for Youth Investment supports state and local efforts to "braid" public and nonprofit funds and create networks or coordinating bodies to promote the "collective impact" of cross-institutional, interagency youth-focused investments. See Forum for Youth Investment, *Collective Impact for Policymakers: Working Together for Children and Youth* (Washington, DC: Forum for Youth Investment, 2014). The collective impact framework builds on John Kania and Mark Kramer, "Collective Impact," *Stanford Social Innovation Review* Winter (2011): 36–41.
20. Based on predicted test scores, Geoffrey Canada had to deal with the wrenching necessity of telling Promise Academy eighth graders that there

would not be a ninth grade as part of a promised four-year expansion; students and their families would have to find another high school. Canada's board, distressed by the apparently poor performance of eighth graders on New York State reading and math tests, would not fund Promise Academy's expansion through high school. As Canada pointed out, this decision paid little attention to the gains that the students made since entering as poorly educated sixth graders two years earlier or to their socioemotional progress and greater attachment to school and goals of high school graduation and possibly college. The board's decision, based on predicted scores, turned out to be misinformed. The official scores released in May 2007 showed significant progress for the Promise Academy kids. Their reading scores jumped from 24 percent on grade level in seventh grade to 33 percent on grade level in eighth grade. Students had improved from being 20 points behind the New York City average to being 9 points behind. And math gains were even more impressive. In seventh grade, 34 percent of the class tested at grade level; their scores in eighth grade put them at 70 percent on grade level, beating the city average by 24 points. See discussion in Tough, *Whatever It Takes*, 234–56.

21. American Youth Policy Forum, *Helping Youth Succeed Through Out-of-School Time Programs* (Washington, DC: American Youth Policy Forum, 2006).
22. Roehlkepartain et al., *Relationships First*.
23. Charles Smith et al., *Continuous Quality Improvement in Afterschool Settings: Impact Findings from the Youth Program Quality Intervention Study* (Washington, DC: The Forum for Youth Improvement, 2012). For case-based discussion of developing and implementing a quality improvement system, see Nicole Yohalem et al., *Building Citywide Systems for Quality: A Guide and Case Studies for Afterschool Leaders* (Washington, DC: The Forum for Youth Investment, 2012).
24. Charles Smith et al., *Preparing Youth to Thrive: Promising Practices for Social and Emotional Learning* (Washington, DC: The Forum for Youth Investment, 2016).
25. For instance, tracking how children spend the hours between 3:00 p.m. and 6:00 p.m., the Afterschool Alliance found that while overall participation in afterschool programs grew by nearly 60 percent in the decade 2004–14, with almost four million children enrolled in afterschool, unmet demand for afterschool opportunities continued to rise across the country. In 2014, more than nineteen-million parents said they would enroll their child in an afterschool program if one were available; the demand for afterschool opportunities, both met and unmet, exceeds 50 percent of the country's school-age children. Although afterschool participation in high-poverty communities is greater than the national average (24 percent

compared to 18 percent), the demand for afterschool programs in these communities is much higher than nationally. More than half of the children growing up in concentrated poverty would be part of an afterschool program were it available to them, and more than two out of three parents in these communities would like their child to participate in a summer learning program were one available. African American families living in high-poverty neighborhoods experience the greatest unmet demand for afterschool opportunities. While surveys show that these children have a higher level of participation than children in more-advantaged communities (30 percent compared to 27 percent), data also show that more than 70 percent of African American children growing up in high-poverty communities would be enrolled in an afterschool program were one available to them. Afterschool Alliance, "America After 3PM: Special Report: Afterschool in Communities of Concentrated Poverty," August 2016, http://www.afterschoolalliance.org/AA3PM/Concentrated_Poverty.pdf.
26. Nicholas Zill, Christine Winquist Nord, and Laura Spencer Loomis, "Adolescent Time Use, Risky Behavior and Outcomes: An Analysis of National Data" (report, Office of the Assistant Secretary for Planning and Evaluation, US Department of Health and Human Services, September 11, 1995).
27. Afterschool Alliance, "America After 3PM."
28. More than two-thirds of black and Hispanic families living in high-poverty neighborhoods report difficulty in finding an afterschool environment for their child. In many cases, an afterschool program simply was not available in their community. In other instances, parents cited logistical considerations of hours, distance, and fees as obstacles. Factors that turned many parents away from available programs included negative perceptions about quality of the program, unsatisfactory care, lack of academic help, access to unhealthy snacks, and an absence of physical activity. Concerns for their child's safety highest among factors affecting parents' choice of an afterschool program: 86 percent said it was "extremely important."
29. See http://datacenter.kidscount.org/data/tables/7753-children-living-in-areas-of-concentrated-poverty-by-race-and-ethnicity#detailed/1/any/false/1572,1485,1376,1201,1074/10,11,9,12,1,185,13/14943,14942ethnicity#detailed/1/any/false/1572,1485,1376,1201,1074/10,11,9,12,1,185,13/14943,14942.
30. The National League of Cities (NLC) identified twenty-seven cities around the country that have made notable progress in the development of citywide OST systems and reported on their efforts to build comprehensive, high-quality programs for their community's children and youth. The NLC report provides survey data about OST opportunities as well as case profiles of participating cities. National League of Cities, "Municipal

Leadership for Afterschool: Citywide Approaches Spreading Across the Country" (report, Institute for Youth, Education and Families, National League of Cities, Washington, DC, 2011).
31. Sharon Daloz Parks, *Big Questions, Worthy Dreams: Mentoring Emerging Adults in Their Search for Meaning, Purpose, and Faith*, rev. ed. (San Francisco: Jossey-Bass, 2011), 133.

ABOUT THE RESEARCH

The research that led to *You Can't Be What You Can't See* departs from usual youth program research in many ways. Perhaps most significantly, it provides a thirty-plus-year follow-up to *Urban Sanctuaries'* account of CYCLE's success with Cabrini-Green youth during the 1980s. This longitudinal perspective made it possible to address questions of sustained effects as seen in life choices made, challenges encountered, and opportunities taken, as well as the intergenerational consequences of being part of CYCLE.

A longitudinal point of view also affords a different stance from which to understand the nature and persistence of youth program outcomes and consideration of how, if, and why program involvement mattered for participants over time. This perspective can bring to light program consequences that might have been missed if outcomes were tallied on program completion. For example, several of the young women involved with CYCLE's scholarship programs would have been counted, in the short term, as disappointments because they did not go on to college after high school or, if they did, soon dropped out. However, a look at their lives several years later reveals that they put off college because of pregnancy and that when their children became of school age, most did go to college and that several completed graduate degrees—outcomes they attribute to their involvement with CYCLE.

This research also differs in its focus. Much youth program research looks at program inputs—such as how much time youth spent on what activities—and their relationship to outputs, or benefits for youth. This correlational perspective can provide useful information to program planners and funders seeking to learn about trends, but it falls short in several important ways as a guide to policy and practice. For instance, researchers often do not (or cannot because of funding or time constraints) consider the *quality* or nature of particular activities. Yet, youth practitioners know well that the quality of any activity, mentoring for instance, varies significantly across youth programs and that the benefits for young people depend on the nature and duration of youth/mentor relationships. Similarly, just knowing that young people had exposure to activities such as tutoring or coaching or life skills provides little evidence about effective or ineffective approaches. Yet, seldom does youth program research take a close look at *how* program activities are carried out and experienced by youth—the "black box." The research reported here draws on retrospective accounts of the black box of program implementation to understand how and why CYCLE involvement mattered for participants' pathways through Cabrini-Green and to their adult lives.

Gaining access to respondents can be a problem for those doing field research. This project benefited enormously from the fact that all of CYCLE's senior staff and many of the individuals participating in various programs still live in the Chicago area and remain in touch with each other and with founding director Greg Darnieder. Greg easily tracked them down and set up interviews. Social media provided an assist to making these connections, as did the ongoing and vibrant relationships among former staff and program participants.

Greg began talking with former CYCLE participants in 2012 about their experiences of growing up in Cabrini-Green, recollections of their experiences at CYCLE, and accounts of their current lives and families. With Greg's scheduling assist, I began interviewing CYCLE-affiliated individuals and alums in 2013. Several of my interviews involved individuals I had interviewed more than thirty years ago as part of the *Urban Sanctuaries* research project. Greg and I talked with staff coordinators and participants from each of the CYCLE programs. Singly or together, we also interviewed former CYCLE board members, local philanthropists, staff, and parents of CYCLE youth. All interviews lasted at least an hour, involved open-ended questions related to a respondent's CYCLE involvement. Questions posed to senior staff focused on their path to CYCLE, what their jobs involved on a daily basis, challenges they encountered, their relationships with other staff and youth, and their experiences with the program. We asked former participants to describe their lives growing up in Cabrini-Green and their CYCLE involvement and to reflect on whether or how CYCLE experiences mattered to who they are today. Interviews with former board members, community leaders, and funders centered on their involvement with the program and assessment of CYCLE's approach to youth programming. We invited all respondents to share their views of CYCLE's strengths and shortfalls.

Collectively these conversations included more than forty individuals (several of whom we interviewed multiple times) and amounted to more than 150 hours of interviews. We also convened three focus groups of former participants and staff to reflect on CYCLE's activities and opportunities, their roles, and the program's place in Cabrini-Green. Most of those conversations were recorded and transcribed; when that was not possible because of ambient noise, records rely on my notes. All quotes provided in this book come from the interviews Greg and I conducted between 2012 and 2017. Exceptions are quotes from *Urban Sanctuaries*, which are noted in the text.

Respondent selection primarily was purposive. We aimed to gather perspective on all aspects of CYCLE's operation—management and development, staffing, program implementation, youth experience, design choices. We contacted most individuals who played a central role in CYCLE to talk about how the program operated on a daily basis, issues navigated, principles of practice. Scholarship program leaders put us in contact with several participants in their programs and arranged for us to speak with them. We also spoke with people who were important to CYCLE's development and support, including founding board members and local philanthropists.

The descriptions provided also incorporate extensive record data: CYCLE's quarterly newsletters and annual reports from 1984 to 1992, articles from Chicago press, and youth-produced poetry and essays from the summer creative writing project. Accounts of two of the scholarship program activities and outcomes draw on the personal files of the I Have A Dream and College Opportunity Program: Class of 1995 coordinators. These files include program materials and descriptions, participants' school transcripts, funder and tutor comments, coordinator observations about family or school issues, school and prom pictures, and notes about post–high school activities. Tami Doig's archives also include kids' initial COP95 sixth-grade application essays and a thank-you book of letters the youth compiled at the end of their senior year.

These files, combined with coordinators' current knowledge of what their program alums are doing, provide detailed and up-to-date information on *all* participants in the IHAD and COP95 scholarship programs—all seventy-eight kids. Coordinators of the Bright Knights (thirty youth) and Education Assistance Limited (twenty-two youth) programs provided information on their participants' high school graduation status: 100 percent graduated from high school. The Bright Knights coordinator remains in touch with many of the kids in his program and could speak to their postsecondary pathways.

Pat Ford, CYCLE's academic director, oversaw the Junior Staff program, which involved around six hundred youth in leadership positions from the early 1980s through the early 1990s. Relying on her memory and existing communication, she believed that 100 percent of the Junior Staffers graduated from high school and about one-third of them went on to college. Junior Staffers' ongoing contacts with each other and their presence on social media buttress Pat's recollections. Within this tight Junior Staff network, relationships remain close decades later. While not as specific as scholarship coordinators' documentation and current information, Pat and Junior Staffers provided consistent accounts of Junior Staff accomplishments and life stories.

Data limitations involve missing or incomplete information. Formal reporting for CYCLE goals, expenditures, or outcomes does not exist since private funders did not require it. Greg kept records of donors' gifts, and annual reports included funding received and spent. He was the record keeper and intentionally kept it to a minimum. Daily participant counts logged the number of kids involved with tutoring or summer camp activities, but individuals' participation was not systematically followed over the years. Nor did counts of youth involved in daily tutoring make note of which kids were scholarship program participants or were part of the Junior Staff and thus required to attend tutoring sessions. My estimate, based on conversations with senior staff, is that approximately one-half of the three hundred kids involved in CYCLE tutoring every week during the school year participated in tutoring only, not in any other CYCLE program.

The positive and consistent conclusions presented in this book raise three possible sources of bias: selection and self-selection effects on outcomes and confirmatory bias on reported data. CYCLE participants' positive stories of their lives—their education, their families, their jobs—are extraordinary, especially when considered in terms of the bleak social, economic, and institutional context in which they grew up. Their outlier status as CYCLE participants while they moved through the threats and negatives of Cabrini-Green and their current lives as successful adults raise questions about how to interpret these reports that depart so considerably from predicted pathways.

Some might ask whether these young people were selected to participate because of their academic potential or other important individual characteristics that could boost positive outcomes. Is there a selection effect operating to inflate CYCLE's success? CYCLE's open-door policy disputes wholesale selection bias; any youth who wanted to join the program could do so, assuming an available spot. However, Junior Staff positions went to youth judged by senior staff to be most responsible, mature, and committed to CYCLE's mission. These young people were chosen to be academic year Junior Staff based on promise, engagement, and senior staff assessment of their performance as part of a larger group of summer program Junior Staff.

Perhaps self-selection bias existed in the type of young person who made the choice to get involved with CYCLE. Were they more motivated than other youth in the housing project? Were they more academically talented? Did they have particularly engaged moms or supportive home lives? Maybe, but *all* Cabrini-Green youth lived in the same impoverished, dangerous environment. Evident to CYCLE alums is that absent CYCLE they likely would have found themselves struggling to stay off the negative paths predicted for them by virtue of growing up in Cabrini-Green.

Confirmation bias presents another threat to the validity of the conclusions presented here. Did I privilege accounts and experiences that confirmed hopes and expectations and ignore those that did not? No. Senior staff records, personal communications, and social media connections provide information about all the youth who participated in the scholarship and Junior Staff programs, but not all the youth who participated in tutoring only. And a few of the youth involved in the IHAD and COP95 scholarship programs were unable to overcome the challenges of Cabrini-Green's poverty, drugs, and gang violence, especially youth from extremely dysfunctional homes. These young people essentially were raising themselves on the streets and fell away from CYCLE. But the vast majority of the more than seven hundred youth participating in the scholarship and Junior Staff programs did achieve and sustain mainstream lives for themselves and their families.

This research does not lend itself to formal reliability checks, such as interrater consistency. I performed all of the interview analysis. I endeavored to address the goal of reliability estimates—providing the reader confidence in the findings presented and conclusions reached—in another way: I involved respondents in manuscript review and sign-off. Former CYCLE staff and participants quoted in the book had the opportunity to vet the statements attributed to them and respond to conclusions drawn about them and the operation and outcomes of CYCLE programs, as well as the description of Cabrini-Green's social and institutional context. More than twenty CYCLE staff and alums met in the fall of 2016 to comment on an initial draft; all had the opportunity to review and comment on the penultimate draft.

A final word on CYCLE respondents. Many social science accounts disguise respondent identity. However, in this instance, each respondent wanted to have his or her name and life story used in the book. They were proud of all they had achieved—both staff and participants—and proud of what CYCLE had accomplished for Cabrini-Green youth. The names provided here are real ones, not pseudonyms. I consider it the ultimate tribute to the CYCLE program that they wanted their involvement and lives acknowledged.

ACKNOWLEDGMENTS

Greg Darnieder imagined, created, and sustained CYCLE, the Chicago program featured in *You Can't Be What You Can't See*. This book celebrates Greg's vision and unconditional commitment to urban youth and to providing them positive but otherwise unavailable out-of-school opportunities. Greg and I spent much time over the years talking about CYCLE, the challenges it faced, the supports it provided, how and why it succeeded. He has been an extraordinarily generous collaborator, spending hours with me, locating program archives, arranging interviews with community leaders and CYCLE participants, and reviewing every chapter draft.

Pat Ford, a Cabrini-Green native and CYCLE's academic director, was the program's heart and soul. Her unwavering support, clear memories, and honest feedback as chapters took shape were invaluable. Her commitment to CYCLE's core principles, values, and beliefs lives on as if it were fully functioning today.

Scholarship program coordinators Craig Nash (I Have A Dream) and Tami Doig (College Opportunity Program: Class of 1995) dedicated significant time to the development of this book. They generously shared the student files, program notes, news articles, and correspondence they had accumulated over the years—essential documentation. I am grateful that they retained these materials and could retrieve them. Both Craig and Tami spent hours with me explaining how they worked with the youth in their programs, the challenges they encountered, and the supports they found most effective for their kids and reviewing their program rosters to provide a life account for each young person in their charge.

Richard Blackmon, coordinator of the Bright Knights scholarship program at Providence–St. Mel, also dug into his files and memory to describe how this program worked and detailed the outcomes for its participants. Bernard McCune, who led the Education Assistance Limited scholarship program, shared his own experience navigating Cabrini-Green, his perspective on why CYCLE made such a positive difference for kids growing up there, and his accounts of EAL youth. Former Young Life directors Harold Spooner and Alvin Bibbs added invaluable insight into the two organizations' collaborative programming.

There would be no book without the generous and wholehearted contributions of many CYCLE participants. Their willingness to participate in lengthy interviews about their experiences and to search through their files, Facebook contacts, and photo collections and to share their life stories provided the book with priceless detail and perspective on how and why CYCLE succeeded in putting youth on positive pathways through and out of Cabrini-Green. In particular, Brian and Carleta Alston; Shree Green; Tamiko Jones and her mother, Liz Lowery; Brenda Taylor; David Gates; Gloria Purifoy and her mother, Sharon Williams, met with me and Greg multiple times to talk about growing up in Cabrini-Green, their CYCLE involvement, and how that experience played out in their lives. Other CYCLE alums also generously shared details about their experiences and lives: Cyril Nichols, Lloyd Rogers, Kim Brown, Don Smith, William Gates, Jennifer Means, Ken Dunkin, Margie Davis, and Amber Darey.

CYCLE volunteer coordinator Michelle McConnell, former board members Bob Best and Tim Huizenga, funders Gary Wood and Anne Kaplan, and philanthropist Harrison Steans spoke with me about their experiences with the CYCLE program, its development, and its place in Cabrini-Green. The enthusiasm of participants, staff, and supporters in telling CYCLE's story animated this project from the outset.

Merita Irby, cofounder and executive vice president of the Forum for Youth Investment and my partner in the *Urban Sanctuaries* book, has been an invaluable adviser and supporter to this project all along the way. In a fundamental way, she shares ownership of this book.

Melissa Roderick, the Hermon Dunlap Smith Professor at the School of Social Service Administration, University of Chicago, gave her wholehearted support to the project from its inception. The book reflects the many hours we spent discussing ways to present the CYCLE story to highlight its contribution to youth programming and policy. Melissa also owns this book through her long-term commitment to the success of kids like those who benefited from CYCLE.

Great thanks and appreciation go to Michael McPherson, former president of the Spencer Foundation. He believed it was essential to document CYCLE's impressive success with Cabrini-Green youth and it make the account broadly available. He generously provided Spencer Foundation funds to support travel, meetings, transcription, and other expenses that go along with a field-based research project and also funded Melissa Roderick's graduate student, Melissa Noe, to assist with gathering historical Chicago data.

Many friends and colleagues have patiently listened to my thoughts about how best to present CYCLE's story, read draft sections, offered useful advice on relevant connections to research and practice, and provided encouraging support—among them, Barton Hirsch, Nancy Goodban, David Cohen, Ray McDermott, Jonathan Rabinowitz, Barry Groves, Karen Strobel, and Graciela Borsato. Larry Klein's sharp editorial pencil improved language and clarity throughout. As someone with limited knowledge of youth policies or issues (he's a lawyer), Larry was especially helpful in pointing out lines of analysis that didn't make sense to him or needed elaboration.

Stanford colleagues Ed Bridges and Larry Cuban have been especially significant collaborators, reading and rereading drafts, noting fuzzy language or incomplete arguments, raising questions requiring attention, and suggesting organizational changes. Their involvement with this project afforded both thoughtful review and essential moral support; a mere "thank you" falls short of my debt to them.

Nancy Walser, my editor at Harvard Education Press, has been an extraordinary partner in the completion of *You Can't Be What You Can't See*. Her good editorial sense and substantive suggestions are reflected in every chapter. It has been a joy to work with her, and the book is much better for her active engagement.

ABOUT THE AUTHOR

Milbrey W. McLaughlin is the David Jacks Professor Emeritus of Education and Public Policy at Stanford University and the founding director of the John W. Gardner Center for Youth and Their Communities, an organization that partners with communities and youth-serving agencies to develop leadership, conduct research, and support policies to improve the lives of youth. She also founded and codirected Stanford's Center for Research on the Context of Teaching, an interdisciplinary research center engaged in analysis of how teaching and learning are shaped by teachers' organizational, institutional, and socialcultural contexts. Prior to joining Stanford's Graduate School of Education, she was a policy analyst at the RAND Corporation.

McLaughlin is the author or coauthor of books, articles, and chapters on education policy issues, contexts for teaching and learning, productive environments for youth, and community-based organizations. Her books since 2000 include *From Data to Action: A Community Approach to Improving Youth Outcomes* (Harvard Education Press, 2012): *Between Movement and Establishment: Organizations Advocating for Youth* (Stanford University Press, 2009); *Building School-Based Teacher Learning Communities* (with Joan Talbert; Teachers College Press, 2006); *School Districts and Instructional Renewal* (with Amy Hightower, Michael Knapp, and Julie Marsh; Teachers College Press, 2002); *Communities of Practice and the Work of High School Teaching* (with Joan Talbert; University of Chicago Press, 2001); and *Community Counts: How Youth Organizations Matter for Youth Development* (Public Education Fund Network, 2000). McLaughlin is a member of the National Academy of Education and the American Academy of Arts and Sciences.

INDEX

Abbott, Andrew, 140
academic performance, 61
accountability, 79, 84–85, 87, 92, 160, 171–172, 190–192, 212
Adams, Paul, 104
adaptive integration, 209
adolescence/adolescents, 5, 34, 38–39, 64, 80, 90, 93, 143, 199–200, 216–217
adult programs, 64–66, 101
African American volunteers, 68–69
afterschool programs, 37
    See also out-of-school time (OST) programs
    impact assessments, 7
    research on, 4–5
agency, 88–90, 171
Alston, Brian, 3, 74–76, 93, 95, 152, 158
Alston, Carleta, 3, 74–75, 86, 152
American Youth Policy Forum, 213
Amoco Oil, 48
anchor relationships, 202
arts/art programs, 89, 98, 105, 118, 129–130, 150, 172

at-risk youth, 5, 33–35
attendance, 61, 62, 69–70, 103, 115–116, 172–173, 202

Bandura, Albert, 169
Battle, Brian, 104
belonging, 165–178
Bennett, William, 17
Big Brothers and Big Sisters program, 38, 156
birth control, 21–22
black migration, 11
Blackmon, Richard, 18, 23, 29, 63, 104–105, 149–150, 161, 163
board development, 48–51
bonding capital, 176–178
boredom, 27
Boyd, Anita, 101, 159, 187, 193
Boys and Girls Clubs, 38, 72, 181, 207
Breakfast Club, 171
bridging capital, 176–178
Bright Knights scholarship program, 96, 103–106
Burnett, Julie, 66
Burnett, Peggy, 66

business professionals, 50, 151–152
Byrd Community Academy, 17–18
Byrd Dream Class, 108, 111–117, 120–123

Cabrini Extension, 11–12, 14
Cabrini-Green public housing project, 1, 2, 48
   dangerous conditions in, 13–16, 20, 22–25, 199, 204
   demographic makeup of, 13
   gangs, 13, 15, 20, 24–29, 168, 187, 199
   graduation rates in, 3
   income eligibility for, 12–13, 32, 199
   lack of positive exposure in, 143–146
   life in, 11–35
   low expectations in, 21–22, 144–145
   negative stereotypes about, 97–98, 171
   neighborhoods of, 14–15
   schools, 16–20
   sense of community in, 29–31
   social and institutional isolation of, 31–33
   social norms in, 21–22
   social stigma of, 25–26, 171
   violence in, 22–25
   volunteer introduction to, 67–68
Calerway, Johnny, 3
camaraderie, 87–88

camping trips, 44, 53, 91, 109, 114, 148, 150, 162, 173
career opportunities, 147–148
care packages, 134, 162
Chicago Cluster Initiative, 192
Chicago Donors Forum, 48–49
Chicago Housing Authority (CHA), 2, 11, 12, 32, 77, 199
Chicago Public Schools (CPS), 2, 144
child care, 117, 118
choices, 140
Club, 61–62
Coleman, James, 176
collective efficacy, 171–172
collective responsibility, 90–93, 190–192
college aspirations, 22
college education, 2, 4, 22, 95
College Opportunity Program: Class of 1995 (COP95), 53, 69, 125–138, 166, 181, 195–196
   fund-raising, 129
   outcomes, 131–138
   student selection, 126–127
   Tami Doig as coordinator of, 126–138
college students
   as Junior Staff, 73
   as tutors, 50, 63, 67
college visits, 54, 131, 148–149
community
   bonding opportunities, 172–176
   lack of businesses in, 31–33

mentoring, 166–167
    of practice, 181–196
    sense of, 29–31, 165–178
concentrated poverty, 12–13,
    32–34, 71, 143, 167, 197–198,
    215–216
condoms, 21
confidence, 146, 147
continuous learning, 83
CRED (Create Your Economic
    Destiny), 122
crime, 5, 6, 15, 24, 34, 145
Crosby, Latisha, 24
Cuban, Larry, 208
culture of poverty, 8, 197, 200–201
CYCLE participants
    graduation rates, 3
    interviews with former, 2
    life stories of, 7–8
    outcomes for, 93–94, 120–123,
        160–164, 198–199, 213–214
    relationships among, 165–178
    success of, 3–4
    turning points for, 139–142
CYCLE program
    adult programs, 64–66, 101
    annual budget, 48
    beginnings of, 41–46
    board development, 48–51
    closing down of, 192–196
    as community of belonging,
        165–178
    community of practice of,
        181–196
    core principles of, 46–47
    costs and expenses, 51–55
    expanded possibilities provided
        by, 146–151
    exposure provided by, 143–153
    fund-raising by, 48–51, 96,
        211–212
    importance of, 34–35
    introduction to, 1–4
    Junior Staff, 2, 73–94, 147–148,
        160, 162, 203–204
    leadership of, 185–187, 192–196
    lessons from, 179, 211–214
    long-term outcomes, 5
    mentoring and, 63–64,
        155–164, 202
    opportunities provided by,
        197–217
    organizational culture of, 182
    outcomes achieved by, 93–94,
        120–123, 160–164, 182,
        198–199, 213–214
    philosophy of, 6–7, 116
    place-conscious approach of, 7
    practices of, 7, 38–39, 189–190
    recreating, 206–210
    scholarship programs, 95–138
    strength-based focus of,
        160–161
    supports provided by, 168–172
    tutoring program, 57–72
    youth-centered approach, 62–64,
        160–161, 188–190, 205

Darnieder, Greg, 2, 3, 5, 29, 165
    on adult programs, 65
    community outreach by, 177
    on core principles, 46

Darnieder, Greg, *continued*
  on dangers of Cabrini-Green, 53–54
  founding of CYCLE and, 41–44
  fund-raising by, 48–51, 96, 211–212
  on Junior Staff, 76, 81–82, 84, 85, 88–90
  leadership by, 185
  as mentor, 159
  on participation, 172–173
  as role model, 152, 153
  on scholarships, 96, 97, 125–126
  on succession, 196
  on tutoring program, 58
  volunteer recruitment by, 66–67
  on youth-centered approach, 188, 190
David P. Weikart Center for Youth Program Quality, 213
Davis, Dantrell, 22–23
Davis, Margie, 64, 89
decision making, 184
developmental approach, 160–161
developmental leadership, 86
developmental supports, 33–35
discrimination, 17, 19–20, 170–171, 202
distributive leadership, 86
Dittmer, Tom, 104
Doig, Tami, 159, 170
  on commitment, 70
  on relationships, 161, 165
  resignation by, 193, 195–196
  as scholarship coordinator, 126–138, 141, 183–184, 187, 191
Door, The, 50
dropout rates, 19
drug-related crime, 24, 33
DuBois, David, 156
Dunkin, Ken, 55, 64, 77, 157, 159, 161, 174–175

economic environment, 26
economic inequalities, 6
economic segregation, 12, 31–33
Edin, Kathryn, 21
Education Assistance Limited (EAL) scholarship program, 17, 96, 101–103, 140, 181
education inequalities, 6
efficacy
  collective, 171–172
  personal, 169–171
Elder, Glen, 169
embedded curriculum, 151–153
emotional safety, 47, 168–169
employment opportunities, 110, 152, 199, 216
empowerment, 175
environmental context, 34, 200–205
environmental risk, 157
expectations, 21–22, 86–88, 97–98, 144–145, 170–175, 202
exposure, 143–153
extracurricular activities, 39

family engagement, 111–112, 136–137
family members, tutoring for, 64–66
family situations, 62–63, 189

fathers, 2, 16, 199
Feldman, Amy, 39
Fellowship of Friends, 45
field trips, 103, 113–114, 130–131, 148–150, 162, 173
Ford, Greg, 89
Ford, Pat, 74, 77, 99, 137, 159, 160, 187, 191
   as academic director, 50, 60, 127
   on community, 145, 167, 169
   as Junior Staffer, 73
   leadership by, 185–187, 196
   on parents, 64–65
   on relationships, 92
   resignation by, 193
   on scholarship philosophy, 96
   on shared commitment, 187–188
   on teen pregnancy, 22
   on youth-centered approach, 62–63, 89
Francis Cabrini Homes, 14
Fullan, Michael, 208–209
fund-raising, 48–51, 96, 211–212
future selves, 139–140, 144–146, 200

gangs
   in Cabrini-Green, 13, 15, 20, 122, 168, 187, 199
   lure of, 26–29
   violence related to, 24–25
Gates, David, 19, 30, 63, 78–79, 98, 146–149, 152, 158, 166, 167, 171–172
Gates, Peggy, 89

Gates, William, 59
GEAR UP program, 64, 74
GED classes, 66
"Girl X," 23
Gladwell, Malcolm, 166
graduation rates, 3, 17, 121, 160, 182, 198–199
grammar schools, 16–20
Green, Shree, 14, 19–20, 107–109, 113, 114, 117–118, 121–122, 144–145, 150–151, 159
grief, 92
group identity, 90–91
group norms, 173–174, 175

herd programming, 205
high school dropout rates, 19, 199–200
high school graduation rates, 3, 17, 121, 160, 182, 198–199
Hirsch, Barton, 72
Hitlin, Steven, 169
Hoop Dreams (film), 79
Huizenga, Tim, 15

I Have a Dream scholarship program, 12, 53, 69, 107–123, 166, 181
   academic progress and, 115–117
   activities, 112–115
   Byrd Dream Class, 111–112, 114–117, 120–123
   Craig Nash and, 109–117, 122–123
   Kaplans and, 117–120
   outcomes, 120–123

impact assessments, 7
incentive programs, 61, 130
individuals
  choices by, 140
  commitment to, 47
inequalities, 6
initiative, 88
institutional isolation, 31–33
interdependence, 174
Irby, Merita A., 219

job opportunities, 110, 152, 199, 216
job placement, 66
job readiness, 66
Job Training and Partnership Act (JTPA), 51, 53
Jones, Tamiko, 14, 18–19, 24–25, 53, 91, 100–101, 144, 147, 149, 160, 163, 169
Joyce Foundation, 48
Junior Staff, 2, 51, 53, 73–94, 203–204
  agency and choice for, 88–90
  collective responsibility and, 90–93
  connections among, 90–92
  feedback for, 88
  life lessons for, 93–94
  as mentors, 157–158, 160, 162
  outcomes for, 73–74, 93–94
  pay for, 75–76
  relationships among, 165–166
  responsibilities of, 61, 78–86, 175–176
  as role models, 71
  rules and expectations for, 86–88
  support groups for, 92
  valuation and, 76–77

Kaplan, Anne, 117–120
Kaplan, Burton, 108, 109, 117–121, 158–159, 165
Katz, Michael, 26
Kefalas, Maria, 21
Kellogg School of Management, 113

Lady Bountiful problem, 69
Lane Technical High School, 18, 99, 110, 203
Lang, Eugene M., 107
Langman, Juliet, 219
LaSalle Street Church (LSC), 43, 66, 188
Laws, Tamara, 164
leadership
  of CYCLE, 185–187
  new, at CYCLE, 192–196
  skills, 74
leadership skills, skills, 78–79, 86
learning opportunities, 44, 202
Leslie, Bill, 43
life circumstances, 62–63
life course perspective, 6, 214
life lessons, 63–64, 93–94, 149
life skills, 80, 152, 153
life story approach, 6, 7
Lincoln Park High School, 17
Little Hell, 11, 14
local advantage strategy, 216

longitudinal assessment, 140–141
long-term outcomes, 5
Lowery, Liz, 100–101
low-income households, 13
low-income students, 17, 25–26

MacArthur Foundation, 192
mainstream society, 31–33,
    151–153, 178, 203
Marshall Field Garden Apartments, 14–15
Marwen, 129–130
Matjasko, Jennifer, 39
McConnell, Michelle, 19, 29, 58,
    60, 67–68, 147, 163
McCune, Bernard, 92, 97, 140–141,
    143, 159, 162, 184, 187, 204
  on Cabrini-Green, 25
  on camping trips, 150
  on commitment, 55
  on EAL, 103
  on gangs, 20, 26–27, 28–29
  on low expectations, 17
  on race perceptions, 146
  on tutoring program, 72
  on the vans, 54
McLaughlin, Milbrey, 219
Means, Jennifer, 76, 77, 80, 83, 87,
    148, 149, 162, 170
mentors/mentoring, 155–164, 202
  community, 166–167
  in CYCLE, 157–164
  as long-term commitment,
    161–163
  meaning of, 156
  outcomes of, 160–164

poor-quality, 156–157
social capital and, 176–177
tutoring as, 63–64
youth-centered approach to,
    160–161
Minyo, Joanne, 129–130
mutual adaptation, 209

Nash, Craig, 3, 54, 159, 172
  on community, 165, 166, 167,
    169
  on community of practice, 184,
    187
  on gangs, 27–28
  impact of CYCLE on, 93, 160
  on leadership of Darnieder,
    177
  resignation by, 193
  as scholarship coordinator, 12,
    109–123, 145
Nash, Jessica, 58–59
national organizations, 210
near-peer strategy, 64, 82–83, 84,
    174–175
negative stereotypes, 68, 69, 71,
    97–98, 167, 171
Nichols, Cyril, 3, 14, 18, 22, 31, 32,
    85, 92, 93, 95, 146, 148, 158
norms
  in Cabrini-Green, 21–22
  group, 173–174, 175
  mainstream, 151–153
Northwestern University, 113

O'Brien, Tom, 41–42
open door policy, 46

opportunities
  employment, 110, 152, 199, 216
  lack of, 197–200
  learning, 44, 202
  poverty of, 8
  power of, 197–217
outings. *See* field trips
out-of-school time (OST) programs, 1, 4–5, 7–8, 37–38, 214–216
ownership, 175–176

parents, involvement of, 64–66, 111–112, 123, 136–137
Parks, Sharon, 166
participation, 172–173
peer tutors, 64, 82–83
performances, 61–62
personal accountability, 92
personal efficacy, 169–171
personal relationships, 58–59, 63–64, 70–72, 90–91, 130, 150, 165–178, 192–193
personal supports, 97
philanthropists, 96, 117–120, 125–126, 177, 211
physical safety, 46–47, 168–169
place-conscious approach, 7
police, 98
positive outcomes, factors affecting, 5
possible selves, 139–140, 144–146, 200
poverty, 2, 5, 33–34
  concentrated, 12–13, 32–34, 71, 143, 167, 197–198, 215–216
  culture of, 8, 197, 200–201
  of opportunities, 8
  structural elements of, 200–205
principles of practice, 189–190
private schools, 17, 99–100, 203
Professional Partnership Program (PPP), 151–152
program effects, 7
program implementation, 206–210
Providence-St. Mel Scholarship, 103–106, 181
psychological safety, 168–169
Purifoy, Gloria, 12, 30, 63, 66, 74, 83, 86, 89, 94, 158

race, 146–147
racial discrimination, 17, 19–20, 202
racial slurs, 18
racial stereotypes, 68, 69, 71
relationships
  anchor, 202
  building, 130, 150, 162, 163, 205
  near-peer, 64, 82–84, 174–175
  personal, 58–59, 63–64, 70–72, 90–91, 130, 150, 165–178, 192–193
relative disadvantage, 92
responsibility
  collective, 90–93, 190–192
  personal, 78–86, 115, 171–172, 175–176
Rhodes, Jean, 156–157
risk factors, 34
Rites of Passage program, 105
Robert Taylor Homes, 13
Rogers, Lloyd, 3, 28, 76, 83

INDEX **265**

role models, 143, 144, 152, 153
Roskam, Swede, 101–102
rules, 47, 61, 86–88, 202

safe environment, 46–47, 168–169
Sampson, Robert, 33
Saturday Knight School, 105
scaffolding, 47, 81, 85, 87
scholarship programs, 51, 53, 69, 95–138, 181–182
  Bright Knights, 96, 103–106
  College Opportunity Program: Class of 1995, 53, 69, 125–138, 166, 181, 195–196
  Education Assistance Limited, 17, 96, 101–103, 140, 181
  goals of, 96
  I Have a Dream, 12, 53, 69, 107–123, 166, 181
  philosophy of, 96–97
  Providence-St. Mel, 103–106, 181
  Schuessler, 96, 98–100, 181–182
school-based extracurricular activities, 39
schools
  Cabrini-Green, 16–20
  getting into high-quality, 99–100, 203
  low expectations in, 21–22, 144–145, 170–171
  private, 17, 99–100, 203
Schuessler, Walter, 98–99
Schuessler scholarship program, 96, 98–100, 181–182
Search Institute, 213
self-confidence, 146–147, 169–171

self-esteem, 76–77
senior staff, 84–86, 149, 159, 174, 186–187, 190–192, 193
  See also specific staff members
service trips, 149
shared experiences, 173, 187–189
shared values, 187–189, 202
shootings, 23, 24
single mothers, 21–22, 116–117, 141, 178, 199
single-parent homes, 13, 34
Smart Girls curriculum, 207
Smith, Don, 3, 23, 25
snipers, 23, 24
social capital, 176–178
social events, 173
social isolation, 31–33
social networks, 29–31
social roles, 176
social stigma, 25–26
soft skills, 65, 203
spirituality, 188–189
staff reporting, 194
Steans, Harrison, 109, 120
Steans Family Foundation, 192
stereotypes, 68, 69, 71, 97–98, 167, 171
stigmatization, 25–26, 171
St. Joseph's, 17, 18, 19
Stokes, Andre, 3
St. Philip Benizi School, 45
street survival skills, 24
strength-based focus, 160–161
students
  of color, 17
  low-income, 17, 25–26

summer lunch program, 52
summer programs, 52, 82–83, 91, 105, 131, 150, 172
Sunshine Gospel Mission, 43
supervisory skills, 83
support groups, 92, 166

Taylor, Brenda, 126, 133–135, 137–138, 151, 208
teamwork, 188
teen moms, 21–22, 116–118
teen pregnancies, 21–22, 116, 132–134, 141, 199
test scores, 127
Thomas, Nate, 102–103
Todd, Janice, 108
Tough, Paul, 205
Town and Garden Apartments, 14–15
transportation, 53–55
Trinity College, 67
trust-me funding model, 211
turning points, 139–142, 176–178
tutoring program, 52, 57–72
    for adults, 64–66, 101
    near-peer strategy, 64, 82–84, 174–175
    outcomes of, 58
    relationship building and, 58–59, 63–64, 70–72
    tutoring sessions, 59–62, 87, 113
    volunteers, 66–70, 71–72
    youth-centered approach, 62–64

UFOs (Unidentified Flying Objects), 31, 32, 74–75, 158
underground economy, 33
unemployment rates, 26, 33
Urban Sanctuaries (Irby et al.), 1, 207, 219

Vale, Lawrence, 26
values
    mainstream, 151–153
    shared, 187–189, 202
value system, 46, 47, 94
vans, 53–55
Variety Club, 45
violence, 22–25
volunteers, 146–147, 158–159
    African American, 68–69
    long-term commitment by, 161–162
    support for, 163–164
    tutoring program, 66–72
Vygotsky, Lev, 81, 83

Wegner, Etienne, 85
Weinberg, David, 125–126
Weinberg Family Foundation, 125–126
welfare recipients, 13
Wells High School, 17
Wheaton College, 67, 149
White, Jesse, 13
White, Juanita, 65
white people, exposure to, 146–147
Whitney Young High School, 99, 203
William Green Homes, 12, 14

Williams, Sharon, 12, 66
Wilson, William Julius, 201

Young Life, 44–45, 47, 75, 111,
    128, 150, 188
youth activities, 38–39, 47, 93
youth-centered approach, 62–64,
    160–161, 188–190, 205
youth development, 46, 86, 96, 125,
    156, 160–161, 166, 181, 209

youth engagement, 81, 84
youth leadership, 74, 78–79,
    86
youth programs, 38, 206–210
    See also afterschool programs;
    out-of-school time (OST)
    programs

zone of proximal development,
    83